Edward M. Curr and the Tide of History

Samuel Furphy

Edward M. Curr and the Tide of History

Samuel Furphy

E PRESS

Published by ANU E Press and Aboriginal History Incorporated
Aboriginal History Monograph 26

This title is also available online at: http://epress.anu.edu.au/

National Library of Australia Cataloguing-in-Publication entry

Author: Furphy, Samuel.
Title: Edward M. Curr and the tide of history / Samuel Furphy.
ISBN: 9781922144706 (pbk.) 9781922144713 (ebook)
Series: Aboriginal history monograph ; no. 26.
Notes: Includes bibliographical references.
Subjects: Curr, Edward M. (Edward Micklethwaite), 1820-1889
 Authors, Australian--Biography.
 Frontier and pioneer life--Victoria
 Aboriginal Australians--Land tenure.
 Native title (Australia)
 Yorta Yorta (Australian people)
Dewey Number: 994.54

All rights reserved. No part of this publication may be reproduced, stored in a retrieval system or transmitted in any form or by any means, electronic, mechanical, photocopying or otherwise, without the prior permission of the publisher.

Cover images: Map of the Runs of the late Edward Curr, of St Heliers, from Edward M. Curr, 1883, *Recollections of Squatting in Victoria* (Melbourne: G. Robertson); Edward M. Curr (c.1880), photograph courtesy of Ian G. Curr; Edward M. Curr's Map of Bangerang territory, from Edward M. Curr, 1886, *The Australian Race* (Melbourne: John Ferres, Govt. Printer), vol III, 566.

Aboriginal History Incorporated
Aboriginal History Inc. is a part of the Australian Centre for Indigenous History, Research School of Social Sciences, The Australian National University and gratefully acknowledges the support of the School of History RSSS and the National Centre for Indigenous Studies, The Australian National University. Aboriginal History Inc is administered by an Editorial Board which is responsible for all unsigned material. Views and opinions expressed by the author are not necessarily shared by Board members.

The Committee of Management and the Editorial Board
Peter Read (Chair), Rani Kerin (Monographs Editor), Maria Nugent and Shino Konishi (Journal Editors), Robert Paton (Treasurer and Public Officer), Ann McGrath (Deputy Chair), Isabel McBryde, Niel Gunson, Luise Hercus, Harold Koch, Tikka Wilson, Geoff Gray, Dave Johnson, Ingereth Macfarlane, Brian Egloff, Lorena Kanellopoulos, Richard Baker, Peter Radoll.

WARNING: Readers are notified that this publication may contain names or images of deceased persons.

Contacting Aboriginal History
All correspondence should be addressed to the Editors, Aboriginal History, ACIH, School of History, RSSS, Coombs Building (9) ANU, ACT, 0200, or aboriginal.history@anu.edu.au. Sales and orders for journals and monographs, and journal subscriptions: Thelma Sims, email: Thelma.Sims@anu.edu.au, tel or fax: +61 2 6125 3269, www.aboriginalhistory.org

This edition © 2013 ANU E Press

Contents

Illustrations vii

Acknowledgments ix

Prologue: 'Claim Sunk by Pen of a Swordsman' xi

1. From Sheffield to Van Diemen's Land 1

2. 'Troubles of a Beginner' 23

3. 'A Station Formed at Tongala' 37

4. Claiming the Moira 57

5. Decline and Fall 75

6. Rebuilding a Reputation 93

7. Recollections of Squatting 109

8. 'The Native is a Child' 127

9. The Australian Race 145

10. Ethnographic Rivalries 157

11. 'My Sable Neighbours' 173

12. The Tide of History 185

Epilogue: 'The Ghost of Edward Curr' 201

Bibliography 207

Index 223

Illustrations

Figure 1: Edward M. Curr. Engraving. State Library of Victoria, H15062.	xii
Figure 2: John Curr's rails and corves. John Curr, 1797, *The Coal Viewer and Engine Builder's Practical Companion* (Sheffield: John Northall). Gale, Cengage Learning, *The Making of the Modern World*, 2012.	2
Figure 3: Van Diemen's Land Company's establishment at Circular Head. John Arrowsmith. Lithograph. James Bischoff, 1832, *Sketch of the History of Van Diemen's Land* (London: J. Richardson). Australian National Maritime Museum, 00048295.	8
Figure 4: Van Diemen's Land. Map by Peter Johnson.	9
Figure 5: Elizabeth Curr (c.1850). Photograph courtesy of Ian G. Curr.	14
Figure 6: Highfield, Circular Head. William Purser. Watercolour. National Library of Australia, nla.pic-an4911681.	21
Figure 7: Port Phillip District. Map by Peter Johnson.	33
Figure 8: Edward M. Curr's Map of Bangerang territory. Edward M. Curr, 1886, *The Australian Race* (Melbourne: John Ferres, Govt. Printer), vol III, 566.	38
Figure 9: Map of the Runs of the Late Edward Curr, of St Heliers. Edward M. Curr, 1883, *Recollections of Squatting in Victoria* (Melbourne: G. Robertson).	42
Figure 10: Aboriginal Fishing Camp on the River Murray, Near Lake Moira (1872). Samuel Calvert. Engraving. State Library of Victoria, IAN21/05/72/117.	59
Figure 11: Warrie. William Thomas [?]. Sketch. State Library of Victoria, R. Brough Smyth papers, MS 8781 Box 1176/7(a).	69
Figure 12: Edward M. Curr's Mediterranean tour. Map by Peter Johnson.	78
Figure 13: New Zealand. Map by Peter Johnson.	84
Figure 14: Eastern Australia. Map by Peter Johnson.	90
Figure 15: E.M. Curr (1872). Thomas Foster Chuck. Photograph. State Library of Victoria, H5056/235.	104
Figure 16: Edward M. Curr. Painting. Edward M. Curr, 1965, *Recollections of Squatting in Victoria*, edited by Harley W. Forster. Abridged (Carlton, Vic.: Melbourne University Press).	123
Figure 17: The Aboriginal Settlement at Coranderrk (1865). Charles Walter. Engraving. State Library of Victoria, H4082.	128

Figure 18: Mr. John Green (1865). Charles Walter. Engraving. State Library of Victoria, IAN25/08/65/13.	129
Figure 19: Albert Le Souëf (1872). Thomas Foster Chuck. Photograph. State Library of Victoria, H5056/567.	130
Figure 20: William Barak (1876). Photograph. National Archives of Australia, A1200, L22062.	135
Figure 21: General view of Aboriginal Mission Station, Coranderrk (1880). Fred Kruger. Photograph. State Library of Victoria, H2006.123/9.	138
Figure 22: Extract from a vocabulary of the Kamilaroi, Leichardt River, supplied by Montagu Curr. Edward M. Curr, 1886, *The Australian Race* (Melbourne: John Ferres, Govt. Printer), vol. II, 320.	146
Figure 23: Title Page of *The Australian Race* signed by Edward M. Curr. Menzies Library, The Australian National University.	150
Figure 24: R. Brough Smyth (c.1880). George Gordon McCrae. Drawing. National Library of Australia, nla.pic-an6312205.	158
Figure 25: R. Brough Smyth's 'fish-hook'. Edward M. Curr, 1886, *The Australian Race* (Melbourne: John Ferres, Govt. Printer), vol I, 146-47.	159
Figure 26: James Dawson (1892). Johnstone, O'Shannessy & Co. Photograph. State Library of Victoria, H2998/84.	161
Figure 27: A.W. Howitt (1895). Johnstone, O'Shannessy & Co. Photograph. State Library of Victoria, IAN01/08/95/4.	167
Figure 28: Edward M. Curr (c.1880). Photograph courtesy of Ian G. Curr.	202

Acknowledgments

This book began its life as a doctoral thesis in the School of Historical Studies at the University of Melbourne. I was extremely fortunate to be supervised by Patricia Grimshaw; her dedication to mentoring is renowned and her support, advice and encouragement were crucially important. My two associate supervisors – the late David Philips, and Ann Genovese from the Faculty of Law – also deserve particular thanks. I am indebted to the many other staff members and fellow students who helped shape the project with their comments and support, including Joanna Cruickshank, Fiona Davis, Penny Edmonds, Julie Evans, Don Garden, Felicity Jensz, Rob McArthur, Claire McClisky, Erica Millar, Marg Stephens, Shurlee Swain, Patrick Wolfe and Bart Ziino.

My more recent colleagues in the School of History, Research School of Social Sciences, The Australian National University, provided a highly stimulating intellectual environment that helped me transform my thesis into a book. The school is home to both the National Centre of Biography and the Australian Centre for Indigenous History, both leading centres in disciplines so closely associated with my topic. Particular thanks must go to Nicholas Brown, Karen Fox, Paul Irish, Rani Kerin, Shino Konishi, Ann McGrath, Melanie Nolan, Maria Nugent and Martin Thomas.

I received valuable assistance from the staff of numerous research libraries, including the State Library of Victoria, the State Library of New South Wales, the National Library of Australia, the British Library, the Baillieu Library, and the ANU Library. I also owe a debt to the Public Record Office of Victoria, the National Archives of Australia, the Royal Historical Society of Victoria, and the National Archives of the UK.

I thank warmly Wayne Atkinson, a Yorta Yorta elder, and playwright Andrea James, both of whom generously offered their views on the significance of Edward Curr to their people. I was also privileged to meet several of Curr's descendants, who shared their thoughts and their family archive, including Pamela Curr, Ian and Elinor Curr, and Andrew and Belinda Curr.

To the board of Aboriginal History, and in particular to the monographs editor Rani Kerin, I offer my sincere thanks for recognising the value of my work and agreeing to publish it. Thank you also to the reviewers of my manuscript, Ann Curthoys and Russell McGregor, whose insightful comments were crucial to the completion of the book.

Rebecca Bennett and Erica Millar did a wonderful job proofreading my thesis, and I thank Geoff Hunt for his thorough work on the book manuscript. For assistance with images I am indebted to the various institutions acknowledged in the text, to Christine Fernon and Maxim Korolev, and to Peter Johnson, who designed the maps. For cover design and production I am grateful to the staff of ANU E Press, particularly Lorena Kanellopoulos and Duncan Beard. Publication of this book was also supported by a subsidy from The Australian National University.

My family and friends have been unerringly supportive of this project over a long period, particularly my parents, Cate and Clem Furphy, but none more so than my wife, Rebecca, to whom I offer my most profound thanks.

Prologue:
'Claim sunk by pen of a swordsman'

When the High Court of Australia rejected the final appeal in the Yorta Yorta native title case in December 2002, a headline in *The Age* announced: 'Claim sunk by pen of a swordsman'.[1] The man in question was Edward M. Curr (1820-1889), who was certainly fond of fencing in his youth, but is better known as the author of *Recollections of Squatting in Victoria* (1883), an engaging account of his early life as a pastoralist on the Goulburn and Murray rivers. In 1841 Curr was among the first squatters to occupy land belonging to ancestors of the Yorta Yorta people, described by Curr as 'the Bangerang Tribe'.[2] His nostalgic memoir is one of very few written accounts of Indigenous life in the early years of the pastoral invasion of northern Victoria. The apparent failure of Yorta Yorta people to maintain traditions identifiable with those that Curr had described was a key reason for the defeat of their native title claim.

Born in Hobart in 1820, Curr was the first son of English-Catholic immigrant parents. His father was an influential businessman and politician, who played a prominent role in the early colonial affairs of Van Diemen's Land and the Port Phillip District of New South Wales (later Victoria). Curr himself was educated in England and France before managing his family's squatting runs for a decade. His pastoral endeavours were highly successful and the dispossession of the Indigenous owners was swift. He later experienced financial failure but recovered to forge a successful career as a government official in Victoria, rising to the senior position of Chief Inspector of Stock. From 1875 he was an influential member of the Board for the Protection of Aborigines during a highly controversial period; he doggedly pursued the closure of the Coranderrk Aboriginal reserve near Healesville, publicly displaying a profound paternalism and disregard for the wishes of the Indigenous people concerned. In the same period, he pursued an interest in Aboriginal languages and ethnology.

---

1   Fergus Shiel, 'Claim sunk by pen of a swordsman', *The Age*, 13 December 2002.
2   Throughout this book I use terms for Indigenous groups that were common among nineteenth century writers, notably those preferred by Edward M. Curr, including 'Bangerang', 'Towroonban', 'Wongatpan', and 'Ngooraialum'. Other terms such as 'Aboriginal', 'Indigenous', 'Maori', and 'Native' are used advisedly, recognising both their conceptual limitations and their broad utility.

Figure 1: Edward M. Curr.

Engraving. State Library of Victoria, H15062.

Curr's life is a remarkable enough example of a colonial career to warrant investigation: his broad experience of pastoralism, public administration and Indigenous-settler relations ensure that his life is relevant to several major themes of historical interest. Yet it is his literary legacy that provides the most compelling case for a detailed biographical study. Curr wrote with humour, insight and flair, regularly quoting classic works to illustrate his points in an engaging literary style. It was his ability to write well that established his reputation as a man of ability. He published four major works in his lifetime, including a prize-winning essay on scab in sheep, a treatise on horse breeding, his memoir of squatting and a four-volume ethnological work, *The Australian Race*, which was published by the Victorian Government. His best-known work is *Recollections of Squatting in Victoria*, which has had an enduring influence on Australian historiography. Scholars frequently consult Curr's memoir for an account of Victoria's early colonial history, including the lives of Australian squatters, the social world of the pastoral frontier, the environmental effects of pastoralism, and the prominent role of fire in Australian ecology. Curr's work has also been consulted for its detailed descriptions of the Aboriginal people he encountered during his squatting years.

The considerable influence of Curr's writings on Australian historiography first attracted my attention when I was a student of history at the University of Melbourne in the mid-1990s. I was already well aware of Curr's memoir, as it touched on the history of the region in northern Victoria where I spent most of my childhood. When taking university courses on environmental history and Aboriginal history, I discovered Curr's legacy was broader than I had earlier surmised. His influence was most clearly apparent in the late 1990s when the Yorta Yorta native title case was going through the courts; it was then that I realised a biographical study of Curr might be a productive contribution to what was then quite a passionate debate about history and the law of native title.

The sources available to a biographer of Curr are extensive, although they are certainly biased towards his public persona. Curr was a regular correspondent to newspapers and his views on many prominent issues have survived as a result of his public appointments. He gave evidence to commissions and inquiries and published several works of non-fiction. Less evidence remains, however, to provide an insight into his private world, his home life and relationships, making an intimate personal portrait elusive. The key exception is a family memoir written in 1877, which includes an account of his ancestry and a short outline of his life to that point. A copy is now held in the La Trobe Library in Melbourne. A variety of other documents are lodged with the Mitchell Library in Sydney, including a diary Curr wrote in France in 1838 and some of his later ethnological records. Curr's descendants have retained other valuable items, including photos, letters and heirlooms. It is not known if Curr collected personal correspondence, but it is possible that valuable material was lost when his son Ernest destroyed a large portion of the family's papers in the early twentieth century.[3] Nevertheless, by assembling a range of sources it is possible to paint a detailed picture of Curr's life.

The principal source for any biographer of Curr is, of course, *Recollections of Squatting in Victoria*, which provides a vivid account of his decade as a pastoralist, particularly the eventful years of the early 1840s when he established his family's squatting enterprise. As Curr wrote this account in the 1880s, however, it presents certain challenges to the biographer, particularly if a broadly chronological life story is the goal (as it is here). Curr wrote a memoir not a diary: his recollections are the product of a mature mind looking back on his youthful experiences. In many passages they reveal as much about his interests and preoccupations later in life as they do of his daily activities in his twenties. This is particularly true of his descriptions of Aboriginal people, their manners and customs. Moreover, his memoir can only occasionally be weighed against independent corroborating evidence, making it difficult to detect the potentially corrupting influences of both a fallible memory and a nostalgic outlook. Finally, *Recollections of Squatting in Victoria* is first and foremost a work of literature aimed at a British colonial readership. Curr's principal purpose was to write an engaging book. He apologised in his preface for publishing 'mere personal matters ... possibly of not a very representative sort', suggesting that he was conscious of the need to shape his recollections to please a broad readership.[4]

Curr's excuse for the publication of personal recollections was 'the contrast their relation exhibits between the past and the present state of things in Victoria'. This was no doubt a valid defence in the 1880s and remains so more than a century later. The historical value of Curr's work was recognised in 1965 when Melbourne University Press published an abridged edition of *Recollections of Squatting in Victoria*. Three years later the full work reappeared as a facsimile edition published by the Libraries Board of South Australia. These publications increased Curr's prominence among a new generation of historians and general readers. Unlike much nineteenth-century writing, Curr's prose remained easily accessible: a review of the new abridged version in the Hobart *Mercury* noted Curr's 'considerable powers of evoking a telling mental picture in words' and suggested that his recollections were 'as fresh and readable today as doubtless they were when first published'.[5] By 1980, Paul de Serville had concluded that

---

3   Curr, Edward A. 1979: 25.
4   Curr 1883.
5   Book Review, 'Recollections of Squatting in Victoria', *Mercury* (Hobart), 29 September 1965: 4.

the work was quite unique: 'As an historical record and as an unaffected work of art Curr's memoir stands alone – not even Boldrewood managed to capture the essence of a squatter's life in the 1840s'.[6]

Although scholars with a broad range of interests have found Curr's writings illuminating, those interested in environmental history have been particularly impressed. Curr's descriptions of landscape are vivid and compelling and his insightful descriptions of the effect of fire and pastoralism on the Australian continent have attracted praise. Stephen Pyne observed in 1991 that 'Edward Curr thought that it would be difficult to "overestimate" the consequences of the Aboriginal firestick'.[7] More recently, Bill Gammage looked to Curr before any other to provide a clear statement of his key thesis in *The Biggest Estate on Earth: How Aborigines Made Australia*. On the second page of his comprehensive book, Gammage quoted Curr's bold claim that 'it may perhaps be doubted whether any section of the human race has exercised a greater influence on the physical condition of any large portion of the globe than the wandering savages of Australia'.[8]

As we shall see, Curr's reception among scholars in the field of Aboriginal history has been more ambivalent, largely due to his role in Aboriginal administration. The entry for Curr in the *Australian Dictionary of Biography*, written by Harley W. Forster in the 1960s, does not record Curr's membership of the Board for the Protection of Aborigines. Forster relies primarily on Curr's memoir when he asserts that his 'approach to [Aboriginal] people … reveals sympathetic understanding'.[9] This is not a view shared by Diane Barwick, who insisted that Curr's approach to Aboriginal administration was characterised by 'ignorance and profound paternalism'.[10] Among those more directly interested in Curr's ethnographic writings, a surprisingly wide range of views have been expressed: in *Triumph of the Nomads* (1975) the historian Geoffrey Blainey described Curr as 'one of the sharpest observers of tribal life'; three decades later the legal scholar Ben Golder argued that Curr provided 'as perfect an example of crude racist stereotyping as it is possible to find among early colonial accounts of Indigenous people'.[11] A similar variation of views is evident among anthropologists: *The Australian Race* was roundly criticised by Curr's contemporary and rival A.W. Howitt, but nearly a century later A.P. Elkin numbered Curr (with Howitt) among 'the founders of social anthropology in Australia'.[12] Curr's legacy in this regard is clearly a complicated one and defies easy description.

---

6   De Serville 1980.
7   Pyne 1991: 103-104.
8   Gammage 2011: 2; Curr 1883: 189-190.
9   Forster 1969: 508.
10 Barwick 1998: 114-115.
11 Blainey 1975: 97; Golder 2004: 51.
12 Howitt 1889; Howitt 1891: 30-104; Elkin 1975: 1-24.

In the wake of the *Yorta Yorta* case, the value of Curr's writings on Aboriginal people became a major point of contention. The trial judge in the *Yorta Yorta* case, Justice Howard Olney, strongly favoured Curr's written account, arguing that he 'clearly established a degree of rapport with the local Aboriginal people'.[13] He posited Curr's writings as the principal yardstick against which legitimate Yorta Yorta tradition must be measured. In contrast, the judge largely rejected the credibility of Yorta Yorta oral testimony, which he viewed as inherently unreliable. The oral testimony was crucial to the claimants' argument that, while their traditions had evolved, they had nonetheless been continually observed since Curr's arrival in 1841. Justice Olney's rejection of the oral evidence and reliance on Curr thus played an important role in his final conclusion, which was that 'the tide of history' had 'washed away' Yorta Yorta native title rights.[14]

The idea that Curr's writings posthumously defeated the *Yorta Yorta* native title claim has a chilling irony about it, given his earlier appropriation of Yorta Yorta lands for pastoral purposes. Some Yorta Yorta people imagined a role for the 'Ghost of Edward Curr' in the failure of their claim.[15] Meanwhile, a wide range of scholars in law and history commented unfavourably on Curr's influence. The outcome of the case highlighted the extent to which the written word is granted special status as evidence. It was a stark demonstration of the narrowly defined approach to historical inquiry that prevails in the native title courts. Furthermore, the case epitomised a clear disjuncture between historians and lawyers regarding their methodological and theoretical approaches to knowing the past; it led many to question the possibility of sophisticated and nuanced historical inquiry in the native title context. During the long *Yorta Yorta* claim, therefore, Edward M. Curr became something of an historical celebrity, highlighting the need for a detailed appraisal of his life, his biases, his opinions, and his attitudes towards Aboriginal people. This book responds to that need by offering a biography of a man who more than a century after his death became a crucial witness in a major native title case.

---

13 *Members of the Yorta Yorta Aboriginal Community v Victoria* (1998) FCA 1606, [53].
14 *Yorta Yorta v Victoria* (1998), [129].
15 See, for example, the play by Andrea James: James 2003.

1. From Sheffield to Van Diemen's Land

Edward Micklethwaite Curr was born into an upwardly mobile middle-class English-Catholic family, which rose to prominence in Sheffield in the late eighteenth century. Family sources speculate that the Currs might have come to England from Scotland in the seventeenth century with the Court of James I, but very little is known for certain.[1] The family's rise in social status was principally due to the ingenuity and resourcefulness of John Curr, who was born in Durham in 1756. Edward M. Curr recorded that his grandfather trained as a civil engineer and, according to family reports, 'was a man of considerable ability, self-reliant, original, and hard-headed'.[2] As a young man John Curr found employment in the collieries of Sheffield, a coal-rich town on the brink of industrial transformation. Curr's abilities as a mining engineer were quickly recognised and in 1781 he was appointed 'Superintendent of the Coal Works of his Grace the Duke of Norfolk'. His rapid rise was attributable to his talents as an engineer and inventor.[3]

In 1776 John Curr was one of the first engineers to utilise flanged iron rails in a coalmine. The transportation of coal carts ('corves') along these rails was considerably more efficient than earlier methods. Curr also invented elaborate hauling machinery, which greatly increased the potential output of each pit. The people of Sheffield were initially suspicious of Curr's improvements, reflecting their general resentment of the House of Norfolk's tight control of the coal supply.[4] Furthermore, when Curr introduced his iron rails, the innovation was strongly resisted by the colliery workers, who perhaps suspected improvement in efficiency would threaten their jobs. According to Edward M. Curr, his grandfather's plan 'created such a feeling amongst the colliery population, that they threatened to take his life, so that he hid himself in a wood for three days, until the ferment had somewhat subsided'.[5]

---

1 Curr, Edward A. 1979.
2 Edward M. Curr, 'Memoranda Concerning Our Family' (1877), State Library of Victoria (SLV), La Trobe Library Manuscripts Collection, MS 8998.
3 For a detailed account of John Curr's career in the Sheffield collieries see Medlicott 1983: 51–60. See also Mott 1969: 1–23.
4 Leader 1901: 84.
5 Curr, 'Memoranda Concerning Our Family' (1877), SLV, MS 8998.

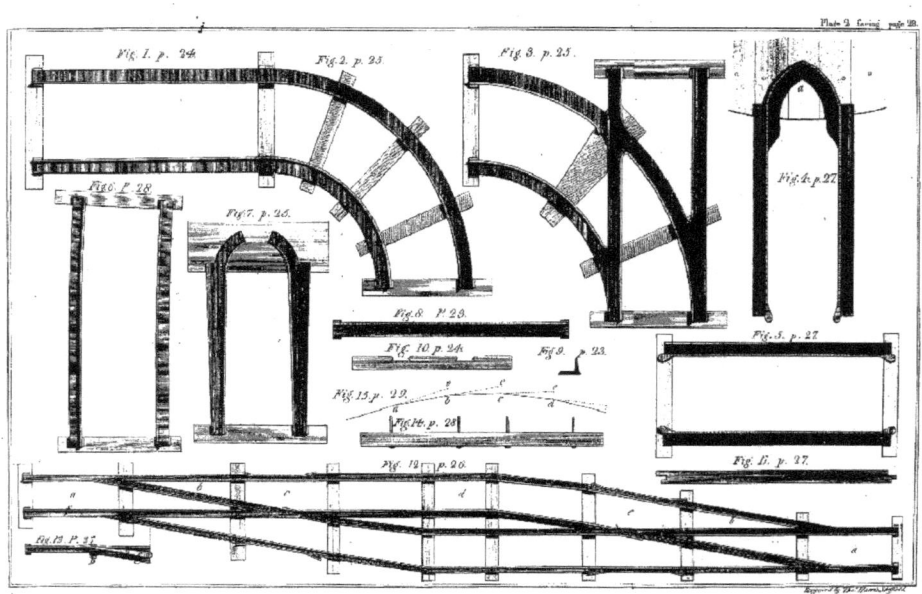
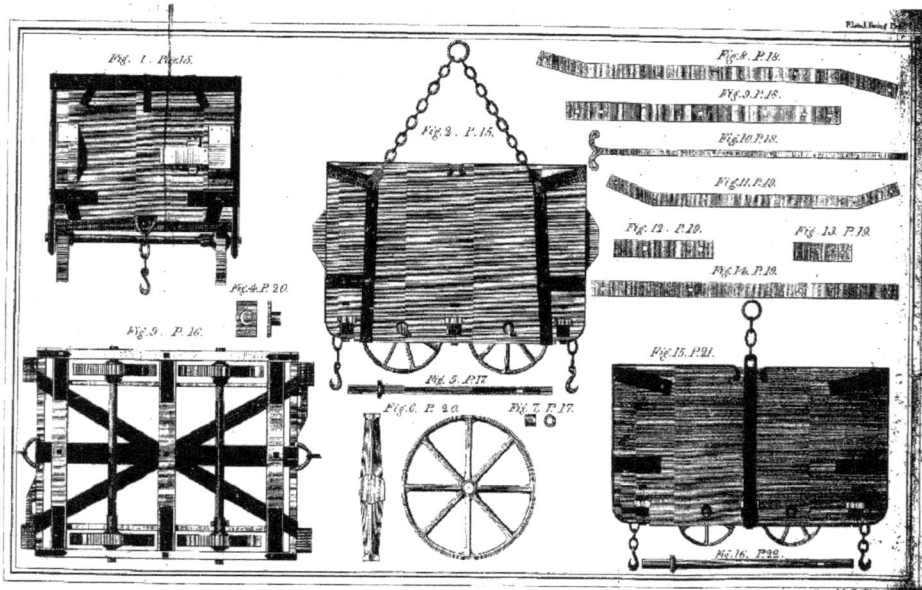

Figure 2: John Curr's rails and corves.

John Curr, 1797, *The Coal Viewer and Engine Builder's Practical Companion* (Sheffield: John Northall). Gale, Cengage Learning, *The Making of the Modern World*, 2012.

1. From Sheffield to Van Diemen's Land

Despite considerable opposition John Curr's technological improvements helped transform the British coal industry.[6] He took out a patent on his haulage technique, which proved highly lucrative as other collieries adopted the ingenious system.[7] At the height of his success, he published *The Coal Viewer and Engine Builder's Practical Companion*, which is now recognised as a significant text in the history of mining and engineering.[8] Despite his undoubted talents, John Curr was dismissed from his position as Superintendent of the Sheffield Collieries in 1801. During the early years of his management the mines' profitability had increased exponentially, but in the 1790s this trend reversed due to an economic depression in Sheffield and increased competition from new and existing collieries inspired by Curr's success. By 1801 the Sheffield collieries were working at a financial loss, prompting Curr's dismissal after more than 20 years' service.[9] Curr continued to apply his talents to various projects. He was the proprietor of the 'Queen's Foundry' in Duke Street, Sheffield, where he experimented with further improvements in mining technology. Between 1788 and 1813 he took out ten patents, most relating to the manufacture of rope and systems for its use in mines, on ships and for catching whales.[10]

The success of the Duke Street business and the royalties from his various patents enabled him to keep his family very well. On 1 May 1781 at the Cathedral of St Peter, Sheffield, John Curr had married Hannah Wilson. The couple raised six daughters and three sons and resided at Bellevue House, Sheffield Park, to the south-east of the town. The premises were extensive, reflecting the wealth and social standing of the Currs in Sheffield.[11] Clearly, John Curr can be credited with the rise in social status and financial security of the Curr family, which in turn laid the foundation for his descendants' business and pastoral successes in the Australian colonies. Edward M. Curr later recorded that his grandfather might have bequeathed more money to his descendants were it not for the foolish actions of a naïve priest named Pére Ductiône. Shortly before his death, John Curr apparently entrusted 30,000 pounds to the priest, with instructions to invest the sum 'in the French funds'. According to family legend, Ductiône 'took upon himself the responsibility of investing the whole sum in some mercantile bubble which he thought would be more profitable'. When the entire investment was lost in a shipwreck, the priest returned to face the late John Curr's executors, offering only a silk pocket-handkerchief as recompense. The episode became folklore for the family of Edward M. Curr:

---

6   The great value of John Curr's innovations was affirmed in a report by consultant the John Buddle in 1787. See John Buddle, 'Arundel Castle Manuscript', quoted in Medlicott 1999: 67.
7   Medlicott 1999: 74.
8   See Curr, John 1970.
9   Medlicott 1999: 73.
10 Bland 1930–31: 121–130. See also Medlicott 1999: 76.
11 Medlicott 1999: 77.

> Years afterwards when I was a young man this handkerchief was in the possession of my mother, who said to me telling the story, 'Eddie my boy, this handkerchief is all that your grandfather's family got for thirty thousand pounds'. God willed it should be so![12]

John Curr had died in January 1823 and was buried in Sheffield at St Marie's Church, which he had been instrumental in establishing.[13] Edward M. Curr never met his grandfather, but described him as 'a very exemplary and sterling Catholic'. He spent some time with his grandmother as a young boy: 'She was an old lady, benevolent, strict and starch.' He had very little to do with his six aunts, but his two uncles, John and Joseph, all figured more prominently in his life. Curr described his uncle John in the following terms: 'Unlike the rest of the family, he was a little man but a good horse man, painted well and had studied engineering, in which science he was well read.'[14] In about 1833 he migrated to Van Diemen's Land and later to New South Wales, but according to Edward M. Curr he 'married beneath him' and became poor in the colonies. In the 1840s he travelled back to England to promote his theories on steam powered ocean navigation; although he published his views in 1847, his suggested techniques were not adopted by shipowners.[15] Joseph Curr, like two of his sisters, chose a life in service of the church; he was a well-respected Catholic priest whom Edward M. Curr often saw during his education in England. Curr described his uncle as 'a very exemplary man'.[16] In 1829 Joseph had written a book on the sacraments and the duties of Catholics titled *Familiar Instructions in the Faith and Morality of the Catholic Church*, which was published in at least three editions.[17] He spent some time as a priest in his native Sheffield. In 1847 he moved to Leeds to minister to victims of a typhus epidemic and subsequently fell victim to the disease himself.[18]

Edward Curr senior (the father of Edward M. Curr) was born at Bellevue House on 1 July 1798. He received a first class Catholic education in England and according to his son 'was well up in the classics and a good mathematician'. To round out his education, he was placed in the service of a merchant's office in Liverpool for two years. Due to the success and fortune of his father, Edward Curr senior did not lack opportunity: apart from his fine education, he was given 'three or four thousand pounds … to begin the world with' and 'the choice of any business or profession which he might elect to follow'.[19] A budding man of Empire, Curr formed the view that the colonies offered the best chance to

---

12 Curr, 'Memoranda Concerning Our Family' (1877), SLV, MS 8998.
13 Hadfield 1889: 32.
14 Curr, 'Memoranda Concerning Our Family' (1877), SLV, MS 8998.
15 Curr, John 1847.
16 Curr, 'Memoranda Concerning Our Family' (1877), SLV, MS 8998.
17 Curr, Rev. Joseph 1829.
18 'Rev. Joseph Curr', <http://www.newadvent.org/cathen/04573b.htm> (Accessed October 2005).
19 Curr, 'Memoranda Concerning Our Family' (1877), SLV, MS 8998.

develop his career and expand his fortune. In 1817 he sailed to Brazil, where he stayed for several months and learnt to speak Portuguese. Edward M. Curr recalled his father 'made some long trips inland, and saw a good deal of the country'; he also met the celebrated naturalist Charles Waterton. Edward M. Curr's sister Elizabeth recorded that Brazil made a lasting impression on her father: '[he] often told me of the gorgeous flowers, the magnificent trees and the beautiful pacing horses'.[20] Ultimately, Brazil did not sufficiently appeal to Curr. His son Edward later wrote 'the state and customs of the country were not to his liking', while his daughter Elizabeth was more specific: 'the laws of the country pertaining to slavery were very distasteful to him'. Accordingly, Edward Curr senior returned to England to ponder where else he might venture.

In 1819 Edward Curr increased his fortune by marrying Elizabeth Micklethwaite, 'with whom he received a considerable amount of money'.[21] Elizabeth was a granddaughter of Richard Micklethwaite, the 4th Lord of Ardsley, whose family had resided for generations near Barnsley in Yorkshire.[22] She was the posthumous child of Benjamin Micklethwaite, whom Edward M. Curr later described as 'a dashing horseman, good shot, practical joker, and a rather hard drinking squire'. Benjamin had married Sarah Lister in 1795, but died in January 1798, four months before the birth of Elizabeth. Curr recalled that his mother 'was noted in youth for a dignified and friendly manner, and great personal beauty'. She married Edward Curr senior at Bellevue House on 30 June 1819 in a Catholic ceremony, but the service was repeated in a Protestant church the following day to satisfy English law.[23] His pockets filled with 'three or four thousand pounds' from his father and 'a considerable amount of money' from the family of his new wife, Edward Curr was ready to embark on his next colonial business venture.

Hobart Town

Soon after his marriage, Edward Curr entered into a business partnership with a London merchant, John Raine, who was about to sail for Van Diemen's Land. Curr arrived in Hobart in February 1820 and purchased a home in Davey Street, which he named 'Bellevue House' after his father's Sheffield residence. Curr subsequently found it difficult to dispose of his merchandise in Hobart and soon fell out with his business partner. Raine became insolvent in 1822 and Curr was only partially successful in recovering his debts. In the meantime, Curr visited Sydney and formed a new partnership with Horatio William Mason, an innkeeper

---

20 Elizabeth Pennefather, 'In the Early Days', (1911), Murrumbogie Papers.
21 Curr, 'Memoranda Concerning Our Family' (1877), SLV, MS 8998.
22 *Burke's Landed Gentry*, 17th edition, 1952.
23 Curr, 'Memoranda Concerning Our Family' (1877), SLV, MS 8998.

and merchant.[24] He developed an advantageous association with the lieutenant governor of Van Diemen's Land, William Sorell, and was appointed to Sorell's council in October 1820, when only 22 years of age.[25] He also served in the Deputy Judge Advocate's Court and on several committees of inquiry. Like his father in Sheffield, Curr became a leader in the Catholic community, hosting services in his store after the arrival of Father Philip Conolly in 1821. He was the treasurer of a fund to build a church and a home for Conolly in Harrington Street.[26]

While in Hobart, Edward Curr senior showed the first outward signs of a proud, tough and uncompromising demeanour, which, although certainly a factor behind his many business and political achievements, had the tendency to alienate his fellow citizens. He brought several actions for repayment of money lent by him in 'notes of hand'. He also appeared in court in July 1822 charged with assaulting his assigned servant, Frederick Davis, for failing to attend to his duties: 'He had beaten Davis insensible with blows from an axe handle.'[27]

Following his father's death in Sheffield, Curr dissolved his partnership with Mason and returned to England. Evidently, John Curr had funds invested in his son's activities, so his death might have released Edward from a familial obligations to remain in Hobart. Edward M. Curr later recorded that his father 'had not found Van Diemen's Land to his liking' and was happy to leave with his young family in June 1823.[28] While in Hobart, Elizabeth Curr had born two sons: Edward Micklethwaite was born on Christmas Day 1820 and William Talbot on 7 March 1822. A third son, Richard, was born off the coast of New Zealand on 22 June 1823 as the family was returning to England. Edward M. Curr later recalled how his brother Richard earned his nickname: 'After a New Zealand Chief, well known to fame at the time, my little brother was long called Shungy.'[29]

Edward Curr senior utilised the return journey well by writing *An Account of the Colony of Van Diemen's Land*, which was published in London in 1824.[30] Curr's book advocated the recreation of a model British society in the Antipodes, but pessimistically concluded that such an ideal was rarely achieved. He was not entirely dismissive of the colony's potential, but rather suggested that it provided a challenging opening for the respectable English immigrant with capital to invest. Curr did admit, however, on presenting a copy of his book to the Colonial Secretary, Lord Bathurst, in 1825, that 'it gives what might be considered rather an unfavourable and discouraging account of the colony'.[31]

---

24 Pike 1966: 269–272.
25 Von Stieglitz 1952: 17.
26 Robson 1983: 124.
27 Von Stieglitz 1952: 24.
28 Curr, 'Memoranda Concerning Our Family' (1877), SLV, MS 8998.
29 Curr, 'Memoranda Concerning Our Family' (1877), SLV, MS 8998.
30 Curr, Edward 1824.
31 Edward Curr to Lord Bathurst (Colonial Secretary), 31 March 1825, PRO, CO 280/1, Colonial Office: Tasmania, Original Correspondence.

Curr had 'many tiffs' with a rival author, George Daniel, who was preparing his own work on Van Diemen's Land, but Curr confided in Daniel that he was very proud of his 'little work': 'I send it like the Dove from the Ark and I wait anxiously to see if it returns with a green branch in its mouth.'[32] His hopes were soon realised.

The Van Diemen's Land Company

The influence of his book and the continuing patronage of Colonel Sorell ensured that Curr caught the eye of the Van Diemen's Land Company, a newly formed agricultural company in London that hoped to obtain a large grant of land in the distant colony. According to Edward M. Curr the undertaking 'was considered at the time to be the most important of anything of the sort, south of the equator'.[33] Recently returned from Hobart, Colonel Sorell was a personal friend of at least one of the directors of the new company and was invited to advise the board on conditions in Van Diemen's Land. Sorell enlisted the assistance of Curr, who met the board in December 1824. Curr subsequently became a significant shareholder in the new venture and was appointed Agent with an impressive salary of £800 a year. He was integrally involved in lobbying the British Government for the necessary land grant.[34] That Curr was appointed to this position at such a young age says much for his ability and for the quality of his business and political connections.

The growing Curr family returned to Van Diemen's Land via Spain and Brazil, arriving in Hobart in March 1826. Curr senior quickly made his mark as a significant new power in the colony; he carried letters of introduction and despatches from Lord Bathurst, which he delivered to the lieutenant governor, George Arthur. As D.H. Pike later observed: 'The company was powerfully backed, and with great caution Arthur invited Curr to join the Legislative Council.'[35] Curr recorded that he was ambivalent about the appointment and that his loyalties lay first and foremost with the Van Diemen's Land Company, not Arthur's council. K.R. Von Stieglitz, historian of the Van Diemen's Land Company, has explained that Curr aligned himself with commercial interests in the colony: 'He considered himself to be a link between the Hobart Town merchants and the Governor, as commercial men were not generally received at Government House.'[36]

---

32 Pike 1966: 269–272.
33 See Curr, 'Memoranda Concerning Our Family' (1877), SLV, MS 8998.
34 See correspondence between Curr and the Colonial Office on 4 February 1825, 22 March 1825, 31 March 1825, 15 April 1825, 18 April 1825, 31 August 1825; PRO, CO 280/1, Colonial Office: Tasmania, Original Correspondence.
35 Pike 1966: 269–272.
36 Von Stieglitz 1952: 19. Curr did resign from the Legislative Council in 1827.

Figure 3: Van Diemen's Land Company's establishment at Circular Head. John Arrowsmith.

Lithograph. James Bischoff, 1832, *Sketch of the History of Van Diemen's Land* (London: J. Richardson). Australian National Maritime Museum, 00048295.

By September 1826 Curr had selected Circular Head (modern-day Stanley) as the company's headquarters, but lobbied for the company's grant of 250,000 acres to be made in separate blocks, rather than the one contiguous square that the charter stipulated. Arthur opposed this course bitterly and wrote to Lord Bathurst in November that 'scarcely less than one fourth of the whole island' would satisfy Curr.[37] The company soon became the subject of considerable jealousy among the general populace. On 9 December 1826 the *Colonial Times* published a hostile report of both Curr and the company, to which Curr strongly objected; the newspaper was subsequently forced to print a reluctant apology.[38] By 1840, when David Burn wrote an account of the company for *The Colonial Magazine*, the negative feelings regarding the company were well established:

> The colonists entertained sanguine hopes that the large capital, said to be at this company's disposal, would tend greatly ... to the general improvement of the island. Such, however, did not prove to be the case,– the company took their overgrown grant at Circular Head – became settlers upon an extensive scale – attempted no beneficial

---

37 Pike 1966: 269–272.
38 Von Stieglitz 1952: 18.

public measure,– contributing even less than others to the general advancement,– in fact, were scarcely even heard of save as large landed monopolizers.[39]

This resentment derived partly from the company's extensive rights and privileges, but also from Edward Curr's overbearing manner. One of Curr's official roles was magistrate for the north of the colony, a position that gave him significant power and autonomy. Von Stieglitz has described the company's land as a 'colony within a colony, with Edward Curr as its Governor'.[40] A critical *Hobart Town Almanack* once described him as 'the Potentate of the North'[41] and disagreements between Curr and the administration in Hobart were frequent.

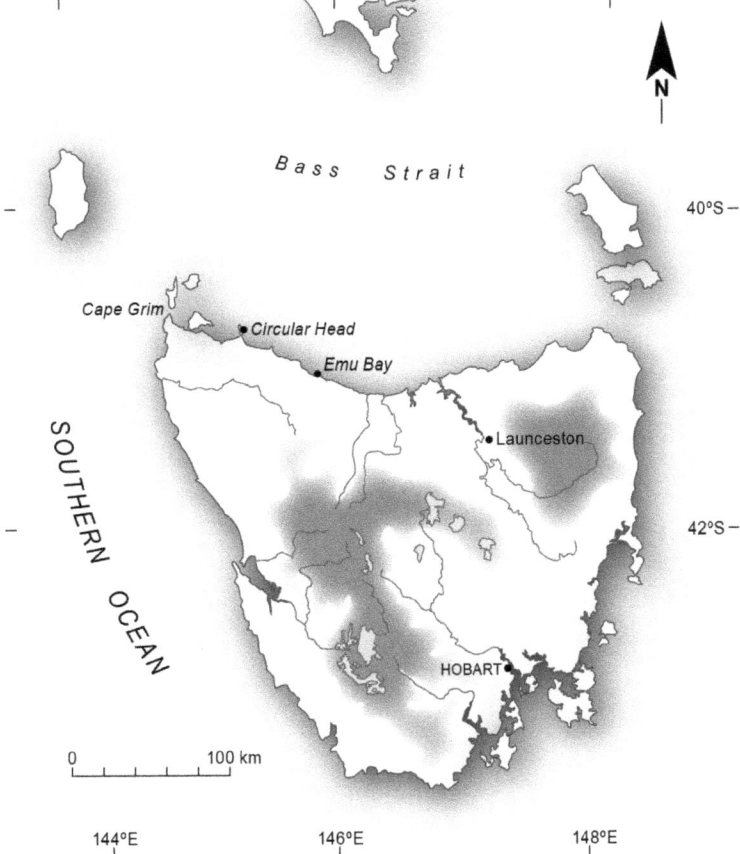

Figure 4: Van Diemen's Land.

Map by Peter Johnson.

---

39 Burn 1973: 27.
40 Von Stieglitz 1952: 7.
41 Von Stieglitz 1952: 29.

Edward Curr reputedly became a very good judge of sheep during his time with the Van Diemen's Land Company. He convinced the directors to spend over £40,000 introducing Saxony merino sheep to the colony. A newspaper later reported: 'From these, the leading Australian flocks have drawn much of their blood.'[42] Curr must have passed his good judgement of stock to his son Edward M. Curr, who later became Chief Inspector of Sheep for the Victorian Government. The introduction of sheep was, however, extremely disruptive to the traditional Indigenous economy; consequently, the company's poor relationship with Indigenous people was a prominent feature of its early years.

The Cape Grim Massacre

Over a period of three months from late 1827, several employees of the Van Diemen's Land Company were involved in a series of violent clashes with Aborigines culminating in the 'Cape Grim Massacre' in February 1828. The revisionist historian Keith Windschuttle has attempted to downplay the extent of violence at Cape Grim.[43] In a well-researched response, however, Ian McFarlane successfully refuted Windschuttle's claims, providing a shocking account of this troubled period.[44] A key source of evidence is the journal of George Augustus Robinson, who recorded that sexually exploitative behaviour by the company's men provoked a response in December 1827: 'The aboriginal females said that the Company's shepherds had got the native women into their hut and wanted to take liberties with them, that the men resented it and speared one man in the thigh.'[45] Shortly afterwards Aborigines speared some of the company's sheep and threw them off a cliff. Employees then mounted an attack on the Cape Grim Aborigines from the company's ship the *Fanny*, during which 12 Aborigines were killed. The 'Cape Grim Massacre' itself occurred in the remote north-west on 10 February 1828. Robinson's key source was a convict, Charles Chamberlain, as he recorded in his journal in 1830:

> Interrogated a man of the name of Chamberlain, one of the four men who shot the natives. 'How many natives do you suppose there was killed?' – 'Thirty'. 'There appears to be some difference respecting the numbers'. – 'Yes, it was so. We was afraid and thought at the time the Governor would hear of it and we should get into trouble, but thirty was about the number'. 'What did you do with the bodies?' – 'We threw them down the rocks where they had thrown the sheep'. ... 'What had they

---

42 State Library Victoria, *Historical Press Cuttings*, Vol 4a, 135. See also Massy 2007.
43 Windschuttle 2002: 249–287.
44 McFarlane 2003: 277–298.
45 George Augustus Robinson, 21 June 1830, in Plomley 1966: 181–182.

done to you?' – 'They had some time before attacked us in a hut and had speared one man in the thigh. Several blacks was shot on that occasion. Subsequently thirty sheep had been driven over the rocks'.[46]

The fine details of the debate surrounding the massacre (including the number of Aborigines killed during the various encounters) are well canvassed by McFarlane, but it is worth considering further the role played by Edward Curr senior. The available evidence suggests that, although Curr was not personally involved in the violence and expressed written disapproval of at least one incident, the conflict had his tacit support. His written reports (to both his directors in London and to the authorities in Hobart) consistently downplayed the extent of violence and the culpability of the company. Furthermore, he clearly neglected his role as a magistrate by failing to investigate the Cape Grim Massacre and other incidents.

Curr's inaccurate reporting of events was first evident in his account of the raid mounted from the company's ship in early January 1828. Curr wrote to his directors on 14 January that the crew of the *Fanny* 'were obliged to retreat without firing a shot', thus concealing 12 Aboriginal deaths.[47] In contrast, a disinterested visitor at Circular Head and guest of the Curr family, Rosalie Hare, wrote in her diary on 19 January 1828: 'The Master of the Company's cutter *Fanny*, assisted by four shepherds and his crew, surprised a party and killed twelve.'[48] Regarding the Cape Grim Massacre itself, Curr never recorded casualties remotely approaching a figure of 30, but in fact revised his tally downwards from six to three when he belatedly reported the events to George Arthur in Hobart.[49] As McFarlane has argued, any uncertainty regarding the number of Aborigines who died at Cape Grim can be blamed on Edward Curr's negligence as a Justice of the Peace: 'there was no trial, no investigation nor even a rudimentary investigation into the incident'.[50] That an event as horrific as the Cape Grim Massacre could occur, yet remain unknown to the authorities in Hobart for nearly two years, is clear evidence that Curr was not fulfilling his duties. There seems only one plausible reason for his lack of action: he believed the violence against the Aborigines at Cape Grim constituted legitimate defence of company property, but lacked the confidence to test this theory by informing the lieutenant governor.

News of the Cape Grim Massacre eventually reached George Arthur in a letter from a senior company employee, Alexander Goldie, who was under pressure to explain his alleged role as an accessory to the murder of an Aboriginal woman

---

46 George Augustus Robinson, 16 June 1830, in Plomley 1966: 175.
47 Quoted in McFarlane 2003: 280.
48 Lee 1927: 41.
49 McFarlane 2003: 289–291.
50 McFarlane 2003: 281.

at Emu Bay on 21 August 1829.[51] Goldie, who had responsibility for the alleged murderers, reported the incident to Curr in a letter dated 16 September 1829. Curr was outraged: 'That the killing of this woman amounts to murder in the moral sense, I have no doubt whatever, and as little that you are a guilty accessory to the crime.'[52] Within two months Goldie wrote to Arthur in an attempt to justify his actions. He outlined the general state of violence, including the Cape Grim Massacre, and explained that Curr had never investigated any incident, even those preceding the declaration of martial law in November 1828. Goldie explained that many Aborigines had been shot by company servants and added: 'On one occasion a good many were shot … and although Mr Curr knew it, yet he never that I am aware, took any notice of it although in the Commission of the Peace'.[53] Goldie was taking the 'Nuremberg' defence to his indictable actions: he hoped to show that he (and the other men involved) were only ever acting in the best interests of their employer and had the tacit support of Curr until the events became public and the company needed a scapegoat.

As it was, Curr was still quite reluctant to investigate the murder at Emu Bay. He wrote to his directors: 'it is apparent that I cannot escape the painful duty of investigating that occurrence myself as I sincerely hoped I might have done'.[54] His inquiry was consequently very brief: he visited Emu Bay in December 1829 and took a statement from the storekeeper, Thomas Watson, but he did not interview any of the men actually involved in the murder. Ultimately, he concluded that the recent proclamation of martial law prevented him from charging the perpetrators with murder, a conclusion supported by the Solicitor-General.[55] Nevertheless, the Emu Bay murder drew George Arthur's attention to the wider issue of violence in Van Diemen's Land Company territory. Curr's subsequent correspondence with the Governor reveals his view that violence against Aborigines was justified when it involved protecting company property:

> They have pilfered a little, it is true, but this I freely forgive, for it is probable they see no difference between us taking their kangaroos and their taking our flour and sugar. … I certainly will not sanction their being fired upon in retaliation for such an offence. If they attack our flocks again I should consider the case to be quite different. To steal what is of use to them may be consistent with notions of amity, and I think it is, but if they should commit a wholesale slaughter of our stock it can have no other motive than our expulsion and it will justify our taking strong measures in our defence.[56]

---

51 For details of the murder, see the journal of G.A. Robinson, 4 August 1830, in Plomley 1966: 192.
52 Curr to Goldie, 30 September 1829, in Plomley 1966: 235, note 133.
53 Alexander Goldie to Governor Arthur, 18 November 1830, quoted in McFarlane 2003: 285.
54 Lennox 1990.
55 Plomley 1966: 235, note 133.
56 Edward Curr to Governor Arthur, quoted in Lee 1927: 180.

While Edward Curr senior condemned certain acts of violence towards Aborigines, he justified others on the grounds of self-defence or the protection of company property. In a submission to the Aborigines Committee of 1830 in Hobart, he wrote: 'The Crown sells us lands, and is therefore bound to make good our titles and possession against previous occupants and claimants.'[57] In this way, Curr laid the blame for the 'Aboriginal problem' squarely at the feet of the British Government and asserted the primacy of the property rights of his company. As later chapters will show, these views were not dissimilar to those of his son, Edward M. Curr, who expressed regret at unnecessary acts of frontier violence, but ultimately saw conflict as an inevitable and justifiable consequence of colonial invasion.

A Privileged Childhood

Edward M. Curr's earliest recorded memory concerns his family's voyage from England to Van Diemen's Land, during which he visited Madeira and Rio de Janeiro: 'None of my recollections of life are half so enchanting as those which refer to foreign countries in which I landed ... in my early childhood'.[58] Arriving in Hobart in March 1826, the Curr family first resided at Bellevue House, their former home in Davey Street, which they rented from its new owner. For nearly two years, while Edward Curr senior established his company's headquarters at Circular Head, Elizabeth Curr remained in Hobart with her growing family. She was to bear 15 children: her nine sons were Edward, William, Richard, Charles, Walter, Arthur, Marmaduke, Julius and Montagu, while her daughters were Agnes, Augusta, Julia, Elizabeth, Florence and Geraldine.

In November 1827 the family sailed to Circular Head and moved into a small cottage known as Highfield House, which should not be confused with the later manor house of the same name. An early visitor of the Curr family was Rosalie Hare, the young wife of a ship's captain, whose vessel delivered fresh supplies and new employees to the Van Diemen's Land Company. Rosalie Hare was a guest of the Currs from January until March 1828 and recorded many details of her visit in her diary.[59] She observed that many of her husband's passengers were not enthusiastic about their new working conditions: their 'fancy visions' were dashed as they were greeted with 'tents, bark huts and huge mountains', rather than 'comfortable houses as they had been used to see in England'. Hare's description of Circular Head itself displays considerable ambivalence; the signs of civilisation the young woman could readily identify balanced its undeveloped and wild prospect:

---

57 Edward Curr, Submission to the Aborigines Committee, AOT CSO 1/323/7578, vol 8, p 374, quoted in McFarlane 2003: 290.
58 Curr, 'Memoranda Concerning Our Family' (1877), SLV, MS 8998.
59 Lee 1927: 33–43.

Figure 5: Elizabeth Curr (c.1850).

Photograph courtesy of Ian G. Curr.

> This was indeed a new scene! The Head justly called Circular presented a rather desolate sight … Mr. Curr's house, equal to a genteel English farm-house, stood on the top of a hill called Ladder Hill on account of a rude narrow path with here and there a few steps dug out of the earth leading to the house.
>
> Near the house is a garden which supplies the settlers with vegetables – a fine piece of ground neatly laid out and very flourishing, vegetables every season … Round the house are cornfields and we had the satisfaction of seeing the first harvest gathered in. There are also beautiful plains not far distant called Western, Eastern and Lovely Plains, where most of the sheep are kept in good pasture. The large number of snakes in the grass prevented my going to see them.
>
> This part of the settlement is very woody, and I was much pleased with the beautiful little parrots and cockatoos constantly flying about; the kangaroos skipping on their hind legs are also very curious … They are very fine stewed into what is here called a steamer. I had an opportunity of frequently tasting them. Mrs. Curr's son had a small kangaroo, tamed in some measure, about the house.

Hare does not mention Edward M. Curr specifically apart from her brief reference to his pet kangaroo, but she later wrote: 'Many cheerful hours have I spent at Highfield House with my friend (Mrs. Curr): many pleasant rambles have we had together with the interesting little children.'

As has been noted, Hare recorded important details regarding company relations with Aborigines in this period. It is impossible to say what knowledge seven-year-old Edward had of these events; he might have been shielded from many details, but must surely have learned something of the conflict when he grew older. In her diary Hare also described visits to Highfield by Aboriginal women, one of whom warranted an entry of several lines:

> She had learned a little English and appeared more intelligent than most of her race. She was astonished at all she saw, particularly at the chairs, tables and beds, never before having seen any other dwelling-house than a hut of the bark of trees made over a hole dug in the earth with a fire at the entrance. She insisted, much against my inclination and Mrs. Curr's also, upon kissing us and the children.

Hare was also appalled to observe the result of cruelty to Aboriginal girls by sealers in the region: 'How was my very soul shocked when two of these girls took off their kangaroo-skin coats and showed the inhuman cuts these European monsters had given them.' She reported that Mrs Curr's 'feelings were instantly aroused' for the youngest girl and that she had contemplated recruiting her to take care of the children. According to Hare such a course was deemed too dangerous, 'as they have been frequently tried as servants, but universally proved traitorous'.

Edward M. Curr himself recorded virtually no details of the two years he spent at Circular Head. In 1829 he and two brothers, William and Richard, were sent to England to commence their formal education. Curr later recalled the excitement of the voyage, during which the ship was hit by a fierce storm and pursued by pirates.[60] In December 1829 the three Curr boys arrived at Stonyhurst College, Lancashire.[61] Their new school was a Jesuit institution that traced its origins to the College of St Omer's, which was founded in northern France in 1592. St Omer's was set up as one of the 'seminaries beyond the seas' during the anti-Catholic Elizabethan period in England. Nearly two centuries later a tumultuous period for Jesuit institutions saw the College driven north to modern-day Belgium. By 1794 Protestant fervour in England had waned, allowing the College to open at its present site in Lancashire. A former pupil provided a neglected mansion called 'Stonyhurst', where the College has been located ever since.[62]

In the 1820s Stonyhurst housed up to 250 students and approximately 50 clergy.[63] Curr and his brothers commenced their education at the preparatory school 'Hodder', which was a short distance away from the main campus and concentrated on the basics of spelling, reading, writing and grammar. Once they were admitted to Stonyhurst College proper, the boys progressed through six year-long classes, which were designated Abecedarians, Figuritians, Grammar, Syntax, Poets and Rhetoricians. A College Prospectus from the period states first and foremost that 'the Scholars are instructed with great care in the duties of religion and morality'. It also outlines the secular curriculum including 'a full course of Classical Education, ... Reading and Elocution, Writing, English, French, Arithmetic, and Geography'. The more advanced students received tuition in 'History, Algebra and Geometry ... Logic, Natural Philosophy ... Chemistry, and the Higher Mathematics'.[64]

Discipline at the College was firm: the children rose each day at 5.30am and washed before chapel at 6am; the day was carefully divided between study, instruction, meals and leisure time, before bed at 8.30pm. Holidays lasted for only five weeks each summer and children were forbidden from leaving the College at other times; the College even discouraged trips home during the vacation period, as 'such visits have been too often found to be followed by

---

60 Curr, 'Memoranda Concerning Our Family' (1877), SLV, MS 8998.
61 'Edward Curr (O.S. 1829)', *The Stonyhurst Magazine* 266 (1926): 67.
62 Gerard 1881.
63 'Stonyhurst College', *Monthly Magazine* (1823); copy supplied by Mr David Knight, College Librarian and Archivist.
64 'Stonyhurst College Prospectus' c.1844, supplied by David Knight. Mr Knight stated that in almost all respects the curriculum would have been the same in the 1830s.

idleness and discontent'.⁶⁵ The gravest punishment at Stonyhurst was known as 'a discipline' and consisted of 25 lashes from 'the cat'; it was apparently quite a rare occurrence and reserved for those on the verge of expulsion.⁶⁶

In addition to its academic curriculum, Stonyhurst fostered interest in the arts. The College reported in 1823: 'Each Superior unites to his official and academic duties some pursuit of taste; painting, sculpture, electricity, astronomy, mechanics, botany, herbiculture, agriculture, etc.'⁶⁷ Furthermore, tuition in music, drawing and dancing was made available to those who wished.⁶⁸ Edward M. Curr later recalled that his particular interest was literature, which he satisfied by 'writing reviews of works and also novels, poems, sermons and so forth'.⁶⁹ It was a privileged education for the Curr brothers, which cost their parents up to 50 guineas for each child per annum.⁷⁰

Edward, William and Richard spent eight years at Stonyhurst. Although they were very remote from their parents during this time, they were not altogether isolated from family. They had regular contact with their clerical uncle Joseph, who often visited Stonyhurst, and were contemporaries of their cousins John and Charles Curr (sons of their elder uncle John). Edward M. Curr also recalled vacation visits to his ageing grandmother Hannah Curr in Sheffield: 'She kept a pretty good house in Sheffield … we used to amuse ourselves by ringing all the bells in the house, the old lady fancying she heard a noise, but unable to make out what it was'. Despite these antics Curr remembered his grandmother fondly: 'The poor old lady was always very kind to me [and] took care not to flatter my vanity.'⁷¹ In 1833 the boys' parents briefly returned to England and took a house in Sheffield while Edward Curr senior reported to his company directors. Two more brothers, Charles and Walter, commenced schooling at Stonyhurst that year, while sisters Agnes and Augusta began their schooling at Preston, 14 miles away. The summer of 1833 was to be the last time Edward M. Curr saw his parents for over five years.

A Year in France

In August 1837 Edward, William and Richard Curr departed Stonyhurst and enrolled at St Edmunds College, Douai, in the north of France. The aim was

---

65 'Stonyhurst College Prospectus' c.1844.
66 Personal Communication, Mr David Knight, 6 November 2001.
67 Henderson 1986: 62.
68 'Stonyhurst College Prospectus' c.1844.
69 Curr, 'Memoranda Concerning Our Family' (1877), SLV, MS 8998.
70 The fees outlined in a College Prospectus for c.1844 were 40 guineas for boys under 12 and 50 for those over 12.
71 Curr, 'Memoranda Concerning Our Family' (1877), SLV, MS 8998.

for the boys to become fluent in French and after nine months of study they boarded with a family in the village of Quincey for several more months. Their hosts were Monsieur and Madame Delhay, whose son Henri was of a similar age to Edward. Henri Delhay had recently begun studying to be a Notaire, in which profession Edward M. Curr believed he would succeed because he had the necessary 'duplicity, tact and cunning'. Although Curr might have been glad of the company, he was not particularly enamoured of Henri: 'He thinks that I am extremely attached to him, but it is not so. I know his interested duplicity better than he is aware of; if he deceives himself, let him do so.'[72]

Curr recorded these and other thoughts in a journal, which he commenced in October 1838. The journal (only part of which survives) is both a record of daily events and a series of reflections on French literature, which he was reading as part of a seemingly independent course of study. The opening page of the journal sets a somewhat serious tone:

> When we consider the object of all the labours of man, we cannot but acknowledge, that if they are not all well directed, they all at least preserve that tendency which the Lord has chosen to give them. That tendency is to Happiness.
>
> When these pages are swelled to hundreds, let me again peruse them; that thus seeing the follies into which youth must certainly fall, I may correct the inclinations which are bad within me, and which have brought evil and may thus profit by the past. In a word may I thus learn to house the Supreme Being according to his heart, and conduct myself as he has ordered me to do with regard to my neighbour.[73]

There is very little in Curr's extant writings that reveal the impact of his religion on his life; this passage from his youthful journal is the principal exception. As well as alluding to his religious beliefs, Curr's introduction to his journal displays an early commitment to a routine of reading, writing and reflection that would characterise his life. The journal contains observations on his daily reading, which included a French translation of Sterne's *A Sentimental Journey*, Lady Morgan's *The Life and Times of Salvator Rosa* and Florian's translation of *Don Quixote*. The earnest tone of the introduction continues in parts, but is regularly broken by more light-hearted passages, including his observation that it is 'droll' that the comic *Don Quixote* was written by a man in prison:

---

72 13 November 1838, Edward M. Curr, 'A Journal' (1838), in 'Curr Family – Papers and Station Records, 1838–1937', State Library of New South Wales (SLNSW), Mitchell Library, MLMSS 2286.
73 Curr, 'A Journal' (1838), SLNSW, MLMSS 2286, Title Page.

'It has often been the case that men in mournful situations have produced comic works, and that men in the most flattering circumstances have written the most melancholily [sic].'[74]

While studying the French language, Curr developed some patriotic views on the superiority of English poetry: 'I do not … think that their verses in any respect equal ours. Though they may sometimes make a high sounding verse, we can … pour the very soul of melody into our strains'.[75] He expanded this thesis five days later:

> For if in life and liveliness the French are far our masters, if their conversation is more brilliant and their elasticity of spirit more unbroken; we at least can claim a language more adapted to melancholy subjects, and a way of thinking which is more sincere and affectionate. Our language too is more formed for describing grief as well as for comforting it. For if it is high and elegant; it is also warm and simple: and thus to comfort more effectual for 'Honest plain words best pierce the ears of grief.'[76]

Curr's youthful journal reveals a fascination for language and a commitment to developing his abilities as a writer. On 14 November 1838 he reported that he had commenced writing his 'Opinions, Recollections and Anecdotes of my friends at Stonyhurst', which has unfortunately not survived. From time to time he broke his self-imposed study to practise fencing with students from St Edmunds and other suitable acquaintances. He later wrote in a family memoir 'whilst in France we became excellent swordsmen'[77] and his journal seems to bear this out. On 24 October he 'fenced "en salle" for the first time with a sub officer'. On 26 October he wrote: 'I was interrupted in what I was writing yesterday evening by the arrival of the two Mons Guillards the elder of whom was come to fence with me. In the course of the evening shivered three foils.' In his published recollections Curr later revealed that he had a childhood fascination with Napoleon and had read 'perhaps fifty volumes' on the French General. He explained that, when in France as a youth, he had practised his fencing with veterans of many of Napoleon's campaigns.[78]

It was clearly a stimulating time for a young man, but Curr was not immune to the effects of homesickness, which had been building for many years. On 5 November 1838 he wrote in his journal of his impatient desire to return to Van Diemen's Land:

---

74 9 November 1838, Curr, 'A Journal' (1838), SLNSW, MLMSS 2286.
75 24 October 1838, Curr, 'A Journal' (1838), SLNSW, MLMSS 2286.
76 29 October 1838, Curr, 'A Journal' (1838), SLNSW, MLMSS 2286.
77 Curr, 'Memoranda Concerning Our Family' (1877), SLV, MS 8998.
78 Curr 1883: 366–367.

> Oh with what anxiety do I not wait for that moment? When shall I jump on the ship's deck which is to bear me away? Five years have already elapsed since I have seen my dear parents. Five years have run, heavily, most heavily on. But when I finally do arrive, all the pains of those years shall be instilled into one instant and changed into bliss, that instant shall be – when I fall on the neck of my mother.[79]

Curr's journal has not survived intact beyond 15 November 1838, as unfortunately 40 pages are torn from the bound volume. It is possible that these pages contained observations from the remainder of his time in France, and perhaps from his subsequent sea voyage to Van Diemen's Land. The next surviving page of the journal contains an undated entry consisting mainly of a quote from Milton. Intriguingly, the following pages include details of a droving trip Curr and his brothers undertook 18 years later in the Australian colonies. The potential that the lost pages might have contained records of Curr's thoughts and experiences over an 18-year period rather depressingly presents itself. When or how the pages were lost remains a mystery.

Curr and his brothers left France in November 1838. They spent Christmas in England before departing for Van Diemen's Land aboard the *William Bryan*. They arrived at Circular Head in May 1839 where Edward M. Curr would have observed the expansion of the Van Diemen's Land Company's settlement, including the construction of his family's new 24-room manor house. He would also have observed the expansion of his own immediate family and met four new siblings – Elizabeth, Marmaduke, Julius and Montagu. Sadly, he could only pay his respects at the grave of his sister Julia, who had died in 1835 at the age of two after a tragic accident in the garden at Highfield.[80]

Edward M. Curr's childhood was by any measure a remarkable one: he sailed four times between Britain and Van Diemen's Land, experienced foreign countries and remote colonial outposts, completed a rigorous education in Britain and France, and developed a keen interest in reading and writing that would shape his life. His childhood was certainly one of privilege, but it was also one of diverse experiences that would open his eyes to a world of possibilities. His upbringing provided the perfect preparation for a varied and remarkable colonial career.

---

79 5 November 1838, Curr, 'A Journal' (1838), SLNSW, MLMSS 2286.
80 Von Stieglitz 1952: 28–29.

Figure 6: Highfield, Circular Head. William Purser.

Watercolour. National Library of Australia, nla.pic-an4911681.

2. 'Troubles of a Beginner'

The Van Diemen's Land Company did not provide rapid or extensive returns to its shareholders. During its first 15 years of operation, the company spent £250,000 on its antipodean venture, yet no dividend was paid for the first 11 years and the few that were subsequently paid were small.[1] The slow progress increasingly troubled the London-based directors, who also became concerned about Edward Curr senior's 'frequent and acrimonious disputes' with the authorities in Hobart. In the late 1830s these issues reached crisis point due to Curr's 'persistent refusal to pay part of the salary of the police magistrate stationed at Circular Head'. The dispute greatly hindered the progress of land exchange negotiations between the company and the government, so the directors ordered Curr to pay the salary in 1839. When he refused 'on the ground that compliance would injure his dignity' he was given a year's notice to vacate his position.[2]

There were many in Van Diemen's Land who were not disappointed to see the back of Edward Curr senior, as he had a reputation for poor treatment of those under his charge. He was known to physically assault his indentured servants on the regular occasions that they tried to escape; he also sentenced assigned convicts to floggings at twice the rate of other magistrates in Van Diemen's Land.[3] When Curr eventually departed, a local newspaper reported 'unusual joy' in the Circular Head community: 'the result will be no less beneficial to the affairs of the company, we trust, than pleasing to its tenants and servants'.[4] In contrast, local historians Kerry Pink and Gill Vowles grant Curr considerable credit for his management of the Van Diemen's Land Company, which they suggest was financially doomed from the outset. They argue that a lack of support from the London directors contributed to Curr's 'increasingly autocratic and belligerent dealings with the Hobart bureaucracy'.[5] For his own part, Curr senior pointed to the 'singular circumstances' of his being most likely 'the sole survivor of the hundreds of chief agents of companies which date from the memorable 1825'. Curr believed this record deserved more respect from the directors, who, he argued, had 'practically for years disregarded every word of [his] advice'.[6]

Interestingly, the acrimonious nature of Edward Curr's departure from the company is not consistent with the version given by his son in 1877. In his 'Memoranda Concerning Our Family', Edward M. Curr wrote of his father:

---

1   Von Stieglitz 1952: 18.
2   Pike 1966: 271.
3   Duxbury 1989: 49–51.
4   *Cornwall Chronicle*, 19 March 1842, quoted in McFarlane 2003: 296.
5   Pink and Vowles 1998: 18.
6   Edward Curr to Van Diemen's Land Company Board, quoted in Pink and Vowles 1998.

> Though much attached to Circular Head, which with its singular bluff, beautiful bays, pleasant beaches, unsurpassed climate, and those green fields which had been as it were his own creation … he gave up his position there in 1841, and betook himself with his family to Port Phillip … He parted with the company whose lands he had selected, and whose affairs he had managed for many years on the best terms.[7]

It is possible (if unlikely) that Edward M. Curr was unaware of his father's poor relationship with the company directors; it is more probable that he chose to hide the fact from his descendants when writing his family memoir.

In August 1839 Edward M. Curr accompanied his father on a trip across Bass Strait to the booming Port Phillip District of New South Wales. Curr senior had long been interested in the economic potential of the mainland; he had not only urged the Van Diemen's Land Company to push for land grants at Western Port, but in 1827 had personally applied to Governor Darling for a grant, along with such men as John Batman and Joseph Gellibrand.[8] Edward M. Curr later observed that his father 'formed a very high opinion of the colony' during his visit in 1839 and made several town allotment purchases.[9] Clearly he was laying the foundations of a new life for his family.

After his visit to Melbourne, Edward M. Curr spent approximately a year working for the Van Diemen's Land Company at Surrey Hills and Emu Bay. This was the only pastoral apprenticeship he served before his ten years of squatting in Victoria, where his impressive Stonyhurst education would surely have been of limited use. In January 1841 his father bought a small sheep station called Wolfscrag (later Wild Duck Creek), which was situated approximately 70 miles north of Melbourne. Barely 20 years old, Edward M. Curr was sent by his father to manage the station.

'Journey to Wolfscrag'

Curr's years as a squatter are documented in great detail in his published memoir. It is important to recognise, however, that *Recollections of Squatting in Victoria* is not a contemporary record of Curr's early life, but a nostalgic memoir written 40 years after the events it recalls. The perspective of an older man certainly shapes Curr's engaging narrative of his youthful experiences. Curr recalled that as a young man he had 'little inclination' to be a sheep farmer, but acting under paternal instruction he sailed to the Port Phillip District to take delivery of

---

7 Edward M. Curr, 'Memoranda Concerning Our Family' (1877), SLV, MS 8998.
8 Shaw 1996: 37–38.
9 Curr 1883: 22.

2,300 sheep and his father's new station. His father had directed him to engage an overseer, 'from whom I should be able to learn sheep-farming, of which I knew nothing'. He employed the existing manager of the station and instructed him to return to Wolfscrag and await his arrival. Conscious of his inexperience, Curr hoped to find friendly company for his own journey north and was glad to encounter two men (one known to his father) who offered to join him. After a few days in Melbourne, Curr and his companions rode out of town on a hot afternoon, making their way towards the 'Bush Inn', 35 miles to the north: 'we rode slowly, and did not reach the inn until a couple of hours or more after sundown, when my experience of Australian bush life began'.[10]

After two more days of leisurely riding, Curr and his companions arrived at Wolfscrag shortly before sunset. Curr found his new situation to be 'anything but inviting' and his companions offered no congratulations on his prospects. Wolfscrag consisted of 'a mass of barren quartz ranges, between which were a few long narrow flats, watered by small creeks, and very poorly grassed'. The station headquarters comprised two small slab huts located in a grassless valley. When writing *Recollections of Squatting in Victoria*, Curr undoubtedly emphasised the lack of potential for narrative effect, but his description of the unpromising establishment is worth recounting:

> From the huts no grass or herbage could be seen; the dust from the lately yarded flocks slowly drifted in a cloud down the desolate valley, and the whole scene, from a sheep-farmer's point of view, was as disheartening as could well be imagined.[11]

After dismounting, Curr entered the overseer's hut – his new home – 'the interior of which was scarcely an improvement on its outward appearance'.[12] With barely concealed irony, Curr derived considerable amusement from the pride shown by the overseer as he handed over the hut to its new owner:

> [He] formally put me in possession of the premises, with the air of one who was relinquishing what he evidently looked on as a very complete little establishment. Of the correctness of his views on this subject it hardly needed the smile, which I thought I detected on the faces of my friends, to remind me that some diversity of opinion might exist.[13]

Curr's friend assured him the hut was adequate, explaining 'we don't think this bad in the bush'. Recalling his poor first impression, Curr was able to highlight his rite of passage to experienced bushman: '[The hut] was clean in

---

10   Curr 1883: 23–24.
11   Curr 1883: 29–30.
12   Curr 1883: 30.
13   Curr 1883: 32.

its way, but very comfortless as I thought then; later on I got used to things still rougher'. Curr and his friends were then served a simple meal by the overseer's servant, which became an additional source of amusement in Curr's memoir: '"*Messieurs, vous êtes servis!*" said one of my friends, laughing, as we began our meal; probably some hotel on the *Boulevards* suggesting itself to his mind as a contrast!'[14]

Curr spent only a few days at Wolfscrag before he concluded: 'my father's seemingly cheap purchase was in reality a very bad one'. Apart from the lack of grass, the station was under-resourced, possessing no horses, bullocks or dray; moreover, the sheep were of dubious quality, undernourished, diseased and one in three were worn out. Curr anticipated a loss of at least £800 in his first year as a sheep farmer and concluded that 'very vigorous measures would have to be taken to put matters on a proper footing'.[15] He was quickly convinced that abandoning Wolfscrag in favour of better country was the best possible course. He delayed this plan, however, until he could consult with his father and consider the legality of moving scabby sheep.

In the meantime, the only option available to Curr for limiting his father's financial loss was to hire three new shepherds at a reduced rate of pay (down from £52 per annum to £45). He later recalled that the task of hiring new labour in Melbourne in 1841 'was not by any means an agreeable job'. In fact, his account of visiting a public house to find expiree convict labour was the first of many examples Curr later provided to illustrate the 'Troubles of a Beginner'.[16] Entering a rowdy public house for the first time in his life, Curr encountered 30 patrons in various stages of inebriation: 'from maudlin imbecility to that of a maddened bacchanal, vigorous and rampant, in the first stage of his debauch'. A 'burly ruffian' soon threatened the youthful Curr:

> [He] accosted me in a savage and impertinent tone with 'What the --- devil do you want, bloke, eh?' 'A bullock driver,' I replied, looking him in the face, and grasping firmly the hunting-whip which I held in my hand. My answer elicited from the company a roar of laughter, with oaths, yells, and imprecations.[17]

Curr was rescued from the threatening mob by the publican, who ushered him into a separate room and presented various candidates for work, 'whose money being spent, were no longer of any use to him'. Curr selected his new and cheaper labour force from among these 'worthies' and returned to Wolfscrag, where he set about trying to be a sheep farmer. He initially had some difficulty convincing

---

14   Curr 1883: 32–34. *Messieurs, vous êtes servis!* – Gentlemen, you have been served!
15   Curr 1883: 39.
16   Curr 1883: 40.
17   Curr 1883: 41–42.

his new employees to complete their allocated tasks, as they (like Curr) soon took a dislike to the conditions at Wolfscrag: they particularly objected to the difficulties associated with supervising sheep or bullocks which strayed far in their search for decent grass. Curr later noted that his employee's grievances were 'a matter requiring some tact' and that any attempt at '*compelling*' the men to do their work would have been pointless.[18]

With the help of his overseer, Curr slowly began to adapt to a new and unfamiliar lifestyle. As he later recalled, these first weeks presented many challenges for an inexperienced young man:

> To me a squatter's life was a great change from my previous experiences; my not very delightful occupations at this period being helping to dress the sheep for scab and foot-rot, a little bullock-driving, learning to find my way about the bush (an art which had been sadly neglected in my education), getting used to the ways of my men, and in the evening reading Youatt's book on 'The Sheep.'[19]

Curr's poor ability to navigate through the bush was soon exposed when four of his six bullocks 'absconded'. Each day for a fortnight Curr searched the surrounding country and he quickly discovered the challenge of navigation: 'For my part, whilst attempting to find the missing animals, it was only with great difficulty that I managed not to lose myself.'[20] In the narrative of *Recollections of Squatting in Victoria* the loss of the bullocks becomes a seminal event with two critically important consequences: first, as Curr recorded, 'it was the means of making me a bushman'; and secondly, as we shall see, the search for the truant bovines eventually led Curr to 'the well-grassed plains of Tongala and the ever-flowing Goulburn'.[21]

The search for the bullocks was initially unsuccessful and was abandoned after two weeks. Nevertheless, matters at Wolfscrag improved slightly when Curr's overseer suggested that the increasingly hungry sheep should be moved to a patch of well-grassed country further north, which Curr later found was part of a neighbour's lease. Despite sinister behaviour from his overseer, who apparently knew moving the sheep north would amount to trespass, Curr and his men shifted the starving flock and set up a simple outstation. The shepherds' spirits rose immediately, as they knew the sheep would not stray far from the new pastures.[22] Soon afterwards the overseer's three-month contract expired and Curr chose not to renew it, having found his assistance underwhelming.

---

18   Curr 1883: 43–44.
19   Curr 1883: 45.
20   Curr 1883: 45–46.
21   Curr 1883: 69.
22   Curr 1883: 47–51, 73.

The overseer and his servant were paid off and returned to Melbourne with the bullock driver, who was sent for more supplies. As the three shepherds were happily ensconced at their new outstation six miles to the north, Curr found himself alone at Wolfscrag for the first time.

'Alone At My Hut'

When recalling his first visit to Melbourne in 1839, Curr had observed the morbid interest of the town's populace in the expedition of Joseph Hawdon and Alfred Mundy, who sought an overland route between Melbourne and Adelaide:

> The uncertainty of whether these explorers would succeed in passing through several hundred miles of unexplored country beset with blacks, or whether they would get their brains knocked out on the way, was, of course, the principal feature of interest in the affair.[23]

Eighteen months later, when Curr spent a night at the Bush Inn on his way to Wolfscrag, he heard news of more immediate import to his new situation. He met a man whose brother, an overseer at a station only ten miles from Wolfscrag, had recently died 'from a wound received in an encounter with the Blacks'. Curr learnt that some station employees had been killed in the encounter, and that soldiers had been sent from Melbourne for the protection of those who survived. Given this prior knowledge, not to mention the earlier fatal encounters between his father's employees and the Aborigines at Cape Grim (of which he surely would have been aware), there is little wonder that the departure of Curr's overseer from Wolfscrag represented a major moment in his life to that point (or, as Curr put it, 'one of the little epochs in my reminiscences').[24]

Forty years later, in accomplished prose, Curr vividly recollected sitting on a log and watching as the overseer, servant, bullock-driver and dray passed first from sight and then from sound:

> What appeared to me an unusual stillness and loneliness then seemed to settle around me. Afterwards I got used to being alone, and very indifferent on the subject, but it was not so then; and I don't know whether it will strike the reader that the position in which I was placed was a nervous one, bearing in mind that with very little experience of

---

23   Curr 1883: 19.
24   Curr 1883: 28, 52.

> the bush I was suddenly left by myself, probably for three weeks, in an unfrequented spot, and in a neighbourhood in which a considerable number of exasperated and hostile Blacks were known to be.[25]

That Curr later described the local Indigenous people as 'exasperated' (not merely 'hostile') indicates an understanding of their predicament. His narrative suggests he viewed Aboriginal resistance as an inevitable consequence of British invasion, but this belief did not undermine his faith in the righteousness of the colonial endeavour. As a 20-year-old, Curr's attitudes to racial relations were likely less developed than those that motivated him as an author 40 years later. In 1841 his mood was dominated by fear and anxiety, as he readily admitted.

Curr explained his anxiety by identifying his youth and inexperience, the fact that he was 'indifferently armed', that he had 'never seen the Blacks, except in Melbourne' and that he was 'totally ignorant of their ways'. Consequently, his first day of solitude at Wolfscrag 'weighed a good deal on [his] spirits' and heightened his senses in response to unexplained sounds from the bush:

> The wind, the noise of a falling bough, the cawing of a crow, or the whistle of a hawk – which yesterday failed to attract attention – made me now look carefully around ... If a flight of cockatoos passed screaming over the valley, I used to wonder whether they had been disturbed by anyone; and if so, by whom – by a White man or Black? and look carefully around to see if I could descry anyone coming.[26]

His fear was exacerbated when, after a few days of solitude, a passing trooper reported that 'Blacks had been committing depredations' in the neighbourhood of Wolfscrag. The trooper suggested Curr be on his guard, warning him that Aborigines sought revenge for the shooting of some of their people 15 miles away, 'on the banks of the Campaspe'.[27] In *Recollections of Squatting in Victoria* Curr spends six pages describing the growing sense of foreboding that he felt during his isolation at Wolfscrag. The narrative serves to raise the tension as the seemingly inevitable encounter draws near. The encounter itself occupies a further six pages.[28]

When dressing one morning after sunrise Curr noticed 'some wild ducks alight in a water-hole'. He consequently took one of his two guns and 'sallied out' in the 'drizzling rain' to stalk his prey; the ducks eluded him and he returned to his hut with a damp firearm. When the ducks returned a little later, he ventured out again with his other gun, suspecting the first would misfire due to moist

---

25   Curr 1883: 51–52.
26   Curr 1883: 52–54.
27   Curr 1883: 54–55.
28   Curr 1883: 55–61.

gunpowder; unsuccessful for a second time, Curr returned to his hut to cook breakfast. Some time later his kangaroo dog alerted him to an intrusion and Curr spotted a small dog, which he assumed in his inexperience to be wild:

> I levelled my carbine and was about to fire, when something which moved amongst a clump of bushes a few yards off attracted my attention. Quick as thought, I turned the muzzle of my gun from the dog to the bushes, at which, though I could distinguish nothing for the instant, I nevertheless held it pointed, keeping myself still partly covered by the hut. This proceeding, I have no doubt, saved my life, for the next moment I caught sight of a pair of spears quivering amongst the boughs, from which, after a moment's delay, lowering their weapons, there stepped two Blacks, stark naked, and in all the beauties of war-paint.[29]

In Curr's account, the stand-off which followed was tense and drawn out – the Indigenous visitors protested benign intentions, while Curr grew more certain of his peril: 'The hatred which their looks could not hide disconcerted me.' Curr apparently remained calm and vigilant, never lowering his weapon as he retreated to the door of his hut: 'I drew a long breath of relief when I reached my strong-hold.' The episode becomes a key moment in Curr's passage to manhood:

> My visitors, I fancy, still entertained hopes that being young and evidently unused to their ways, I should sooner or later expose myself, when they would kill me. If so, however, they reckoned without their host, for I had made up my mind to trust myself with them no more, but to fight it out, when the time came, at the doorway, where I should have the assistance of a dog, and where two could not get at me at once.[30]

Despite a threat from Curr that 'if they came an inch nearer my door I would shoot them', and a corresponding intimation from Curr's visitors that they would spear him, the encounter ended in a stalemate. Curr was not confident of the reliability of his damp firearms and surmised that if they misfired he would be attacked: 'Had it not been for my doubts on this score, I should have shot one of them at once in self-defence, as it seemed to me that blows were inevitable. Ever afterwards I was glad that I had not done so.' The stalemate ended when, according to Curr, 'the prudence of the two worthies got the better of their valour' and they 'disappeared into the scrub'. When danger had passed, Curr tried his guns, which both failed to fire: 'I had had a narrow escape, and took it as a warning which never required repeating, being from that time scrupulously attentive to the state of my fire-arms.'[31]

---

29 Curr 1883: 56–57.
30 Curr 1883: 58–59.
31 Curr 1883: 59–60.

Curr's recollection of this undoubtedly memorable event provides considerable insight into both his youthful inexperience and the preoccupations of his later life. On the one hand, Curr's account shows how luck (or 'Divine Providence') enabled the young squatter to overcome his early inexperience. The event was also a lesson in vigilance – to keep your guns loaded and well maintained. On the other hand, Curr's account must be read as a product of the 1880s, penned by an older man looking back on his youth. The older Curr's position on the Board for the Protection of the Aborigines is surely relevant when considering how he constructed the narrative of his early inter-racial experiences. Importantly, by emphasising that he did not shoot an Aborigine he affirms his self-professed status as a protector of Aborigines. Nevertheless, Curr did not condemn frontier violence: while he regretted the death of Aborigines by the rifle, he also saw it as occasionally inevitable and unsurprising. Curr believed that Aborigines were bound to resist the invasion of their lands, but was convinced that their dispossession was justified. Consequently, after his close call at Wolfscrag, he prepared himself for possible future conflict: 'When next in Melbourne I also purchased an excellent pair of pistols, which I learnt to use well, and had constantly at hand for several years'.

Curr was alone at Wolfscrag for about three weeks until his bullock driver returned with the dray full of supplies. The driver was accompanied by a married couple, who joined Curr's workforce as a shepherd and a servant. While Curr was glad to be relieved of his solitude, the apparently lowly status of the new arrivals did little to overcome his sense of social isolation: 'I had still no one to converse with.'[32]

'Removal to Tongala'

After his period of solitude, Curr hoped to commence his search for a more productive squatting run, but first returned to the problem of his lost bullocks. The passing trooper, who had warned Curr to beware of 'hostile blacks', had also provided the welcome news that four stray bullocks had been seen on the Goulburn River. Serendipitously, the renewed search for his escaped bullocks eventually led Curr to 'unoccupied country' that suited his purposes nicely. A few days after the return of his dray, Curr set off in search of his bullocks, accompanied by his bullock driver. They followed the 'Major's Line', the route marked by the dray tracks of Major Thomas Mitchell's 'Australia Felix' expedition of 1836, until they reached the Goulburn River at the 'Old Crossing

---

32   Curr 1883: 61.

Place' north of Seymour. In *Recollections of Squatting in Victoria* the description of this journey provided Curr with the perfect opportunity to proffer his views on the inevitability and desirability of European dominance:

> The stillness, so common a feature in the Australian woods, I constantly noticed during my ride. Equally characteristic was the sinuous creek, and not a bit like what I had seen in Tasmania. I saw nothing to remind me of the Blacks, and yet they must have wandered along the creek, built their huts on it, killed opossums along its banks and ducks on its waters for who shall say how many ages? whilst the single party of white men who had passed that way had left a road behind them which one might follow unaided.[33]

Leaving the Major's Line at the Old Crossing Place, Curr followed the Goulburn River downstream where he encountered an Overlanders' camp, with 5,000 sheep bound for South Australia. He continued north for several days, passing the recently claimed pastoral runs of Baillieston, Toolamba, Ardpatrick and St Germains. He also spent a night at the Goulburn River Aboriginal protectorate station, his first experience of a government institution he would greatly influence later in life. Curr finally recovered his bullocks at the Wyuna cattle station, which, at the time, was the farthest down the Goulburn River that European pastoralists had extended their range of occupation.

Apart from retrieving cattle, the journey was useful to Curr for two additional reasons: first, he met an able (but unemployed) man on the road and hired him as his new overseer; secondly, and more importantly, a station hand showed him the plains west of Wyuna, where 'excellent unoccupied country' adjoined the Goulburn River near its junction with the Murray River. Already predisposed to abandoning Wolfscrag, Curr immediately decided to relocate his sheep and 'take up' a new run, a course that faced 'no hindrances of any sort'.[34] Limited only by the quantity of sheep he proposed to graze, Curr applied for a lease over 50 square miles of land on either side of the Goulburn River. To qualify for the lease, he was simply required to be the first to place stock on the relevant country, which he immediately set about achieving. He instructed his new overseer to accompany the bullocks and driver back to Wolfscrag, returning by the same route along the Goulburn River and Major's Line. Curr himself journeyed 'across entirely unexplored country', scouting the most direct route for his proposed northward migration of sheep. Three days later he was back at Wolfscrag: the flocks were assembled in yards near his hut and a letter was

---

33 Curr 1883: 63.
34 Curr 1883: 68.

sent to Melbourne making a formal application for the new pastoral lease. When the overseer returned with the bullocks the final preparations began; Curr commenced his journey two days later, a little after sunrise.

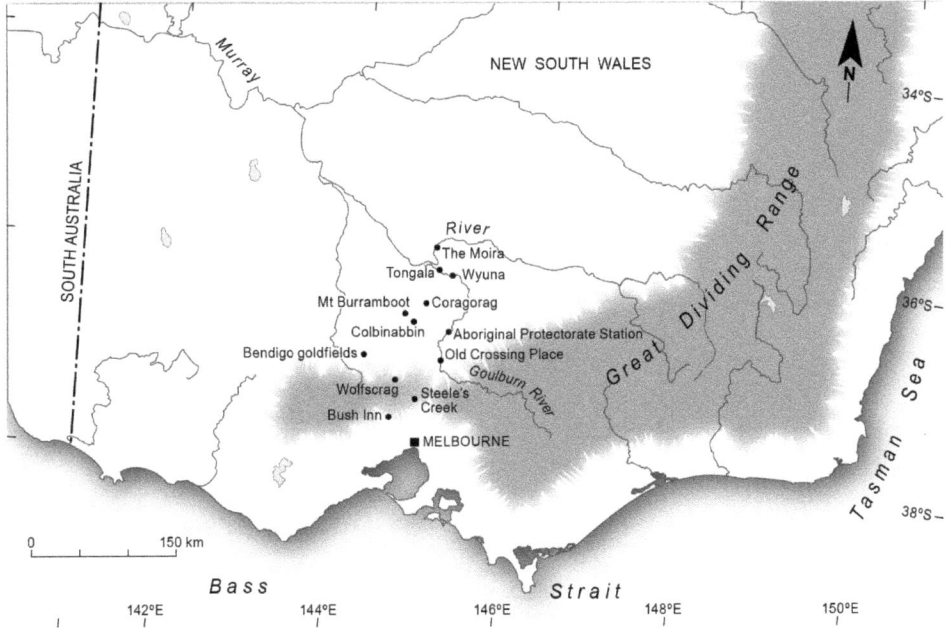

Figure 7: Port Phillip District.

Map by Peter Johnson.

Curr's party totalled eight, including the overseer, four shepherds, the bullock driver and a cook. Being 'in the most hopeful of moods', Curr initially underestimated the effect his plans might have on his employees: 'I had almost forgotten to notice that my servants, from fear of the Blacks, were exceedingly averse to the journey I was beginning.' He recalled that most of his servants were expiree convicts from Van Diemen's Land 'where the Blacks were a very hostile race, and much dreaded'. Interestingly, in his own account of the journey north, Curr appears free from any anxiety: perhaps he comforted himself with the knowledge that 'shepherds ... as a rule are the persons who get speared in new country'. Whatever the case, *Recollections of Squatting in Victoria* creates the distinct impression that the 20-year-old Curr had quickly mastered any fear of Aboriginal attack and now faced his next challenge: managing and assuaging the fears of his servants.[35]

---

35   Curr 1883: 74–75.

Curr armed each of his men with a carbine and six cartridges: 'as much perhaps to give them confidence as from any likelihood of a collision with the Blacks'. Despite his best efforts, Curr recalled that he only narrowly avoided a mutiny by his shepherds. After four days of droving through the foreboding scrub, the four shepherds formally complained and asked to be paid out and released. Although Curr believed he could manage the immediate task of droving without his shepherds, he also knew that finding new staff would be difficult and that their absence would preclude shearing, building of huts and other important tasks. Tellingly, Curr also considered a reduction in numbers to be detrimental to the safety of his group: 'it was most desirable to meet the Murray and Goulburn Blacks, who bore the reputation of being numerous and troublesome, with a fairly strong party'. In other words, Curr privately recognised that the fears of his shepherds were legitimate.[36]

According to Curr's account, he managed with poise and tact to master a threatening situation and control his fractious workforce. First, he attempted to reason with them and chided them for their 'groundless timidity'. Later he covertly confiscated the shepherds' firearms and prepared his own for possible use, should the 'gaolbirds' resort to violence. In the morning, Curr issued an ultimatum, instructing his shepherds 'to proceed with me on my journey, or to leave my camp without arms, food, or wages'. Curr then ordered his loyal staff (the overseer, bullock driver and cook) to prepare for the day's droving. According to Curr, 'threatening speeches were made, and there was loud grumbling, but no violence'. As the party moved off the shepherds reluctantly returned to their duties. The following evening Curr 'held out the olive branch' by offering the men release from service as soon as he could hire replacement labour.[37]

Curr's account of this episode serves, of course, to portray his raw yet effective abilities as a master of men: Curr painted himself as firm but fair – able to exert authority as well as tact. He continued by recording that the fear of his men was shortly alleviated when the party emerged from the 'scrubby country' on to the 'beautiful plains of Colbinabbin and Coragorag'. It seems likely that Curr's own courage was boosted by this welcome change, although he does not say as much in *Recollections of Squatting in Victoria*, where intimations of cowardice are reserved for his expiree convict labour.

While crossing the plains of Colbinabbin, Curr was encouraged by the rising spirits of his men and rode west to the Burramboot ranges to survey the scene:

> The features of the landscape were sunshine and stillness; my little party, now and then discernible amongst the lines of trees on the banks of the

---

36 Curr 1883: 75–78.
37 Curr 1883: 79–81.

creek, was creeping slowly on in a northerly direction; here and there a flock of emus, or a few bustards, were feeding on the green herbage; and on the eastern side of the plain, fifteen or twenty miles away, I could just make out a faint line of smoke, rising, no doubt, from a native encampment on the edge of the forest.[38]

Here Curr's description conveys a sense of the untapped potential of the land: importantly, the 'stillness' of the scene is not disturbed by the clear signs of an Indigenous presence 'on the edge of the forest'.[39] Curr had no difficulty in characterising the land as simultaneously 'unoccupied' and frequented by Aborigines; the Indigenous encampment was simply part of the scenery and did not represent the effective use of productive land by a rival group. Curr explained that, if not for the lack of water, he would happily have ended his journey on the plains of Colbinabbin. Three years later he returned to occupy these fine grasslands with his expanding flocks; but for the time being he drove his sheep northward to the reliable flow of the Goulburn River.

---

38   Curr 1883: 82.
39   Curr regularly refers to the 'stillness' of the bush. See for example, Curr 1883: 51, 63, 124.

3. 'A Station Formed at Tongala'

In July 1841 Edward M. Curr arrived at his new 50-square-mile squatting run, which he named 'Tongala'. He later recalled the derivation of his station name: 'The name was not by any means an apt one, as it is the Bangerang name for the River Murray.' Tongala in fact straddled the Goulburn River; Curr set up his station headquarters on the river's southern bank, about eight miles from its confluence with the Murray. He did not record the reason for his inappropriate usage of the name; it might have been the result of a misunderstanding, or perhaps Curr chose it for its aesthetic value, as he later opined that Aboriginal words were 'frequently very euphonious'. When researching Aboriginal vocabularies several decades later, Curr noticed that many Aboriginal names had been 'retained by the whites', but noted their generally 'mutilated condition'.[1]

At Tongala Curr encountered for the first time the Indigenous people who are the ancestors of the Yorta Yorta claimant group. According to Curr's classification, his squatting run encompassed the traditional land of at least two clans: the Towroonban lived predominantly on the sandhills between the Goulburn and Murray rivers, while the more numerous Wongatpan congregated further north in the region known as the Moira. As Curr described it, these two clans constituted the true 'Bangerang' tribe, although they belonged to a wider tribal federation linked by language. Curr described various other related clans in surrounding areas, with which he was less familiar, including the Wollithiga, Kailtheban, Boongātpan, Pikkolātpan, Angōōtheraban, Ngarrimōwro, Moītheriban and Toolinyāgan. He noted that the linguistically distinct Ngooraialum tribe, which occupied country to the south, commonly referred to all these clans as 'Bangerang'. Based on information from other squatters Curr surmised that in 1841 'the whole Bangerang race numbered not less than twelve hundred souls'.[2] In most cases, however, when Curr referred to the Bangerang, he meant the two principal clans that resided on his own pastoral runs: the opossum-hunting Towroonban and the fish-loving Wongatpan, who numbered 50 and 150 respectively when Curr arrived.[3]

---

1   Curr 1883: 68, 83, 220–221; see also Furphy 2002: 23–38.
2   Curr 1883: 234.
3   My usage of the names of clans and tribes reflects Curr's usage and is not intended to imply that these designations were or are necessarily accurate.

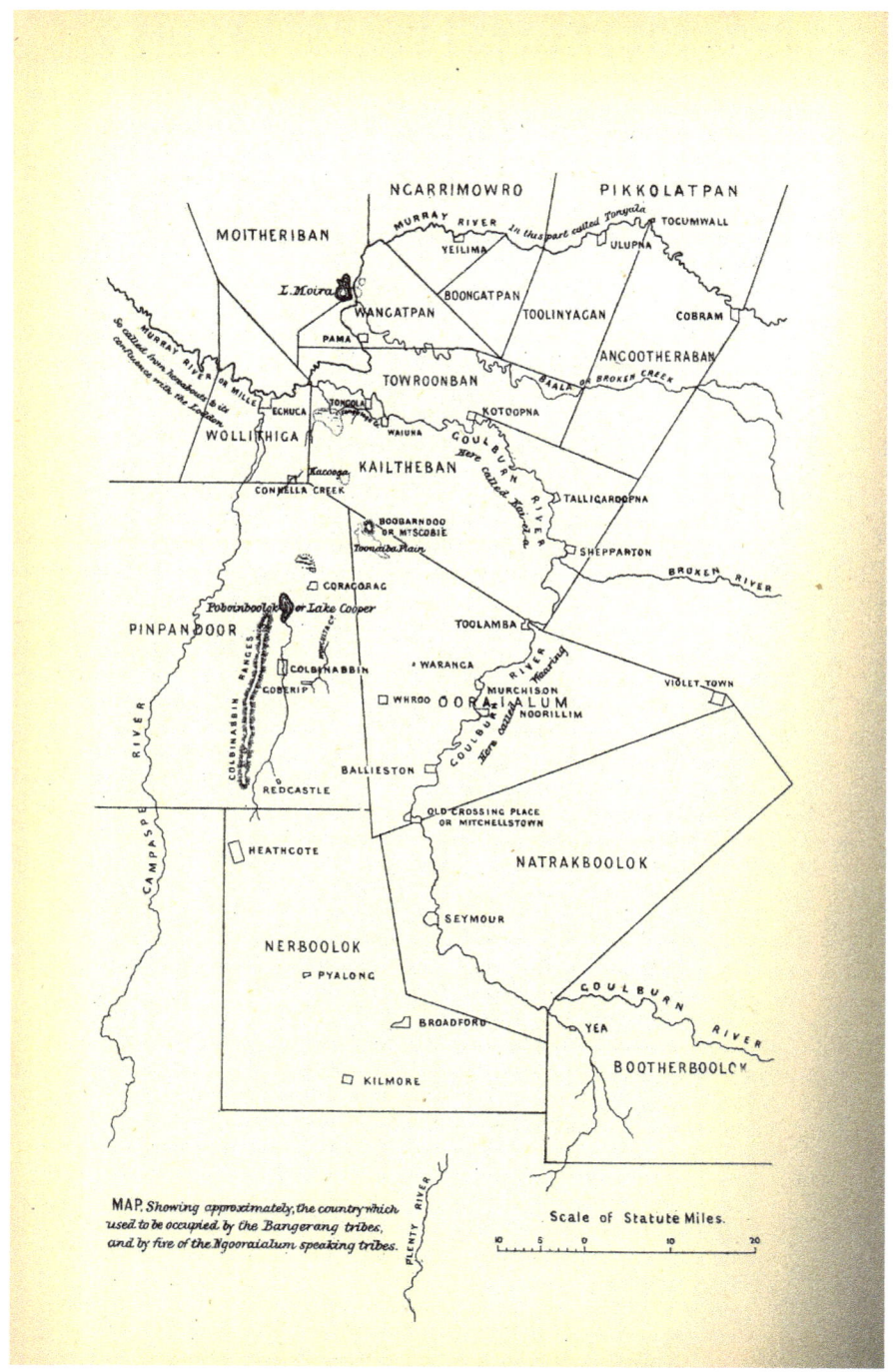

Figure 8: Edward M. Curr's Map of Bangerang territory.

Edward M. Curr, 1886, *The Australian Race* (Melbourne: John Ferres, Govt. Printer), vol III, 566.

3. 'A Station Formed at Tongala'

Curr's first encounter with Bangerang people occurred soon after he arrived with his sheep in July 1841. As his memoir relates, he set his men to work building yards for the sheep, but his arrival was soon noticed:

> Whilst engaged at this work, my attention was attracted by a cooey, and … we saw three Blacks on the opposite side of the stream. Their appearance on the scene caused some little trepidation in my old Tasmanians, whose idea, as I heard one of them express it, was 'to kid (entice) them over and shoot the lot.'[4]

Curr described the violent attitude of his shepherds with typical frankness; importantly, however, the episode enabled him to establish his own apparent benevolence. Curr explained that one of his men, who was 'accustomed to the Blacks', greeted the Bangerang men with a more friendly manner and they were soon invited to cross the river and join Curr's party. Describing the visitors in some detail, Curr noted the 'not ungraceful folds' of their decorated opossum skin cloaks. He also recalled the reaction of the three men to his party's invasion of their territory:

> The crash of the trees falling on the edge of the little plain which had so long been their property, and of which we were unceremoniously taking possession, and the general devastation which accompanies the white man, naturally attracted their attention. Their eyes seemed to take in what was being done, and every strange object around them, but neither word nor gesture of curiosity or surprise escaped them.[5]

The reserved and non-committal mood of the three men apparently required some tact on Curr's part. Forty years later, Curr constructed for himself a role as a calm and rational negotiator:

> After they had come to comprehend that I was going to remain permanently at Tongala, and heard what I had to say about the heinousness of sheep-stealing and shepherd-spearing, the power of fire-arms, and the beauty of my kangaroo dogs – which they much admired – I thought it best to address myself to the better feelings of my guests by directing the cook to give each of them as much meat, tea and damper as would serve two ordinary whites for a meal.[6]

This passage in Curr's *Recollections* reveals not only his belief in the righteousness of colonial acquisition, but also his paternalistic approach to Aboriginal management – a firm show of authority accompanied by a simple but generous gesture. Curr argued that Aborigines were well suited to the type of discipline

---

4 Curr 1883: 84.
5 Curr 1883: 86.
6 Curr 1883: 86.

that he practiced at Tongala: 'the Black very easily accommodated himself to the routine of stations; discipline, if not too severe, rather meeting with his approval'.[7]

The three Bangerang men provided useful assistance to Curr, helping ferry his sheep across the river in a specially made canoe and stripping bark for the roof of his hut. During the fortnight that Curr and his men spent building the requisites of a station, the utilisation of Indigenous labour served a dual purpose:

> Of the Blacks ... considerable numbers gradually made their appearance and camped at the station, which I encouraged them to do, both because I found their services useful, and thought them far less likely under such circumstances to attack the shepherds, or steal my sheep, than if I drove them away and placed myself in a hostile attitude towards them.

Nevertheless, Curr added that he kept his party armed to ensure there was 'no temptation to violence' among the Aborigines he dispossessed: 'In this course I persisted for several years – in fact, until danger was at an end.'[8]

Curr's conception of Aborigines as childlike was firmly established by the 1880s when he penned his memoir and likely shaped his memory of his first encounter with the Bangerang:

> What struck me, on first acquaintance, was their freedom from all the business cares and responsibilities of the white man. They constantly reminded me of children, whose anxieties were about matters to which the average white man is not called on to pay much attention. Besides, they had but little care for the future, their existence being literally from hand to mouth.[9]

Crucially, by portraying the Bangerang as childlike, Curr created for himself a paternalistic role. In the settler colonial relationship, the childlike Aborigine is quickly placed in a subordinate role to the white man, whose 'business cares and responsibilities' mark him out as racially superior. This paternalism is expressed in a variety of ways, not least by Curr's recollection that he 'christened' the entire Bangerang tribe:

> It was not long after our arrival at Tongala until the Bangerang began to find the want of names very inconvenient in their intercourse with

---

7 Curr 1883: 264.
8 Curr 1883: 92.
9 Curr 1883: 92–93.

us. They were, of course, aware that their Ngooraialum neighbours had all got white names, so they took the matter up, and several came to me daily to be named.[10]

Curr subsequently found it 'very amusing' to hear his Bangerang neighbours rehearsing their names and 'returning several times in the day to hear it repeated'. He also recalled with mirth the names he gave to some men, such as 'Plato', 'Jolly-chops' and 'Tallyho'. After observing the customs surrounding an exchange of women between the Bangerang and the Ngooraialum, Curr even considered the idea of 'giving away' Aboriginal brides: '[I] should probably have moved in that matter had not my very imperfect knowledge of aboriginal tongues prevented me'.[11]

Shortly after Curr established Tongala, his brother Richard arrived to assist him. The following year his parents resettled in Melbourne, where Edward Curr senior became a prominent businessman and politician. Curr senior purchased a second pastoral station called Steele's Creek, which was located closer to Melbourne near the recently gazetted town of Kilmore. Edward M. Curr managed this station for several months while Richard oversaw activities at Tongala. Meanwhile, a number of Curr's younger brothers joined the family's pastoral empire: by 1843 there were five Currs involved, including Edward (22), William (21), Richard (20), Charles (16) and Walter (15). With rapidly expanding sheep flocks the Curr brothers quickly acquired pastoral leases over vast areas of land in northern Victoria.

---

10   Curr 1883: 270–271.
11   Curr 1883: 270–271, 130.

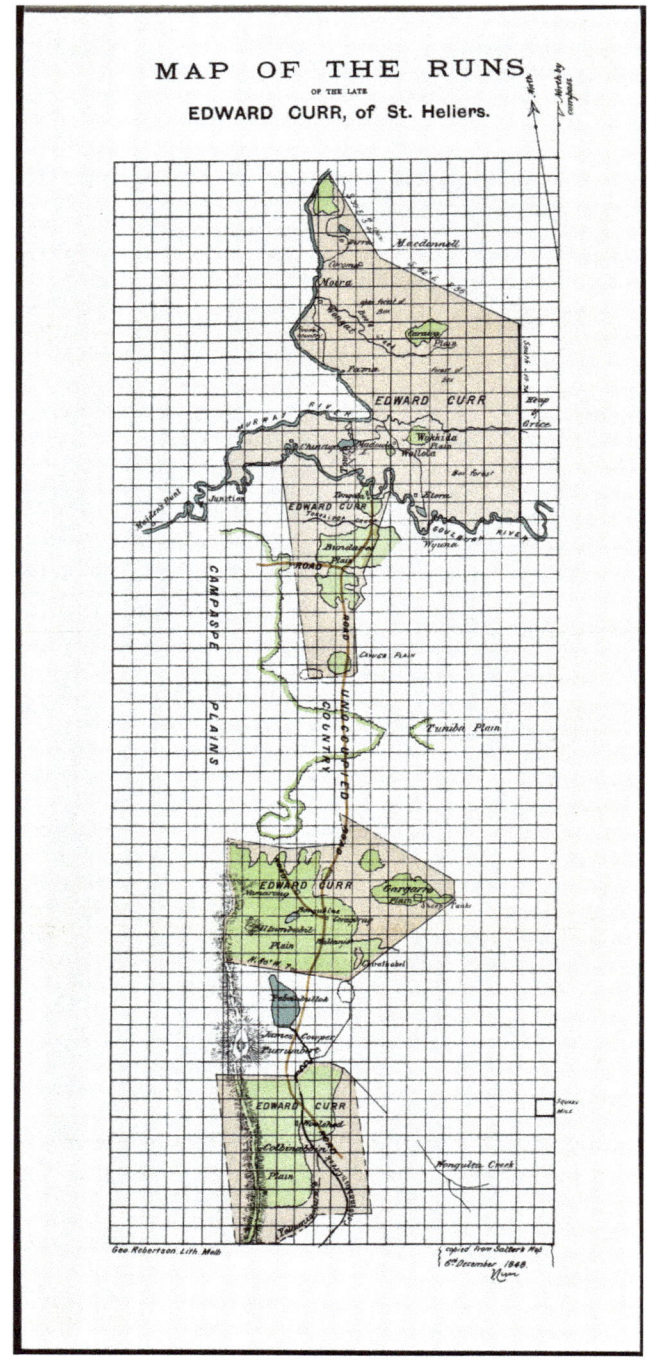

Figure 9: Map of the Runs of the Late Edward Curr, of St Heliers.

Edward M. Curr, 1883, *Recollections of Squatting in Victoria* (Melbourne: G. Robertson).

In *Recollections of Squatting in Victoria*, Curr gives a detailed account of the rapid growth of his pastoral enterprise. A prominent character is the Commissioner of Crown Lands, whose authority in the remote squatting districts was supreme. The commissioner for the Western Port District (which included Tongala) was F.A. Powlett, whom Curr described as 'a pleasant, chatty person' who was 'popular and highly respected'. The commissioner had the power to grant pastoral leases throughout his district and, according to Curr, often did so in a casual or summary manner. Curr recalled a ride he took with Powlett in early 1842, during which Curr took a fancy to some pastures north of the Murray River:

> I applied on the spot for a block of five miles' frontage to the river by eight miles back, which was granted without difficulty, the Commissioner and myself both forgetting that we were actually in a district to which his authority did not extend.[12]

While the Currs never officially leased the portion of their squatting run north of the Murray River, they soon obtained leasehold title to ample pastures in the Port Phillip District. In December 1842 Edward M. Curr moved 2,000 sheep from the overstocked station at Steele's Creek to Tongala, where he and Richard sought to expand their territory. The Currs applied for the massive Moira lease, which was north of Tongala between the Murray and Goulburn rivers. The lush summer pastures of the flood-prone Moira greatly appealed to Edward M. Curr, but the land was also highly valued by the local Aborigines: 'its extensive reed-beds were the great stronghold of the Bangerang Blacks'.[13] Despite concerted resistance from the Bangerang (downplayed by Curr but examined more fully in the next chapter of this book) the Currs subsequently leased 100 square miles of the Moira country.

The success of the Currs' pastoral venture plunged into uncertainty with the widespread financial collapse of 1843. When recalling the circumstances of the economic downturn, Curr described it as the inevitable consequence of past imprudence: 'the results of the extravagance of the colonists were at hand … the general bottled beer and champagne bill of the community was about to be settled'.[14] The short-term effect was highly detrimental to the Australian pastoral industry: sheep previously worth 40 shillings were sold for one shilling; Curr's horses, purchased at nearly £40 each, dropped in value to less than the price of a common saddle. Stability returned to the industry with the discovery that boiling down sheep for tallow provided a more lucrative alternative to selling them on the depressed meat market. Curr correctly credited Henry O'Brien of

---

12 Curr 1883: 122–123.
13 Curr 1883: 166.
14 Curr 1883: 214.

Yass with inspiring the tallow-led recovery of the Australian pastoral industry: sheep that were virtually unsaleable in April and May were worth up to eight shillings by June 1843.[15] According to the Port Phillip chronicler 'Garryowen' (Edmund Finn), Curr's father also played a role in the emerging trade in tallow: 'Edward Curr opened a boiling down establishment at Port Fairy'.[16]

Despite the economic downturn, the Currs further expanded their pastoral holdings in 1843, moving south in search of drier land for winter grazing. Edward M. Curr was not initially aware that both the Tongala and Moira runs were inclined to flood in the wetter months, but a clue was provided when his brother Richard made a startling discovery near the Goulburn River: 'my brother noticed a large log of wood which hung in the fork of a tree some six feet from the ground. ... The log was old and charred by fire, and must have weighed two or three tons.'[17] Edward and Richard were sceptical of Bangerang explanations that the log had been floated there by floodwaters, as this would have involved the inundation of large areas of land, which were then arid. Their doubts were shattered by the floods of 1843, when 'the greater portion of our run (*entre rios*) became inundated, much of it to the depth of several feet'. Curr described the flood as 'unpleasant ... difficult and inconvenient', the only solution to which was expanding his lease to include higher ground away from the rivers.[18]

In August 1843 Curr set out on his chestnut mare to scout the land between Wolfscrag and Tongala, through which he had often passed. This 40-mile stretch of 'undulating and sparsely-timbered country' was 'at that time entirely unoccupied'. The land had been 'waterless ... though well grassed and handsome' on previous visits, but the heavy rains had rendered the country desirable.[19] Forty years later, Curr recalled vividly the wet night he spent camping on these valuable grasslands: 'I slept soundly and comfortably until about midnight, when in a gradual sort of a way I became sensible that rain was falling in torrents.'[20] He described in detail the saturated plains on which he camped: 'so desolate and dank just then, so handsome and cheery at other times'. Nevertheless, the nostalgic lens of recollection tempered the discomfort: 'The chops of course were delicious, and champagne now-a-days is not the nectar that quart-pot tea was at twenty'. Curr's mood was surely further boosted by the fact that he had found a new squatting run of 50 square miles, which he called Coragorag – 'a sonorous appellation in the mouth of the Pinpandoor'.[21]

---

15   Scott 1967: 292–293.
16   Finn 1888: 116.
17   Curr 1883: 216.
18   Curr 1883: 217; *entre rios* means 'between rivers' in Portuguese.
19   Curr 1883: 220.
20   Curr 1883: 225.
21   Curr 1883: 220–222.

3. 'A Station Formed at Tongala'

Harley Forster has explained that the 'efficient squatter' established a seasonal routine for grazing, 'influenced in his decisions by possibilities of drought on the plains and floods on the rivers and creeks'.[22] Curr certainly introduced such a regime and moved two flocks to Coragorag shortly after his visit. With his flocks still expanding, Curr subsequently looked further south to the plains of Colbinabbin, but on this occasion the environmental effects of fire influenced his movements. In November and December of 1843 a widespread fire had swept the Colbinabbin area and was followed by extensive rains. With the creek full and fresh grasses growing, Curr resolved to lease the Colbinabbin plains, which he had admired since first crossing them in 1841. He later recalled that while in Melbourne for a holiday, he encountered by chance the Commissioner of Crown Lands and made a verbal application for the country. He was frustrated when the commissioner became unusually attentive to legal procedure and insisted Curr must be the first to put stock on the relevant country if any lease were to be granted. Curr recalled that his frustration at these conditions derived principally from the fact that his planned sojourn of several weeks in town was cut short by the immediate need to move sheep to Colbinabbin before any of his neighbours did so. He wrote that he 'considered himself entitled' to make the verbal application and surmised the commissioner knew of another (perhaps favoured) pastoralist who was interested in the Colbinabbin country.

Curr rode quickly to Tongala and prepared to relocate a 'flock of scabby sheep' to Colbinabbin. Richard Curr took charge of the sheep, while Edward packed a dray with supplies for a new station and followed behind. Once again, Curr had a diverting tale to tell: in this case it involved the competing claim for Colbinabbin by a neighbouring squatter, whom Curr managed to outmanoeuvre. When he arrived at Colbinabbin with the dray he was pleased:

> I was delighted to find my party in undisturbed occupation, and that the little serpentine creek, embosomed in trees, now full to overflowing, and the green rolling plains and picturesque ranges were indeed possessions of my father. Of course, only squatting possessions, which, however, before the discovery of gold it was generally thought would last our time at least. As for the value of the country thus secured, it could easily have been sold for a thousand pounds even in those times, so that we had every reason to be pleased.[23]

Curr's contentment was broken a few days later when his neighbour arrived, hoping to scout out the location for his own station at Colbinabbin. He was extremely frustrated to find Curr already there: 'It rather amused me that my neighbour, having no one else to make a confidant of, in a very complaining

---

22 Forster 1965b: 15.
23 Curr 1883: 337–338.

sort of way sought my sympathy in his disappointment.' After sharing a pot of tea the rival squatter got up to leave, an expression on his face betraying his intention to dispute Curr's claim by placing a flock of his own sheep on the same country:

> Not appearing to notice his words, I said carelessly, 'How I regret that I cannot, like you, leave this rough work behind me and ride home. However, in another fortnight the sheep-dressing will be over and I shall be at liberty.' 'What,' said he, 'are your sheep scabby?' 'Oh yes,' I replied, 'this flock is a little so, and I have brought it here to be out of the way.' This answer rendered his bringing his sheep near mine, for the purpose of disputing my possession, out of the question, and was, I think, the last drop of bitterness in his cup that day: at all events he turned his horse's head and rode away without a word in reply.[24]

The irony that Edward M. Curr, Victoria's Chief Inspector of Stock, had earlier gained possession of a squatting run worth 'a thousand pounds' by stocking it with scabby sheep would certainly not have been lost on his 1880s readership. In fact, Curr honestly confessed to scabby sheep at various points in *Recollections of Squatting in Victoria*. If nothing else, he showed that his prize-winning essay on scab in sheep, published in 1865, was informed by personal experience.

By the end of 1844 the Curr brothers had successfully occupied four valuable squatting runs: Tongala, the Moira, Coragorag and Colbinabbin. They subsequently added smaller pockets of land to the various leases and all received Indigenous names, including Cócoma, Dírra, Wóllenjo, Gargárro, Námerong and Ullumbúbbil. At the full extent of their pastoral empire the Currs held over 300 square miles of land in northern Victoria.[25] The pastoral leases were all held in the name of Edward Curr senior, with the exception of the Gágarro run, which was later known as Corop. Edward M. Curr leased the Corop run in partnership with his brother William and they stocked it with 1,500 ewes given to them by their father. When William died in 1846 he left his share of the venture to Edward. Although it was a small part of the Currs' extensive pastoral holdings, the Corop run gave Edward M. Curr some financial independence from the wider family business. Nevertheless, for most of the 1840s he lived at the head station at Tongala.

---

24   Curr 1883: 339–340.
25   Curr 1883: 331.

'The Father of Separation'

During the 1840s the Curr family revolved around the prominent, controversial, antagonistic and imposing figure of Edward Curr senior. He was the head of a large family and exerted considerable control over the lives and fortunes of his many children. Apart from directing his sons in their squatting ventures, Curr senior was a prominent businessman and investor, but he is best remembered for his significant public role in the emerging Port Phillip District. Edward M. Curr described his father as a big man, who was over six feet tall and weighed 17 stone: 'He had a fine head, large and square, a massive jaw, and abstracted looking grey eyes.'[26] After moving to Melbourne in early 1842, Curr had established a home for his large family on the Yarra River at Abbotsford, which he named St Heliers. His daughter Elizabeth, who was eight-years-old when she arrived in Melbourne, later wrote that St Heliers was a picturesque property, comprising 20 acres of shrubberies, lawns, flower gardens and fruit gardens; she recalled that visitors from the Melbourne township 'seemed to look at the garden as a sort of promised land, and many a basketful of fruit was sent to them by one of the gardeners'.[27] Elizabeth also recalled that her father acquired two roan horses and a carriage from London, which he used to travel into town for his business and political activities.

Edward M. Curr later explained that his father moved to the Port Phillip District because it 'offered to his young and numerous family, advantages incomparably greater than any presented by Van Diemen's Land'. Despite this, Curr senior soon immersed himself in public affairs and, according to his son, neglected his family's interests: 'from the day of his arrival in Port Phillip [he] seemed almost to forget that he had any family, as he busied himself heart and soul with politics'.[28] Curr senior's prominent public role was evident within a year of his arrival in Melbourne. Despite courting controversy in a quarrel with temperamental Judge Willis of the Supreme Court, Curr was soon seen as a potential political leader.[29] In January 1843 he was nominated to represent Melbourne at the first elections for the New South Wales Legislative Council, but his campaign was opposed by the prominent Presbyterian John Dunmore Lang, who backed Mayor Henry Condell as a rival candidate. Lang himself also stood for one of the five places on the council allotted to the Port Phillip District, despite the fact that he was a resident of Sydney. Fuelling the sectarian conflict, Curr announced that he would not sit in the council if Lang also won a seat, but was spared this apparent indignity when Condell won the Melbourne election by 295 votes to 261. The result was immediately followed by riots, as Catholic supporters of

---

26   Curr, 'Memoranda Concerning Our Family' (1877), SLV, MS 8998.
27   Elizabeth Sarah Pennefather (née Curr), 'In the Early Days' (1911), Murrumbogie Papers.
28   Curr, 'Memoranda Concerning Our Family' (1877), SLV, MS 8998.
29   For details of Curr's quarrel with Justice Willis, see Pike 1966: 269–272.

Curr complained of irregular voting; a contingent of mounted police arrived and Captain Dana read the riot act. Meanwhile, Edward Curr pleaded with the rioters to disperse. In Sydney, Governor Gipps recognised Curr as the superior candidate but did not regret his defeat; he wrote to Superintendent Charles La Trobe three days after the riot that Curr had 'showed no unfrequent signs of a bad and bitter spirit'.[30]

Curr's feud with Lang continued, but his focus soon shifted to the campaign for Port Phillip's independence from New South Wales and its Sydney powerbrokers. As D.H. Pike has noted, Curr 'threw his energies into the cause with such unmatched zeal that, although the movement had begun in 1840, he was later called "the Father of Separation."'[31] Some Port Phillip squatters who favoured the cause of Separation worried that Curr's quarrelsome and ungovernable temper might prejudice the cause.[32] Nevertheless, Curr guided the campaign to a successful conclusion, news of which reached Melbourne from London only days before he died in November 1850. Meanwhile, he served two terms on the New South Wales Legislative Council and became a prominent spokesman on several important issues affecting the squatters.

In 1844 Governor Gipps had proposed new land regulations, which quickly attracted the opposition of squatters throughout New South Wales. Gipps proposed that no pastoral lease should comprise more than 20 square miles and stations more than seven miles apart should be considered separate, each incurring its own £10 annual lease fee. Furthermore, in order to retain their right of occupation, squatters would periodically be required to purchase 320-acre blocks within their lease for not less than £1 per acre.[33] The proposed regulations were particularly distasteful to the larger landholders, so Edward Curr senior was not surprisingly a prominent spokesman against the proposal. He addressed a meeting of Port Phillip squatters on Batman's Hill on 1 June 1844 and contributed to the campaign that ultimately saw the Gipps plan defeated.

While Curr enjoyed the support of his fellow squatters on the issue of land regulations, his support for the importation of penal labour earned the ire of many. When funding for the assisted immigration of free settlers was exhausted in 1843, Curr and others began to seek alternative sources of labour for their business and pastoral enterprises. Perhaps due to his Van Diemen's Land experience, Curr senior was not opposed to the use of convict labour and threw his support behind a proposal to import 'Pentonville Prisoners' to Port Phillip. The Pentonville Prison was opened in north London in 1842 with a reformist ideology that became a model for the penal system throughout the British

---

30   Shaw 1989: 217.
31   Pike 1966.
32   See, for example, Neil Black to T.S. Gladstone, 16 October 1845, quoted in Kiddle 1967: 151.
33   Kiddle 1967: 165.

Empire. The increased focus on prisoner rehabilitation did not assuage the fears of the citizens of Port Phillip, who opposed the introduction of any form of penal labour. Curr justified his support for the scheme with an argument based on pragmatism: he insisted that he would prefer free labour, but that none was available; furthermore, the labour shortage would push up wages, which would in turn encourage 'shoals of expirees' to converge on Port Phillip from both Van Diemen's Land and New South Wales.[34]

Curr's economic argument did not win the support of all squatters with many fearing the social cost of penal labour. The issue was extremely divisive: in January 1847 Melbourne's *Argus* condemned the plan as 'the audacious attempt of a few shamelessly mercenary men to sacrifice a whole community for the sake of alleviating a temporary pressure in the labour market'.[35] Despite considerable opposition, however, Curr and his supporters won the debate and 1,727 Pentonville prisoners arrived in Melbourne between 1844 and 1849. During the same period as many as 2,000 ex-convicts arrived from Van Diemen's Land, ensuring that wages for the Curr family's shepherds remained low.[36] Edward M. Curr later recorded that the annual salary for his shepherds dropped from £45 when he arrived in 1841 to around £20 for most of the 1840s.[37]

Edmund Finn described Edward Curr senior as 'one of the ablest and best known, though not most popular, men of his day'. Although he was unpopular for many reasons, his role in gaining independence for Port Phillip was lauded. This impression must only have gained over time, especially since the new Colony of Victoria was proclaimed shortly before its valuable gold resources were discovered. Finn noted that when Curr died, 'the event was deplored with an universal regret, which was deepened by the singularly melancholy coincidence of the announcement of the victory, and the loss of the commander of the campaigns'.[38] Edward M. Curr was similarly inclined to credit his father as a leading Port Phillip citizen.[39] In a family memoir penned in 1877 he observed:

> It would I think be difficult to find anyone more respected by those who knew him, or more respectable than my father, for he was a man of marked ability, extended sympathies, unimpeachable character, distinguished presence, the head of the patriotic movement then on foot in the colony, and of what were then large pecuniary resources.

Curr was not, however, under any illusions as to the controversy his father courted. He wrote in 1877 that his father 'was decidedly unpopular with

---

34 Kiddle 1967: 152.
35 Kiddle 1967: 157.
36 Kiddle 1967: 153.
37 Curr 1883: 152.
38 Finn 1888: 28, 858.
39 Curr 1883: 151–152.

the gentry' and attributed this fact not to his Catholicism but to 'an imperial manner, which was as natural to him as his skin'. He concluded that his father's manner 'was not relished' and noted that even 25 years after his death it had not been forgiven.[40]

Curr's 1877 memoir gives some insight into what appears to have been a strained father-son relationship. He recalled that his father's overbearing manner was evident not only in his public role, but in his daily life:

> I never saw him in company or conversation, even on the most trifling occasions, when anything but the first place was given up to him. Habitually and unknown to himself, he imposed his will on others, and I have always thought that people treasured up a resentment against what I may call a state of momentary vassalage to which they habitually found themselves reduced in his company or rather, I should say, in his presence, for to that it amounted.

Like Melbourne's early population, Edward M. Curr found his father's manner restrictive and controlling. Furthermore, he formed the opinion that the time-consuming campaign for Separation ('my father constantly laboured for seven years') was ultimately detrimental to the Curr family's best interests:

> The money which he expended keeping house in town with the object of procuring separation which he considered his particular mission, had it been expended in the purchase of property of any kind, would have been worth to his family ten years after his death a quarter of a million of money.[41]

These financial calculations were clearly performed with the benefit of hindsight and Curr's father can hardly be condemned for failing to anticipate the discovery of gold. This is only one of many instances in his 1877 memoir where Edward M. Curr explains how his family might have been richer. Nevertheless, that he wrote as much in a memoir intended for family suggests a degree of filial animosity that should not be discounted.

A Bush Gentleman

While Edward Curr senior pursued a business and political career in Melbourne, his sons set about establishing their position within the social world of the frontier. In his memoir, Edward M. Curr conveyed his perceived status most prominently through his characterisation of the working class. He delighted in

---

40 Curr, 'Memoranda Concerning Our Family' (1877), SLV, MS 8998.
41 Curr, 'Memoranda Concerning Our Family' (1877), SLV, MS 8998.

describing the exploits of his ex-convict employees – an 'average lot of ruffians', who, at least initially, appeared to be universally alcoholic. In one passage he explained the extensive demands of his first crew of shearers, which included four glasses of rum per day: 'I felt myself to be a much abused master, and should, no doubt, have struck employing men entirely, had it been possible to conduct the business of sheep-farming without them.' Curr created humour through irony, but he also reinforced his superior social position. In order to acquire the crucial keg of rum for his shearers, Curr despatched one of his men who 'was not so immoderate a drunkard as the generality of my party' to the nearest publican, 100 miles away. When writing *Recollections of Squatting* Curr clearly enjoyed describing the man's journey, which involved getting all the shepherds on the road drunk and replacing the missing rum with water. Subsequently, Curr was forced to organise the washing and shearing of his sheep with an inebriated or hung-over workforce, until he watered down the rum still further with desirable results.[42]

In *Recollections of Squatting in Victoria* Curr rarely named his employees, who were generally 'a nondescript lot' fitting a predictable stereotype. A notable exception was his first bullock driver, 'Dan', who stood out among Curr's 'motley crew', but whose company involved only 'a little conversation and a good deal of smoking'. Another servant worthy of particular mention was Jimmy-Jack, a young Bangerang man whose services were welcomed at Tongala: 'Of a particularly mild disposition, he seemed to take to civilized ways more easily than his fellows'. Jimmy-Jack fulfilled the role of 'general useful' around the station 'in which capacity his obliging disposition made him quite a favourite'. Jimmy-Jack's tasks included fetching horses, working bullocks and accompanying the dray to town; he would also 'ride with my brother and myself when we went out kangarooing or duck shooting'. Curr was apparently very fond of Jimmy-Jack, although the principal motive for his inclusion in the narrative of *Recollections of Squatting in Victoria* was to describe his death following a 'disgusting assassination' by Aborigines at Colbinabbin. Curr insisted that without descriptions of such events 'the life of an Australian savage would be ill understood'.[43]

Curr noted that his shepherds often became quite eccentric through isolation, but some 'improved their minds a good deal by reading'. Recalling one instance, he explained that he lent a 'trashy romance' to a shepherd, who read it over and over until 'he must have almost known it by heart'. The man subsequently read more widely from Curr's library, and also purchased books from a hawker who visited Tongala. Years later the shepherd asked to borrow the original novel, which he still fancied was 'the finest book that ever was written', but he was

---

42   Curr 1883: 97–98.
43   Curr 1883: 322, 64, 321, 325.

puzzled to find that it now appeared to be 'a poor childish sort of book'. Curr concluded: 'So I saw the man's literary taste had grown, unknown to himself, and his endeavour to read the old book was like trying to put on the boots which had fitted him in boyhood.'[44]

The isolation of station life — free as it was from the temptation of drink and 'anything worth stealing' — had a reforming role among the expired convicts who almost invariably came into his employ. Moreover, Curr believed that the easing of the labour shortage that plagued the early 1840s led to an improvement in the quality of his employees:

> In the case of the working class, the first step towards better things was a great fall in wages, which practically had the effect of transforming them from drunkards and idlers into shepherds and hutkeepers, and, so far as my experience went, eventually into tolerable servants and citizens.[45]

The tight labour market, high wages and predominantly convict labour of the early 1840s required, Curr implied, a tactful approach: he credited his apparently positive relationships with employees to 'the humility which became a master of those times'.[46] Curr thus portrayed himself as one well able to manage the rough working men who staffed his station, whom he described with both irony and affection: 'Truly a heterogeneous lot they were — horse stealers, machine-breakers, homicides, disorderly soldiers, drunken marines, house breakers, petty thieves, and so on.' In keeping with the nostalgic tone of his account, Curr argued that ex-convicts were preferable to free immigrants as employees; the latter, 'though often sober men ... were generally dissatisfied and had a very faint idea of obeying orders'.[47]

Throughout his detailed account of his squatting years, Curr emphasised the charming simplicity of the early days. His memoir suggests that rapid pastoral expansion was achieved with little trouble; there were occasional disputes with rival squatters or disgruntled Aborigines, but none that hindered the success of the venture. Within a very short time, he was able to settle into a pleasantly bucolic existence, which he remembered fondly for the rest of his life. Curr recorded that 'the hard sort of life we led at first did not last more than two or three years' after which two brothers returned from England 'to lessen our labours'. Subsequently, the Curr brothers chose to 'give up work, in great measure, for supervision' and divided their vast runs into manageable portions. They established a second head station at Colbinabbin, which Richard oversaw,

---

44 Curr 1883: 441–442.
45 Curr 1883: 438.
46 Curr 1883: 438.
47 Curr 1883: 443–444.

another at the Moira for a younger brother, and a small substation at Coragorag: 'From this time our chief occupation was riding about the run looking after shepherds and hunting wild dogs.'[48]

Curr's sister Elizabeth later recalled that her brothers adopted pig hunting as an appropriate sport for their leisure time: 'they turned out a special breed of Pigs, and very soon had any amount of Pig Sticking, trading with the Blacks in spears suitable for the sport'.[49] Curr himself also recorded his love of hunting and described the meetings of squatters at Moama in a chapter titled 'Hunting with Fox-Hounds'.[50] He regularly noted the prominent role of horses in his squatting exploits. They were crucial to his account of the unmistakable squatter of the 1840s, 'who strode so gaily up Collins-street in his Hessian boots, with the "action" of one who, even when on foot, could not altogether get rid of the feeling of having a horse between his legs'. Similarly, he described the curious tendency for squatters to acquire a reputation more properly belonging to his horse: 'with the estimate of the rider the capacity and peculiarities of his horse were often whimsically mixed up'.[51]

As time passed, Curr was able to establish himself in the apparently satisfying role of the gentleman squatter. In *Recollections of Squatting in Victoria*, the social status of the Curr brothers is prominently conveyed by their education and love of reading. The arrival of a new book at Tongala was a source of joy, but if there were only one it also presented a dilemma, as it was hard for one brother to enjoy the new volume while another sat opposite 'apparently going through "Hamlet" for the hundredth time'. In a typically nostalgic passage, Curr stressed that the squatters of the 1840s were a highly educated lot; though books were hard to come by, their shelves 'were better provided than at present, and typical of a more educated class'.[52]

Although noting the bookish ways of his family, Curr also described the great pleasure he derived from remote bush life. He confessed to 'a somewhat vagabond turn of mind' and described in detail his 'Rambles in Unoccupied Country'. Each year before lambing in May, Curr habitually passed two or three weeks in the remote country north-west of Tongala. He usually took at least one of his brothers and sometimes 'a couple of Blacks'. Curr described his vagrant existence at these times as 'somewhat savage in its tendency' but nonetheless 'a relief from the sameness of station life'. He also believed his love of rambling was unusual for the time:

---

48   Curr 1883: 358.
49   Elizabeth Pennefather (née Curr), 'In the Early Days' (1911), Murrumbogie Papers.
50   Curr 1883: 380.
51   Curr 1883: 100–102.
52   Curr 1883: 369–370.

> This custom of ours, I may say, was an exceptional one, as bushmen generally took their holidays in town; 'the pleasure of the pathless woods,' of which we have all read, being indulged in no oftener than was absolutely unavoidable. With me the reverse was the case, as I preferred hunting excursions into unoccupied country to visits to the city; hence gradually I came to look on the country of our rambles, which in extent might be a hundred and fifty miles by fifty, as a sort of *plaisaunce*, or grand park, on which I was free to wander, shoot, hunt, fish, and do as I chose, my only care being to escape getting a spear through me.[53]

During his squatting years Curr developed a basic interest in Aboriginal custom and language that would mature later in his life. In *Recollections of Squatting in Victoria* he noted that he immediately had 'a good deal of curiosity about the aborigines' and observed their ways and picked up 'a smattering of their language'. A few pages later, however, Curr notes that he did not occupy his leisure hours with scientific or cultural inquiry; he and his brother Richard were ignorant of 'botany and bird-stuffing' and 'neither did it occur to us to take up the Aboriginal languages, or grapple with the traditions of the ancient and singular race with which we had been brought in contact'. Deferring ethnological pursuits until later in life, Curr and his brother took instead to 'much swimming, throwing spears, [and] climbing trees after the native fashion (by means of tomahawk-notches)'.[54]

Nevertheless, because Tongala was an out-of-the-way place (an *ultima thule* as Curr put it), white visitors were rare; as a result, 'novelty … usually came by means of our black neighbours'. Although not a serious ethnologist during the period he lived among the Bangerang people, Curr was captivated by the surprising novelty of the customs he casually observed. He recalled in considerable detail the first time he witnessed a corroboree in 1842, during a meeting of the Bangerang and Ngooraialum tribes. He was 'strongly impressed' by the scene, which he described variously as extraordinary, singular, ghastly, sinister, thrilling and strange. Curr revealed that at the climax of the performance he had feared for his life when the dancers made as if to throw their spears at the Curr brothers:

> The idea that all was over with us, and an intense longing for my pistols, flashed through my brain. But before I could attempt to move, the climax had been reached, and the performers, dropping their spear points to the ground, burst into one simultaneous yell, which made the old woods ring again, and then hurried at once out of sight, a laughing mob, into the forest's gloom.[55]

---

53 Curr 1883: 419–420.
54 Curr 1883: 92–92, 126–127.
55 Curr 1883: 140.

Certainly, Indigenous custom must have been intriguingly alien to Curr as a young man in the early 1840s. His recollection of the corroboree appears vivid, although it was certainly also shaped by his attempt to produce an engaging narrative for his 1880s readership. This is particularly evident at the conclusion of his description, when he pondered the meaning of the dramatic climax: 'Was that yell, fancy suggested, the farewell cry to pleasant earth of a rabble-rout of fiends hurrying back to subterranean prisons in obedience to some mysterious power?'[56] This passage suggests, along with many others, that Curr's ultimate goal in writing *Recollections of Squatting in Victoria* was to entertain his reader with a diverting account of events long past. We can only speculate as to how different Curr's description of the corroboree might have been had he written it in 1842.

In an engaging literary style, *Recollections of Squatting in Victoria* charts Curr's journey from a novice grazier to an experienced bushman, and ultimately a gentleman squatter. Along the way, his social status and his apparent skill at managing both Indigenous people and the working class are asserted. The rudiments of a conventional upper-class life are present in the form of reading and hunting, even if Curr's living conditions were simple and his love for rambling was 'savage in its tendency'. Certainly, Curr stressed the simplicity of the pre-gold era of Victorian history; nonetheless, his narrative emphasised his role as a pioneer of the squattocracy that became Victoria's upper class.

Towards the end of *Recollections of Squatting in Victoria* Curr describes the success of his pastoral endeavours, which despite an uncertain beginning proved lucrative. When he left the colony in 1851 the family business was well established and highly profitable:

> remembering that the £1,500 so ill invested in Wolfscrag and the £500 worth of sheep received from Steele's Creek had been producing, for several years before I left, a net income ranging from £1,000 to £2,500 a year, I think it will be admitted that the undertaking was brought to a successful issue.

Aside from an enviable annual income, the Currs held pastoral leases over 300 square miles of 'first-class quality' country with 30,000 sheep on the ground. Furthermore, 'with the help of a few tanks' Curr believed the land could support a flock of 100,000 sheep.[57] This substantial and lucrative enterprise was built, of course, on the back of Indigenous dispossession, as the next chapter shows.

---

56   Curr 1883: 140.
57   Curr 1883: 449–450.

4. Claiming the Moira

A common belief that surrounds Edward M. Curr is that he was unusually sensitive to the plight of Australian Indigenous people. Justice Olney implied such a view in his *Yorta Yorta* judgement when he noted that Curr had 'clearly established a degree of rapport with the local Aboriginal people'.[1] Earlier, historians had regularly followed the lead of the *Australian Dictionary of Biography* and asserted Curr's 'sympathetic understanding'. To a certain extent, this view was justified: Curr was both observant and curious, and evidently acquainted himself with Aborigines more than the average pastoralist. He described some aspects of Indigenous culture with a dignity that distinguishes him from many contemporaries, even if he also insisted that Aboriginal life was savage and violent. Moreover, Curr apparently strove to avoid violent confrontations with the people whose land he usurped.

The mainstream view of Curr's attitudes towards Aborigines appears to derive, however, from his own account in *Recollections of Squatting in Victoria*, with little consideration of alternative sources. In certain passages Curr portrayed himself as one who protected the Aborigines wherever possible. He recounted, for example, his visit to a convict hut-keeper at Wyuna, whom he reprimanded for the 'cowardly and barbarous act' of shooting at an unarmed Aboriginal man. Curr surmised that his concern for Aboriginal welfare was unusual for the time: 'Ever after, I dare say, he [the hut-keeper] looked on me as a sort of dangerous lunatic for troubling myself about the lives of a few Blacks'.[2] Harley Forster observed in his introduction to the abridged *Recollections of Squatting in Victoria* in 1965: 'About the white interlopers, [Curr] is usually gently ironic, sometimes shocked, and occasionally angry.'[3] Although Forster provided a good summary of the attitudes to frontier violence expressed by Curr in his 1883 memoir, he did not adequately explore alternative accounts of Curr's pastoral activities. In this way, the view of Curr as sympathetic to Aborigines is primarily a function of Curr's own writings about himself. When *Recollections of Squatting in Victoria* is considered within the context of other primary evidence from the 1840s a more complicated picture emerges.

---

1   *Members of the Yorta Yorta Aboriginal Community v Victoria* (1998) FCA 1606, [53].
2   Curr 1883: 95.
3   Forster 1965a: vii.

The Moira

On Christmas Day 1842 Edward M. Curr arrived at Tongala ahead of a flock of 2,000 sheep, which he was moving north from the Currs' station at Steele's Creek, near Kilmore. Richard Curr, who had been managing Tongala, reported to his older brother that valuable grazing land was unoccupied to the north in the region known as 'the Moira'. In *Recollections of Squatting in Victoria* Curr recounted his first visit to these valuable flood plains east of the Murray River: 'under water for several months of the winter and spring, it abounded in summer in excellent sheep feed … and was usually as green as an emerald from November till March'. Curr briefly noted another crucially important characteristic of the Moira:

> As we learned afterwards, its extensive reed-beds were the great stronghold of the Bangerang Blacks, whom, as will be told presently, my brother had found somewhat troublesome during my absence at Steele's Creek; and owing to the plentiful food supply, it was a favourite place of meeting for all the tribes in the neighbourhood. Hence, it had advantages and disadvantages.[4]

In his book Curr does not immediately elaborate on how his Indigenous neighbours had become 'troublesome'. Two chapters later the reader learns that as many as 200 sheep had been speared by the Bangerang in two separate incidents that Curr characterised as childish naughtiness rather than organised resistance. The sheep spearing occurred about a year after Curr had first arrived at Tongala and preceded his decision to expand his pastoral lease into the Bangerang stronghold. Reading between the lines of *Recollections of Squatting in Victoria*, there appears to be more at stake than Curr suggests; in fact, contemporary evidence confirms an extremely tense relationship between the Currs and the Bangerang.

Shortly after Curr's return to Tongala in late December 1842, he and Richard rode north to the Moira in search of pastures. In Curr's memoir the sense of discovering an untouched paradise is strong. After crossing the Towro sandhill, the brothers passed the Madowla lagoon, where 'an Aboriginal belle' sang joyfully: 'The notes rang clear and silvery on the still morning air; the songstress … infusing into her lay the vivacity and *abandon* of life's springtime.'[5] Continuing north to the Baala Creek, Curr arrived at the Moira for the first time, where a Bangerang presence was evident in the 'camp fires smouldering under the shade of a spreading tree'. He viewed the Moira as a picturesque wilderness and was quite taken with its natural beauty: 'The grass under foot, as yet undefiled by flock or

---

4 Curr 1883: 166–167.
5 Curr 1883: 167–168, emphasis in the original.

herd, was as green and fresh as Eden.' Nonetheless, as Curr later wrote, 'we were just then intent on sheep feed, and not on scenery'; consequently, the brothers found a tall red gum and climbed to its high branches, from where they could view the surrounding country and 'discuss its capabilities at our leisure'.[6]

Returning to the Bangerang camp, Curr enlisted the aid of Tommy, 'a rather civilised Black', who agreed to guide him down the Murray River in a canoe from the Baala Creek (Broken Creek) to Pama (Barmah). In his recollections, Curr delighted in describing this river journey, which took him through unexplored territory: 'Stately and hushed, old Tongala flowed on through his trackless woods!' Tommy explained to Curr the territorial boundaries of the various Bangerang clans: the Wongatpan (Tommy's people) occupied the east bank of the Murray, while the Moitheriban (Moira people) occupied the west bank, 'a numerous tribe, [which] had plenty of fish and thousands of spears'. Curr also recalled in minute detail the information Tommy provided regarding individual ownership of fishing weirs constructed at the mouths of creeks: 'these were evidently very important matters with Tommy'.[7]

Figure 10: Aboriginal Fishing Camp on the River Murray, Near Lake Moira (1872). Samuel Calvert.

Engraving. State Library of Victoria, IAN21/05/72/117.

---

6   Curr 1883: 170–171.
7   Curr 1883: 173–175.

In one of the better-known passages in *Recollections of Squatting in Victoria*, Curr then related his memorable encounter with a Bangerang fishing party. One member of the party, an elder who Curr surmised was 90-years-old, initiated a sustained protest against Curr's invasion:

> His fishing spear quivered in his hand, and, after an abortive attempt at a war-like caper, he howled, abused, and spat at me, in senile fury, asking, as Tommy afterwards explained, why I came to the Moira? What I wanted? That I was a demon from the grave! That the water, the fish, and the ducks belonged to his tribe. That he spat at me and hated me. That I was Pekka (a ghost), but that man or devil he would spear me![8]

Meanwhile, the rest of the fishing party implored their elder to retreat, fearful Curr would raise his gun, 'of which weapon they well knew the use'. According to Curr, a middle-aged man then forced a ten-year-old girl to fetch the old man to safety, clearly assuming that 'white men did not war with children'. According to his recollections, Curr responded in a way that clearly conveys his paternalistic attitude:

> Curious to test the temper of the people, I whispered to Tommy to be silent, that I should not hurt her; and raised my gun to my shoulder. The child, now not many yards off, noticed the action, looked me full in the face, and without altering her course, gathered her opossum-rug tightly about her, and with somewhat stately step, passed close before the gun to the gibbering old savage. Addressing him in a low soft tone, without further notice of me, she took his hand in hers.[9]

Curr watched the girl lead the old man to safety then instructed Tommy to proceed down the river, as he was 'unwilling to annoy these people further'. Rounding the next bend Curr reviewed the incident with his guide:

> 'Well, well!' said Tommy, 'big one stupid ole man! No gammon!' 'What name belong to young girl?' said I. 'Undyărning,' replied Tommy. Good nerves, Undyărning, thought I, and a good representative of her race in that particular; and we again floated silently down our liquid road, between grand old gum trees, abundance of couch-grass, and clumps of reeds, up which climbed convolvuli in waste luxuriance.[10]

In his memoir Curr proceeded to outline in detail the multitude of birds in the area (a sign, no doubt, of its untapped potential) and finally concluded: 'Being satisfied with what I had seen, I shortly after applied for, and obtained about

---

8 Curr 1883: 176–177.
9 Curr 1883: 178.
10 Curr 1883: 178–179.

eighty square miles of Moira country, which turned out very valuable.'[11] For Curr, the furious entreaties of a 'senile' old man to leave his country counted for little alongside the 'wasteful' abundance that, to him, was readily apparent.

Curr's narrative implies that the Bangerang people at the Moira were living in a state of nature, hitherto unaffected by the Currs' pastoral endeavours to the south. He noted that 'they never had the curiosity to have a look at my party, not fourteen miles off'.[12] Curr did not link the protests of the 'tribal grandsire' with the prevalent sheep stealing that preceded his visit to the Moira. A close reading of Curr's text reveals, however, that the elder's son Warri was a 'ringleader' in one of the earlier incidents. The chapter arrangement of Curr's memoir masks the reality of strong Bangerang resistance to his family's pastoral enterprise. In Chapter 16 he refers only obliquely to the Bangerang being 'troublesome', preferring to describe his discovery of the Eden-like Moira flood plains. Chapter 17 consists of tangential observations regarding 'Changes in Connection with Flora and Fauna'. When Curr returns to the sheep spearing incidents in Chapter 18, the strong link with his experience at the Moira is largely obscured. It is nonetheless certain that the hostility of the Bangerang was well known to Curr before his trip down the river with Tommy, and before his decision to expand his run to include 80 square miles of the Moira.

Sheep Stealing

Curr's account of the Bangerang attacks on his sheep is accurate in many of its details, but silent on several issues of importance; furthermore, its light-hearted tone belies the tense relations outlined in other accounts from the period. Curr described two incidents that occurred a few days apart; although he gives no specific date, he implies that they occurred a short time before he returned to Tongala in December 1842. Contemporary press reports reveal, however, that they occurred several months earlier in July 1842.[13] The first incident occurred in the section of Curr's pastoral station north of the Murray River, which was in the vicinity of the Moira lease he subsequently acquired. According to Curr's narrative, an apparently friendly Bangerang man (or 'gentle savage') visited a remotely stationed shepherd ('of an altogether unwarlike spirit') and requested some tobacco; during the exchange the Aborigine took the shepherd's carbine, which Curr explained had been left 'lying against a tree' nearby. A party of 70 Bangerang men, whose safety was now assured, emerged from the scrub and speared one sheep each to carry off for feasting.[14] Curr's recollected account

---

11   Curr 1883: 179.
12   Curr 1883: 175.
13   'Black outrage', *Port Phillip Gazette*, 25 February 1843: 2.
14   Curr 1883: 193–194.

suggests a case of simple trickery of a careless shepherd, but a deposition given by the shepherd at the time suggests that his assailant 'got behind him and took forcible possession of the gun [and] at the same moment another black levelled a spear at him'.[15]

A few days later two troopers from the border police force arrived at Tongala on their usual patrol. The troopers responded to reports of the incident by imprisoning an Indigenous man who happened to be at Tongala. The following day they forced him to guide them in search of the suspected sheep stealers; when the man tried to escape, not wishing to betray his people, the troopers shot him and he died shortly afterwards 'without a word or a groan'. Placing the dead man in a canoe, the troopers sent him down the river, presumably to be seen by his comrades. Curr later wrote: 'I always regretted this catastrophe.'[16] Shortly afterwards the Bangerang took another 120 stray lambs for a feast lasting three days. Curr concluded: 'Such feasting and greasing of heads had never probably been known in the history of the Bangerang, and no doubt the tribe was merry and witty at the expense of the "white-pella."'[17]

Edward Curr had been away at Steele's Creek during these events but heard of them from Richard Curr when he returned several months later. It was in this context that the Curr brothers visited the Moira in late December 1842. Meanwhile, reports of the incidents had reached the highest level of government in the Port Phillip District: on 31 December the Commissioner of Crown Lands, F.A. Powlett, reported the theft of 'a few' sheep from Curr's station.[18] In February 1843 Captain Henry Dana of the Native Police Corps reported the number of sheep stolen as 'upwards of two hundred'.[19]

In March 1843, while visiting the Currs at Tongala, the Chief Protector of Aborigines, George Augustus Robinson, recorded some further information, which helps explain how the animosity between the Currs and the Bangerang had grown. After making inquiries he noted that neighbouring pastoralists had not had any sheep stolen and were 'on good terms with the blacks'. One neighbour also provided an explanation as to why the Currs did not enjoy the same harmonious relationship:

> Mr. Irwin said, 'when Curr first went to the Murry [sic] the natives were friendly and assisted them with the sheep, but one of the natives' dogs got among the sheep and could not get out'. The natives tried to get it

---

15 'Black outrage', *Port Phillip Gazette*, 25 February 1843: 2; see also Committal before Frederick Berkley St John [Police Magistrate], 24 February 1843, PROV, VPRS 30P, Box 186, NCR 77, (reference kindly provided by His Honour Paul R. Mullaly QC).
16 Curr 1883: 196.
17 Curr 1883: 197.
18 F.A. Powlett to Charles La Trobe, 31 December 1842, PROV, CO 201/332, Item 46.
19 Henry Dana to Charles La Trobe, 2 February 1843, PROV, VA 473, VPRS 19, Box 41, 43/293.

out but could not. It at last got out and the elder Curr tried to shoot it. The natives drove it into the river and the young brother shot it getting out. The natives howled and cried for their dog.[20]

Edward Curr did not record his own version of this event, although he mentioned in an earlier chapter of *Recollections of Squatting in Victoria* his shooting of a mangy dingo at 'The Deserted Camp' of his Wongatpan neighbours.[21] Robinson also recorded evidence of conflict between Curr's shepherds and the Bangerang:

> Curr related a story this evening: a native was clearing out a sheep yard, a ruffian white man threw dung at him. The native did the same. The white man then flew in a passion and threw a stick at the native. The native then took a spear. The white man went to his hut got his gun fired but missed the black. The native jumped into the river.[22]

Robinson's diary suggests a level of conflict and disagreement between the Currs and the Bangerang that Edward Curr's own memoir generally avoids.

Captain Dana

Meanwhile, Superintendent Charles La Trobe had responded to reports of the sheep stealing by despatching Captain Dana and his Native Police Force to Curr's station. Dana reached Tongala on 29 January 1843 and explained (according to Curr) that he had been instructed 'to put himself at the head of his present force, apprehend all troublesome blacks, and restore quiet to the disaffected district'. In his recollections Curr derived considerable humour at Dana's expense, although he did not reveal the name of the 'officer' he so mercilessly parodied. He wrote that Dana's manner and general deportment 'tickled my fancy so much … that I have not yet forgotten it'. The historian Marie Fels describes Curr's account as 'witty and erudite … [but] also patronising and distant, leaving him quite definitely on the side of the angels, bountiful and merciful in his relationships with Aborigines in general, and only a little bit just'.[23] It is a reasonable critique, particularly when Dana's official record of his activities is compared to Curr's recollection. While Curr chose to trivialise the events and mock Dana's self importance and military precision, Dana's account to La Trobe portrays a virtual state of war. It is worth reproducing at length:

---

20   G.A. Robinson, Sunday 26 March 1843, in Clark 2000, vol 3.
21   Curr 1883: 148–150.
22   G.A. Robinson, Monday 27 March 1843, in Clark 2000, vol 3.
23   Fels 1988: 159.

Sir,

I have the honor to report that I arrived with the Police under my command at Mr Curr's Station near the junction of the Goulburn and Murray on the 29th Ulto.

Mr Curr informed me that the natives were assembled in large numbers on the southern bank of the Murray in the vicinity of his substation and daily threatening the lives of his men and attempting to take the sheep, and that the three ringleaders of the many, who a short time ago attacked the shepherd and took away his gun and sixty five sheep were among them. I accordingly proceeded on the 1st February in the direction of the native encampment, a distance of about twelve miles, accompanied by Mr Edward Curr, Corporal Rolfe of the Border Police, and Trooper McGregor of Native Police who I ordered to disguise themselves and carry no arms except pistols. We found the natives to the number of about 200 or upwards on both sides of the Murray near to Lake Moira, now an immense plain of high reeds. I sent Mr Edward Curr forward to see if he could identify the three natives who had taken a shepherd's gun and the sheep. He returned to me with a number of the natives following him, and pointed out the men. One of the Ring Leaders named Warri was taken by the troopers after a strong resistance, and in endeavouring to hold one of the others my horse shied, threw me, sprained my wrist. This man and the other escaped into the Murray and swam across. The other natives took to their spears and seemed inclined to attack us, and threw some spears, upon which I ordered Mr Edward Curr and trooper McGregor to fire across the river but the distance was too great to have any effect. The natives then ran into the reeds and thinking they were gone I dismounted and went up the River a short distance alone, but to my surprise a number of the natives rushed out of the reeds and threw several war spears at me, one of which struck me in the thigh, and at the same time Mr Edward Curr had a narrow escape of being speared in the side. I fired a small pistol into the reeds but without any effect. Several of them came on the banks of the river with their weapons in their hands and made violent gestures as if wishing to renew the skirmish. I called to them and told them if they would go away I would not fire on them any more, but they still kept their ground in a very determined manner. I then made a demonstration to swim across the river which had the effect of driving them into the reeds. I remained a short time longer and then returned to Mr Curr's station with Prisoner Warri in charge of the two Troopers.

> Mr Richard Curr informed me that some of the natives attempted to take sheep the night previous out of the yards but hearing the noise he got up and distinctly saw them run away from the folds.
>
> The number of sheep taken by the natives from Mr Curr within these last few months is upwards of two hundred.
>
> I deem it necessary to wait for Mr Curr's dray for a few days, by which I propose sending down the prisoner and the shepherd who can identify him.[24]

In *Recollections of Squatting in Victoria* Curr referred to Dana's official report, which he apparently read before Dana sent it to La Trobe. Curr focussed on some 'omissions' in Dana's account, which mostly related to the apparent ineptitude of Dana and his men and the farcical failure of the whole operation. He recalled the moment when Dana was speared:

> At this juncture, I recollect, the officer, who was leisurely scanning the opposite bank of the river, across which he had driven the enemy in such masterly style, received a slight wound in his sword arm from a spear hurled by a blackfellow from the opposite side. 'Hit at last!' was his laughing exclamation, as he handed me a white handkerchief, the corner of which I had noticed peeping from his shell-jacket, to bind up what he termed the 'scratch.'[25]

While Curr's account is certainly entertaining reading, it omits any mention of his own 'narrow escape' from a spear and the fact that he fired shots across the river upon Dana's instruction. Both Curr and Dana also implied by omission that no Aborigines sustained injuries during the altercation. An alternative account by Assistant Protector William Le Souëf, who visited the Moira a fortnight later, suggests otherwise; he discovered several injured Aborigines hiding in the reed-bed, one of whom was not expected to live.[26]

Continuing his comic account of the events, Curr focussed on the arrest of Warri, the so-called 'ringleader' of the sheep stealers. As mentioned, Curr had earlier identified Warri as a son of the 'gibbering old savage' who had harangued Curr at the Moira a month earlier. Curr recalled that Dana's troopers secured their prisoner by means of a rope 'one end of which was round his neck and the other made fast to a trooper's horse'. The troopers detained Warri at Tongala for three days using 'handcuffs round his ankles' and Curr recalled the 'wonderfully

---

24   Dana to La Trobe, 2 February 1843, PROV, VPRS 19, Box 41, 43/293.
25   Curr 1883: 200.
26   Cannon 1990: 140.

grotesque' manner in which Warri moved about the huts. Remembering these events four decades later, Curr related a conversation he apparently had with Warri:

> Sometimes, too, he would come and seat himself before the door of my hut, when little dialogues like the following would ensue:–
>
> Warri.– 'Well, massa!'
>
> A.– 'Well! Warri, my boy, sit down.'
>
> W.– 'Give me smoke? (I gave him some tobacco). Where police take me now?'
>
> A.– 'I believe to Melbourne.'
>
> W.– 'Melbourne, eh? What will the whitefellows in Melbourne do to me?'
>
> A.– 'Well, can't say. I don't know.'
>
> W.– 'I believe they'll hang me – eh?'
>
> A.– 'I believe so.'
>
> W.– 'Well! (with a loud cluck) well! why are you stupid? Why do you get your own blackfellows hung?'
>
> A.– 'Well! why do the Blacks eat up my sheep?'
>
> W.– 'Stupid! Stupid! Blackfellow.'
>
> Warri would then hobble off in the most comical way, with shortened stride, his pipe in his mouth, to seek sympathy elsewhere.[27]

Curr proceeded to explain why he had deliberately allowed Warri to believe he would be executed: 'My object in frightening the poor fellow was, of course, to impress on him thoroughly, and eventually through him on his tribe, the disagreeable consequences of sheep-stealing.'[28]

---

27 Curr 1883: 202–203.
28 Curr 1883: 203.

The Rehabilitation of Warri

Captain Dana took Warri to Melbourne and on 24 February 1843 he was committed to stand trial for sheep stealing. A magistrate took depositions from William Barker, the shepherd concerned, and from Curr himself, who stated that Warri had confessed his guilt to him.[29] George Augustus Robinson was also present and recorded in his journal that the assigned translator spoke 'not a word of Aborigine'. Robinson further noted that 'Young Curr' provided assistance with translation, an unsatisfactory arrangement given that Warri was charged with an offence against the property of Curr's father.[30] Warri was incarcerated pending his trial. On 16 March he appeared before Justice Willis of the Supreme Court, but the case was adjourned because the intended translator, the assistant protector William Le Souëf, had 'excused himself on the plea of having been bitten by a dog'.[31] Willis recorded in his case notes that Warri was 'not at present of suff[icien]t capacity to understand the nature of the proceed[in]gs'.[32] When Le Souëf again failed to appear on 7 April, Justice Willis dismissed the case on the grounds that it was impossible to instruct the defendant. The judge then placed Warri in the care of the assistant protector William Thomas.[33]

Curr's own account of Warri's trial portrays vividly the peculiar form of justice that surrounded frontier conflict in the 1840s, but once again his tone is light-hearted. Regarding the judge's concern that the accused did not understand the nature of the charges, Curr wrote whimsically: 'the expression of the prisoner's face whilst this point was being discussed was certainly strongly corroborative of the judge's view'.[34] Written 40 years after the events it describes, Curr's account is also inaccurate on a number of points. He wrongly suggests that after the trial was aborted Warri remained in prison, and that in this context he emerged as Warri's saviour:

> Seeing that nothing was done, and that Warri had become a law-point incarnate, and was neither to be tried nor set at liberty, I lost all interest in the matter and returned to Tongala. Being in Melbourne again, however, some three months later, I visited the prisoner in his cell, and found him in bad spirits and ill-health. He was delighted to see me …

---

29 Committal before Frederick Berkley St John [Police Magistrate], 24 February 1843, PROV, VPRS 30P, Box 186 NCR 77.
30 G.A. Robinson, Friday 24 February 1843, in Clark 2000, vol 3.
31 'Supreme Court (Criminal Side), 16 March 1843', *Port Phillip Gazette*, 18 March 1843: 4.
32 John Walpole Willis, 'Case Books, 1838–1843', n.d., no 14, p 120, Royal Historical Society of Victoria.
33 *Port Phillip Gazette*, 8 April 1843: 3.
34 Curr 1883: 204.

> So, as I pitied the poor fellow, thought he had been punished enough, and was of the opinion that his return to Tongala would add to the security of property there, I bestirred myself to get him released.[35]

Curr implies that Warri had been languishing in prison for three months, neglected and forgotten, but on this matter his recollections are at odds with contemporary records. From the day of his committal hearing on 24 February and throughout the court proceedings, Warri was entrusted to the special attention of assistant protector William Thomas, who described his duties in a quarterly report to Robinson: 'I have been engaged, per your orders, visiting and endeavouring to teach the black in gaol, in order to prepare him for his trial, which I feel I am incompetent to accomplish, not knowing a syllable of his language.'[36] For six weeks Thomas attended Warri in prison 'mostly two or three times a day' and he accompanied Warri to the Supreme Court on 16 March.[37] George Augustus Robinson's journal entry for that day reveals that Thomas was quite insistent that Warri 'be instructed and made acquainted with the proceedings against him'.[38] Thomas continued his daily visits to Warri until his second court appearance 8 April, when the court committed Warri to Thomas' care. For the next five weeks Warri accompanied Thomas on his daily duties, residing with him for much of this time at the protectorate station at Narre Narre Warren or at Thomas' son's farm at Moonee Ponds. Thomas firmly believed that Warri would happily have remained with him, if only his wife and children were brought to the protectorate station.[39] Warri's desire to return home prevailed, however, and he left Thomas on 17 May. Describing Warri's departure Thomas recorded: 'he looked back once or twice ere he got out of sight, and in his last look waved his hand, evidently not unmindful of the kindness he had received'.[40]

---

35   Curr 1883: 204–205.
36   William Thomas to George Augustus Robinson, 'Journal of Proceedings from 1st December 1842 to 1st March 1843', PROV, CO 201/344, Item 68.
37   Thomas to Robinson, 'Journal of Proceedings from 1st March to 1st June 1843', PROV, CO 201/344, Item 68.
38   G.A. Robinson, Thursday 16 March 1843, in Clark 2000, vol 3.
39   Thomas grew very fond of Warri and probably drew the sketch reproduced in Figure 11. Strangely, the annotations to the sketch record that the Native Police captured Warri in the Grampians, but in other respects the annotations fit Warri's encounter with Thomas. No other Aborigine named Warri appears in Thomas' personal journal.
40   Thomas to Robinson, 'Journal of Proceedings from 1st March to 1st June 1843', PROV, CO 201/344, Item 68.

Figure 11: Warrie. William Thomas [?].

Sketch. State Library of Victoria, R. Brough Smyth papers, MS 8781 Box 1176/7(a).

By contrast, in *Recollections of Squatting in Victoria* Curr asserted his own central role in Warri's saga. He did not mention Thomas at all, and claimed that he suggested to the authorities that Warri be released from prison. Furthermore, when this decision was reached Curr apparently conveyed the happy news to Warri:

> I visited Warri once more in his cell, and, after a little delicate badinage on the subject of hanging, informed him that he was to be set free … Poor Warri stared at me with all his eyes, and was some time before he could believe that I was in earnest, and that his difficulties were to come to so pleasing an end; and it was only after I had shown him a blanket, tomahawk, and a small supply of food, which I had brought for him, that he allowed himself to believe that what I said was the fact.[41]

---

41   Curr 1883: 205.

Although it is quite possible that Curr recommended the charges be dropped, his account overlooks the fact that Warri's release was the result of proper legal process and the established principle that a prisoner must understand the charges against him. Furthermore, he greatly exaggerates the time Warri spent in prison. Curr recalled that after the court hearing on 16 March he returned to Tongala, but lobbied for Warri's release from prison when back in Melbourne three months later. In fact, Warri had been released into Thomas' care only three weeks after the first trial hearing and had left Thomas to return home on 17 May.

Although Warri's motives and his understanding of the trial are difficult to discern, a Bangerang perspective is apparent in a report addressed to Charles La Trobe and written by a police officer at Narre Narre Warren on 27 April 1843: 'I beg to inform your Honor that yesterday afternoon a large party of Goulburn Blacks arrived here … [and their] intentions are to try and steal away the Black which Mr Assistant Protector Thomas has in his charge'.[42] While this report hints at Bangerang resistance to the legal regime of the pastoral frontier, for the most part any understanding of these events must be gleaned from the self-serving accounts of Edward M. Curr and William Thomas, each of whom asserts his own central role in the rehabilitation of Warri. Their accounts of Warri's trial also serve to convey their views regarding the management of Aboriginal people, Thomas emphasising Christian instruction and Curr focussing on the need for good-natured but firm discipline.[43] Curr concluded his description of the episode as follows:

> Ever after [Warri] and I were the best of friends, as he ascribed his release entirely to me; whilst the sage Bangerang, who firmly believed that unnumbered police troopers and officers in shell-jackets would be sent to the Moira to punish any undue indulgence in mutton on their part, became henceforth quite reclaimed characters.[44]

'The classical account of frontier conflict'

Curr's account of the Bangerang sheep stealing and Warri's arrest and trial was intended, of course, to entertain the readers of his nostalgic memoir, not to provide an accurate and disinterested account of the events. Elsewhere, however, Curr provided a very detailed and valuable description of the typical process of dispossession, which Henry Reynolds has described as 'the classical

---

42 Sergeant Peter Roberts Bennett to Charles La Trobe, 27 April 1843, PROV, VPRS 19, Box 44, 43/735.
43 Furphy 2013.
44 Curr 1883: 206.

account of frontier conflict'.[45] The passage to which Reynolds refers does not appear in *Recollections of Squatting in Victoria*, but rather in Curr's more serious ethnological work, *The Australian Race,* published in 1886:

> In the first place the meeting of the Aboriginal tribes of Australia and the White pioneer, results as a rule in war, which lasts from six months to ten years, according to the nature of the country, the amount of settlement which takes place in a neighbourhood, and the proclivities of the individuals concerned. When several squatters settle in proximity, the country they occupy is easy of access and without fastnesses to which the Blacks can retreat, the period of warfare is usually short and the bloodshed not excessive. On the other hand, in districts which are not easily traversed on horseback, in which the Whites are few in number and food is procurable by the Blacks in fastnesses, the term is usually prolonged and the slaughter more considerable. ...
>
> Hence, the meeting of the White and Black races in Australia, considered generally, results in war. Nor is it to be wondered at. The White man looks on the possession of the lands by the Blacks as no proper occupation, and practically and avowedly declines to allow them the common rights of human beings. On the other hand, the tribe which has held its land from time immemorial ... suddenly finds not only that strangers of another race have located themselves permanently on their lands, but that they have brought with them a multitude of animals, which devour wholesale the roots and vegetables which constitute their principal food, and drive off the game they formerly hunted.[46]

Certainly, this oft-quoted passage supports Reynolds' contention that Curr wrote the best overview of frontier conflict. His summary of frontier violence also included a frank, honest and disturbing description of the massacres occurring in 1880s Queensland at the hands of the Native Police Force. Curr described in clear and insightful language the shocking impact of British invasion on Australia's Indigenous peoples, thus leaving an enduring legacy to Australian historiography. As later chapters will show, he was in a possibly unique position to understand the typical pattern of conflict, due to both the formidable network of remotely stationed correspondents he assembled when conducting his ethnological research and to his own leading role in the pastoral industry of the Australian colonies. Many of Curr's correspondents were pastoralists who were familiar with the hostility of the frontier; as such, they were probably better placed to describe inter-racial violence than they were to

---

45 Reynolds 1982: 50. Reynolds repeated this view seven years later: '[Curr] wrote the best overview of frontier conflict'. See Reynolds 1989: 25.
46 Curr 1886, vol 1: 100–102.

provide the vocabularies and ethnological data that were the principal focus of Curr's project. Nevertheless, it is important to consider why Curr wrote such an excellent summary of the typical pattern of frontier violence. Was it because (as the *Oxford Dictionary of National Biography* suggests) Curr was 'atypically sympathetic' towards Australia's Indigenous people? Or rather, was Curr so committed to the righteousness of settler colonial endeavour that he viewed frontier violence as inevitable and unsurprising? A close reading of Curr's life and published works leads logically to the second conclusion.

In 1968 W.E.H. Stanner coined the term 'the Great Australian Silence' to describe the reluctance of Australians (principally in the twentieth century) to address the reality of frontier violence and the dispossession of Australia's Indigenous people.[47] Curr wrote his books before Stanner's 'cult of forgetfulness' had taken hold of the Australian people, which in part explains their value. Moreover, unlike other more liberal minds of his generation, Curr appears less shocked by the brutal reality of the frontier. This is not to say that he advocated violence, but rather that he found 'well-intentioned' protests against the treatment of Aborigines tedious and irritating. Before he wrote the 'classical account of frontier conflict' that so impressed Henry Reynolds, Curr addressed the general issue of frontier violence in *Recollections of Squatting in Victoria*, where his tone was light-hearted and irreverent. It is here that his personal attitude to colonial violence is more clearly evident. He explained that an important function of the commissioners of crown lands in the 1840s was 'to adjust the frequent differences which occurred between the original lords of the soil and the Anglo-Saxon *parvenus*'.[48] With more than a hint of irony, Curr described the usual way in which such differences were reported:

> Generally the first intimation the Commissioner got of a case was a letter from a stock-owner complaining that after having treated the Blacks with uniform kindness and consideration for a length of time, they had suddenly killed one of his shepherds under circumstances of peculiar atrocity, and roasted and eaten two hundred of his flock.[49]

Although Curr offers this as a fictional but typical example, he subtly suggests a link to his own experience, as 200 was almost exactly the number of sheep taken from his flocks by the Bangerang in 1842. Continuing his summary, Curr painted a vivid picture of the summary nature of frontier justice:

> Strange to say, the Blacks habitually neglected to give their version of the tale, though we know that they had constantly very serious charges to advance against shepherds, in connection with their conduct towards

---

47 Stanner 1969.
48 Curr 1883: 119.
49 Curr 1883: 120.

the females of the tribe. As the Blacks, therefore, neglected to appear before the Commissioner in what might be termed his judicial capacity, nothing was left for him as guardian of the public peace but to appear before them, which he did at a gallop, sabre in hand, surrounded by his troopers industriously loading and discharging their carbines.

In writing this passage, Curr implicitly invites the reader to observe the extra-legal nature of the commissioner's actions, before offering his own views on the matter:

> Now, it may seem strange to the reader that there were a few well intentioned visionaries, at the time, who made the Government policy, as carried out by the Commissioner, a subject for unfavourable comment.[50]

Although he does not identify these 'visionaries', Curr was surely referring to the Aboriginal protectors and the few supporters they had in the settler community. Curr dismissed their various complaints, which included the lack of any statute to govern the troopers' actions, the inability of Aborigines 'to represent wrongs' due to language barriers, and the meagre evidence required 'to condemn a tribe to destruction'. This list of complaints was, according to Curr, 'as tedious to answer as it is trifling in itself'. Curr proceeded to address the charge of mistaken identity, which he confirmed occasionally occurred when white authorities responded to Aboriginal aggression. In a revealing passage, Curr justified the shooting of innocent Aborigines with an ironic reference to 'a law in force in our tribes':

> But though one must always regret occurrences of this sort, it is consolatory to remember now – a fact of which we were ignorant at the time, – that whilst our troopers were busily shooting down in mistake individuals who had not injured us in any way, but whose acquaintances had, that we were absolutely acting – by fluke, no doubt – in accordance with a law in force in our tribes, which makes vengeance fall not only on an offender, but equally on the first of his tribe or kind who may come to hand. From this we see how constantly our busybodies were in the wrong.[51]

Curr's discussion of frontier justice in *Recollections of Squatting in Victoria* hardly evinces a predictable attitude for one who was 'atypically sympathetic' to the Aboriginal cause. It is the Aboriginal protectors and other critics of Empire (Curr's 'busybodies') who most deserve this reputation.

---

50   Curr 1883: 120.
51   Curr 1883: 121–122.

When writing generally about the causes of frontier conflict Curr displayed both considerable insight and a refreshingly frank acceptance of the reality of horrific violence. His account of his personal experiences must, however, be read with caution, as his own involvement in frontier conflict is downplayed. Curr's account of his early years at Tongala implies a rapidly developing ability on his part to manage peacefully his relationship with Indigenous people in the area. The importance of creating such an impression in his memoir derives from the need to boost his credentials as an Aboriginal administrator, a role that occupied much of his time in later life. While Curr does not deny that violent acts took place on his runs (he records two Aboriginal deaths by the rifle), his autobiographical account paints him in the best possible light. He alludes to his strained relationship with the Bangerang at the Moira only obliquely and deflects personal complicity by playfully parodying the government's response to the sheep stealing. Based on the available evidence, there is no reason to doubt Curr's implication that he avoided violence wherever possible; but it must be stressed that his apparent concern for Aboriginal welfare never weakened his resolve to acquire vast tracts of land for pastoral purposes. Moreover, the protection of his sheep flocks always remained his paramount concern. Although he recognised that the pastoral invasion had dire consequences for Aboriginal people, he firmly believed that these consequences were justifiable, because Aboriginal land use constituted 'no proper occupation'.[52]

Curr's interpretation of the Bangerang sheep thefts of 1842 reveals a disjuncture between his general account of frontier violence and his record of his own experiences. He described the spearing of 70 of his sheep as 'probably a trivial matter in their estimation, as no doubt it would appear to them that we white men had far more live mutton than we were able to make use of'.[53] It is not clear why Curr did not interpret these actions as hostile, particularly since he had impressed upon the Bangerang 'the heinousness of sheep-stealing' when he first encountered them in 1841.[54] Furthermore, in his general account of frontier conflict in *The Australian Race* Curr noted the inevitability of Indigenous resistance to the pastoral invasion.[55] In *Recollections of Squatting in Victoria*, on the other hand, Curr portrayed the sheep thieves as no more than 'naughty children, who should have been well flogged and locked up for a month'.[56] In this mood, it was natural that he would parody the military tactics of the government authorities. It must be noted, however, that it was the Currs who requested government intervention against the Aboriginal people of the Moira, and that Edward M. Curr guided Captain Dana to the Bangerang camp.

---

52   Curr 1886, vol 1: 103.
53   Curr 1883: 194.
54   Curr 1883: 86.
55   Curr 1886, vol 1: 102.
56   Curr 1883: 205.

5. Decline and Fall

In *Recollections of Squatting in Victoria* Edward M. Curr gives only a vague explanation for his leaving Victoria in February 1851, noting that he was 'desirous of a change' and wanted to travel through some of the countries 'about which I had interested myself from boyhood'.[1] There seems little doubt, however, that his father's death three months earlier was a major catalyst in his decision; for a decade he had worked at the behest of his overbearing father, but was now free to pursue his own interests. Before he departed, arrangements were made regarding the runs he and his brothers had inherited. Richard Curr leased the southern squatting runs from his brothers and based himself at the Colbinabbin station. The northern runs (including Tongala) were let to a Mr Hodgson, although it appears that one or more of the younger Curr brothers might have assisted him with station management.[2] Meanwhile, Edward, Charles and Walter departed the colony only a few months before the discovery of gold threw the pastoral industry into turmoil.

Curr's younger sister Florence recorded in a memoir that Richard established a home for his mother and younger siblings at Colbinabbin. As the closest station to Melbourne, Colbinabbin had occasionally been a winter residence for the wider Curr family. Richard's principal challenge was maintaining his labour force, as the station was only 40 miles from the Bendigo goldfields. Eleven-year-old Florence later recalled that she had a marvellous time at Colbinabbin, blissfully unaffected by 'the troubles of Richard in finding and still more in keeping shepherds'.[3] The labour shortage is the principal reason why Richard, in consultation with his mother, decided to sell the squatting runs in 1852. Perhaps Richard also yearned to join his elder brother overseas, which he soon did.

In his last will and testament, Edward Curr senior had bequeathed his pastoral leases and livestock to his sons and his city properties to his daughters. Although this might have seemed an equitable distribution in 1850, the subsequent discovery of gold had the dual effect of boosting the value of his daughters' city properties, while rendering it extremely difficult for his sons to manage the squatting runs following the collapse of the labour market. This effect was compounded by Richard's decision to sell the pastoral leases.[4] In his private family memoir of 1877, Edward M. Curr observed that Richard's decision to sell

---

1 Curr 1883: 450.
2 See files for Colbinabbin, Corop, Moira and Tongala, PROV, VA 2878, VPRS 5920 Pastoral Run Files (microfiche). See also Curr, 'Memoranda Concerning our Family' (1877), SLV, MS 8998.
3 Florence Curr, 'Unpublished Memoir' [undated], Murrumbogie Papers. See also Elizabeth Sarah Pennefather (née Curr), 'In the Early Day' (1910), Murrumbogie Papers.
4 Edward Curr's Last Will and Testament, 14 April 1849, PROV, VPRS 7952/P1, Unit 3, Item A/375. See also Curr, 'Memoranda Concerning Our Family' (1877), SLV, MS 8998.

the runs had 'ruined my father's sons'.⁵ He neglected to describe the extenuating circumstances of Richard's decision, simply recording that the stations were sold for £11,000 despite yielding £2,000 per annum. Richard sold the runs to James Murphy and William Looker. Murphy was a successful brewer and wine merchant in Melbourne who was elected to Victoria's Legislative Council in 1853. In 1857 Murphy sold the southern stations to John Winter, whose wealth grew after the discovery of gold on his property near Ballarat. Winter's son built a fine Italianate-style brick homestead at Colbinabbin in 1867, to which Curr refers briefly at two points in *Recollections of Squatting in Victoria*.⁶ It was men like Murphy and Winter that benefited most from the boom in Victoria that followed the gold rush, not Curr and his brothers who found themselves without property. Curr's sense of economic loss was intensified by the ever-increasing value of his sisters' city properties: '£30,000 was refused at one time for St Heliers, and £22,000 for a house in Collins St. nearly opposite the Bank of Australasia'.⁷

Unsurprisingly, Curr did not reveal this financial misfortune in *Recollections of Squatting in Victoria*. He explained in the last pages of his book that upon his return to Victoria in 1854, 'I found the squatters – who, during the first fifteen years of the colony, had established a great trade in wool, and built a thriving city – being denounced as monopolists of land and enemies to the public weal.'⁸ That Curr himself was no longer a squatter, and that the wealth he did acquire in the 1840s was subsequently lost during a drought on the Lachlan River, is hidden from the reader. Ultimately, *Recollections of Squatting in Victoria* served to establish Curr's identity as a Victorian pioneer and to assert the social status of a colonial gentleman, which (as a closer analysis reveals) he had later struggled to maintain.

All of this future misfortune was unknown to Edward M. Curr when he sailed for England in February 1851 aboard the *Stebonheath*, accompanied by his brothers Charles and Walter.⁹ In its voyage across the Pacific the *Stebonheath* ventured unusually far south, encountering strong winds and 'great numbers of icebergs'; she visited Rio de Janeiro for supplies in early May before reaching Plymouth on 5 July. The ship carried a cargo of 500 casks of tallow, 3,038 bales of wool and 27 passengers, several of whom, according to *The Times*, had 'realized handsome competencies in Port Phillip and do not intend returning'.¹⁰ The Currs were not so fortunate, their paternal inheritance being somewhat more modest. Under the original terms of his father's will, Edward M. Curr

---

5   Curr, 'Memoranda Concerning Our Family' (1877), SLV, MS 8998.
6   Curr 1883: 81, 338.
7   Curr, 'Memoranda Concerning Our Family' (1877), SLV, MS 8998.
8   Curr 1883: 450–451.
9   Curr, 'Memoranda Concerning Our Family' (1877), SLV, MS 8998.
10 *The Times* (London), 7 July 1851: 8.

received no share of the pastoral properties left to his seven surviving brothers; this reflected the fact that his father had already gifted him a flock of sheep in partnership with his late brother William, with which they had established their own pastoral station at Corop. Shortly before Edward Curr senior died, however, he altered his will to direct that his eldest son should receive half of the share intended for his youngest son Montague, then 12 years old.[11] Curr senior might have intended that this share be held in trust until Monty reached a more mature age, but whatever the case Edward M. Curr was able to fund extensive travel by selling some of his own sheep and leasing the Corop run for three years at £320 per annum.[12]

Curr arrived in London at the height of the 'Great Exhibition' in Hyde Park. It seems likely that he would have visited the Crystal Palace to marvel at the 'Works of Industry of all Nations', but his short family memoir makes no mention of such a visit, simply noting: 'On arriving in London, I shook hands with my brothers and went to Cadiz, where I remained three months.' Curr spent a further eight months in Seville, after which he had 'learned to speak Spanish with tolerable facility'.[13] Curr clearly hoped to satisfy his fascination for Spain and its history, which began during his schooling and continued through his ten years as a squatter.

At Stonyhurst College Curr had developed a boyhood fascination for the First Carlist War in Spain, fought between liberal royalist forces representing the young Isabella II and politically conservative forces representing her uncle Carlos. Curr's teenage sympathy for the Carlist cause, despite British support for Isabella, probably derived from his Catholic and Jesuit loyalties. In claiming the throne, Carlos enjoyed the support of conservative elements of the church, which opposed the general liberalisation of Spanish politics in the period. Moreover, the stronghold of the Carlist forces was the Basque provinces of northern Spain, where Jesuit founder Ignatius of Loyola was born. Support for the Carlists was thus quite understandable for a student of a Jesuit school, but as Curr later explained, his enthusiasm also derived from the exploits of a famous wartime hero: 'I had myself been possessed by a strong desire to take service … under Zumalacarregui, the great Carlist general.'[14]

Curr's interest in Spain survived beyond a boyish fascination in war and grew into a wide-ranging interest in the history and language of the country. It is significant that, despite having studied French and Italian ten years earlier, Curr chose to focus his new studies on the language and history of Spain. After almost a year's study in Cádiz and Seville, Curr dispensed with his books and

---

11   Edward Curr's Last Will and Testament, 14 April 1849, PROV, VPRS 7952/P1, Unit 3, Item A/375.
12   Curr 1883: 450; Curr, 'Memoranda Concerning Our Family' (1877), SLV, MS 8998.
13   Curr, 'Memoranda Concerning Our Family' (1877), SLV, MS 8998.
14   Curr 1883: 445.

set out on a circumnavigation of the Mediterranean, which lasted approximately eight months, beginning and ending at Seville. This was Curr's own middle-class version of the 'Grand Tour', which had been a popular rite of passage among young and wealthy Europeans since the seventeenth century. Although Curr took in much of the traditional route, his itinerary also had a decidedly Eastern flavour.

Figure 12: Edward M. Curr's Mediterranean tour.

Map by Peter Johnson.

He first visited the southern Spanish towns of Granada and Almeria. His experiences in Granada seem to have been a highlight and feature in an extended aside in *Recollections of Squatting in Victoria*. During the 1840s, Curr and his brothers had possessed an impressive 'Bush Library' featuring novels, poetry, histories and various other texts. The books were read, re-read and endlessly discussed by the brothers at Tongala. Curr noted: 'Of the volumes in our collection, very favourite ones with me were those of Washington Irving, which treat of Moorish times in Spain.'[15] Inspired by Irving's account of the great Moorish palace of Alhambra,[16] Curr sought out the fortress and explored

---

15   Curr 1883: 361.
16   Irving 1832.

its intricate history. He managed to locate Matteo Ximenes, Washington Irving's guide of 20 years earlier, who showed Curr around Granada and shared his memories of Irving's research in the city. Curr later recalled:

> Altogether there was something very pleasant in going over in Andalusia the histories which had occupied our little circle on the Goulburn, as well as in looking back on past discussion and conjecture concerning localities from the vantage-ground of personal experience. Indeed, in re-reading history … on the ground where its scenes were enacted lies one of the great charms of travel.[17]

Curr found the pace of life in Andalusia pleasantly sedate, and later attributed this to a lack of exposure to the single-minded endeavour of British colonialism: 'To me there was also something congenial in the every-day life of a community into which the disquietude, bustle, and hurry of the Anglo-Saxon world had not yet succeeded in forcing themselves.'[18]

From Granada Curr travelled to Almeria before leaving Spain by boat for Southern France in the early summer of 1852. His tour took him to many European cities including Marseilles, Lyons, Geneva, Milan, Venice, Florence, Rome and Naples. He travelled via steamer to Corfu and thence to the Greek port of Patras. He proceeded on horseback along the Gulf of Lepanto to Corinth and then Athens. After spending some time in the Greek capital, Curr travelled on to Constantinople and then Beirut.

For his travels through 'the Lebanon' Curr required the services of an interpreter, commonly known as a 'dragoman', who guided him to such places as Zahlé, Damascus and Tripoli. He later wrote that his guide proved to be inadequate: 'Having had a misunderstanding with my dragoman … I discharged him on my return to Beyroot.'[19] Confident that he could speak a little Arabic, Curr continued his journey alone, travelling south to Sidon, Tyre and Acra. For three weeks Curr stayed at the Franciscan pilgrims' hostel the 'Casa Nova' in Jerusalem, from where he visited the Dead Sea, San Saba and Bethlehem. Completing his circumnavigation of the Mediterranean via Gaza, Cairo, Alexandria, Malta and Gibraltar, Curr returned to Seville at the end of 1852, before travelling via Madrid, Bayonne and Paris to London.

From early 1853 Curr spent a year in Dublin, Paris, Brussels and London. He left no record of how he spent his time, but it seems unlikely he did work of any kind. He presumably spent time with family in England, but he also turned his hand to creative writing. In May 1853 *The Illustrated London News* published Curr's

---

17 Curr 1883: 364.
18 Curr 1883: 364.
19 Curr, 'Memoranda Concerning our Family' (1877), SLV, MS 8998.

account of a bushfire he had earlier observed near Kilmore, north of Melbourne. It is one of his earliest surviving literary efforts and displays the flamboyantly verbose style that characterised his later work. It is worth reproducing a small sample:

> Below us was a station; near the house was a barn and wool-shed, and many stacks of oats and wheat. The fire was creeping gradually and slowly towards them; a thread of fire – if I may use the expression – like a thing endued with life, like a brilliant serpent – was winding its way amongst the grass to the fated stacks and buildings. We at a distance at once saw that the struggles of the proprietor and several of his men to arrest the flames were utterly hopeless … They were as children on the shores of the sea who would fain bar back the tide. In vain they plied their green boughs, beating out for an instance the point of the flames most in advance. The luminous monster, as if forecasting a prey, noiselessly stole on…
>
> In vain were struggles! in vain were hopes! but man will struggle: even death is met with less regret, doing. And the hardy Britons wrestled with their foe; but in every direction it overlapped them, and without a check kept on, and at every point they were beaten back. They did their duty well, and retired slowly, leaving nothing untried. And now the fence which enclosed the stack-yard was almost gained…
>
> The fire had conquered: it leaped on its prey, it reared its gorgeous crest upon the stacks, a dense smoke arose, a mimic volcano spouted its flames, and in two minutes all was reduced to ashes. Without proffering useless condolence, we mounted our horses and pushed on.[20]

The full extent of the conflagration described by Curr suggests it was almost certainly the 'Black Thursday' fire of 6 February 1851, which engulfed one quarter of Victoria and killed 1,000,000 sheep. If this is the case, the fire preceded Curr's departure from Melbourne by only a few days; the finer detail of his account suggests he was riding from Tongala to Melbourne to board the ship and was lucky to negotiate the fire without incident. In 1853 Curr's family back in Australia would likely have noted with pride the publication of his account of the fire. His sister Florence later recorded: 'Mother used to subscribe to the *Illustrated London News* then the only pictorial paper and we used to receive them every month or two.'[21]

---

20   Edward M. Curr, 'A bush fire in Australia: by an Australian squatter', *The Illustrated London News*, 7 May 1853. Although this account is attributed to 'An Australian Squatter', an album later compiled by his daughter confirms that Edward M. Curr wrote it. See Constance Curr album (c.1905), Murrumbogie Papers.
21   Florence Curr, 'Unpublished memoir' [undated], Murrumbogie Papers.

Of all Curr's travel destinations, Dublin was to have the most lasting effect on his future life. It is quite likely that one reason for Curr's return to Europe in 1851 was the poor prospect of finding a wife in the colonies. If this were true, his quest was achieved in Dublin; on 31 January 1854 he married Margaret Vaughan at St Mary's Church in Marlborough Street. Unlike his father, Curr did not receive 'a considerable amount of money' when he married. He later recalled the following details about his bride:

> Miss Vaughan whom I met in Dublin was of a family long resident in Kildare, and her father having run through his paternal inheritance, obtained a situation in a mercantile house in Liverpool, in which city he and his wife died. In accordance with the idea of those times, he made a point of not engaging in business, as he might have done in Dublin as such a course would have been considered derogatory to the family dignity.[22]

Following their wedding Edward and Margaret probably travelled to London to attend the marriage of Edward's brother Richard to his French bride, Maria, on 14 February.[23] Both couples then made preparations to sail for the Australian colonies. It is possible that Curr always intended to return to the Antipodes to invest his inheritance in a profitable venture. It seems, however, that his experiences in London did nothing to dissuade him from such a course. He wrote two years later of the strong recognition accorded the Australian colonies in the London business community:

> the windows of Oxford-street literally were as one mighty signboard, pointing with its hundred fingers towards the provinces of Australia and the ports of Tasmania ... the Strand and Bombard-street were but warehouses and shipping offices for the Southern Seas, and London docks one great terminus whence the Emigrant, poor and rich, shaped their course for lands where energy and enterprise were received and rewarded.[24]

Curr's decision to end his holiday and pursue riches once again was certainly also influenced by his new status as a family man. With his brother Richard and their two wives, Curr sailed from Gravesend, Kent, aboard the *Chouringee* on 14 March and arrived in Melbourne on 30 June 1854.[25]

The Curr brothers then set out to rectify Richard's blunder of selling the family squatting runs by attempting to regain their position as men of property. They

---

22   Curr, 'Memoranda Concerning Our Family' (1877), SLV, MS 8998.
23   Richard Curr married Maria in the French Chapel, London on 14 February 1854. Elizabeth Curr, 'Family Record', Murrumbogie Papers.
24   Edward M. Curr, *The New Zealand Spectator*, 28 November 1855.
25   E.M.V. Curr, 'Memoir' (1872), Murrumbogie Papers.

certainly had reasonable capital behind them (Edward M. Curr's charge that Richard's early sale of their runs 'ruined my father's sons' is an exaggeration) but they were ultimately frustrated by a series of mild successes and dismal failures in business over the following decade. Edward Curr senior's sons inherited squatting runs that were sold in 1852 for £11,000; when divided between the eight surviving sons this is hardly a fortune, but neither is it an insignificant amount. Moreover, Edward M. Curr's own station at Corop fetched £4,000 when sold in 1852.[26]

It is unclear whether Curr initially intended to invest his capital in Victoria. If he did, his resolve was soon broken by the transformation of the colony following the discovery of gold: 'the old order of things' had been 'swept away'.[27] While Curr had been away the population of Victoria had more than tripled from 77,000 in 1851 to 237,000 in 1854.[28] Furthermore, the pastoral industry's contribution to Victoria's economic output had fallen from 28 per cent to seven per cent.[29] Recalling his poor impression of the changes wrought by gold, Curr later recounted the oration of 'a tall, burly, good-tempered looking Scotchman' who held court to an audience of new arrivals and noticed Curr as he stepped off the wharf in 1854:

> 'Here's a man that doesn't know me, but I know him. Three years back there were not three men in the colony who didn't know his father – the father of separation, as we used to call him – or who wouldn't have sworn to his pair of roan horses anywhere. Well now! I'll give this gentleman a week to find a man who ever heard of his father, or of separation either. Why, these new chums, who have overrun the colony, seem to think, by George! that they are the first comers here, and that this wharf, and the houses and bridges we built, and the roads we made, and the stock we brought from other colonies before they ever heard of the place, grew of themselves like the gum trees.'[30]

The invective of the burly Scot punctuates Curr's conclusion to *Recollections of Squatting in Victoria*, and gives us some idea as to why he left the colony so soon after returning with his new wife in 1854.

---

26 Curr, 'Memoranda Concerning our Family' (1877), SLV, MS 8998.
27 Curr 1883: 450–451.
28 Goodman 1994: ix.
29 Dingle 1996: 16.
30 Curr 1883: 451.

The 'Waste Lands' of New Zealand

Less then three weeks after arriving in Melbourne, Curr sailed to New Zealand to scout out a new life for his wider family. He returned after five weeks to collect his wife, with whom he travelled to Auckland in September 1854.[31] Curr's three eldest surviving brothers, Richard, Charles and Walter, joined him in New Zealand. All except Walter had married in 1854 and they travelled across the Tasman Sea with a clear desire to purchase freehold land. Although the Currs spent only a short time in New Zealand, Edward M. Curr's time there was important because he wrote a series of letters to newspapers about land settlement, which clearly state his economic and philosophical justifications for the colonial project.

Prior to the Currs' arrival in New Zealand, Governor George Grey had made significant changes to the land system, which appeared to offer considerable opportunities to those, like the Currs, who had some capital to invest. Most importantly, in March 1853 Grey had issued 'cheap land' regulations, which dropped the price of crown land from £1 per acre to five or ten shillings per acre.[32] Grey believed that the higher price had discouraged the immigration of poorer settlers and his regulations were designed to address this issue; but his policy soon provoked fear in some quarters of an influx of Australian capitalists. The arrival of the Currs in 1854 is certainly evidence that men with capital were attracted by Grey's reforms. By mid-November the Currs had sailed to Nelson, from where Edward and Richard visited Hawke's Bay and the Ahuriri region (Napier). They expected that freehold land in this district would soon be sold for ten shillings an acre, following a government purchase of land from the Maori. Their plans were frustrated, however, by the reluctance of the local authorities to release the land for purchase.

Grey's land regulations had been enacted shortly before the election of New Zealand's first parliament under the 1852 constitution. A prominent member of the new legislature was Edward Gibbon Wakefield, whose influence on New Zealand colonisation had already been great.[33] Even before his election to the House of Representatives in August 1853, Wakefield had opposed Grey's new land regulations. As a prominent theorist on colonisation, Wakefield had previously argued that crown land should be sold at a 'sufficient price' to finance the growth of a colony.[34] Wakefield's theories had been criticised for

---

31   See E.M.V. Curr, 'Memoir' (1872), Murrumbogie Papers.
32   See Lucas 1966. These prices did not apply to land in the Wakefield settlements at Canterbury and Otago.
33   See Morrell 1966. See also Moss 2004.
34   Wakefield 1829.

setting this 'sufficient price' too high, but as a member of the new parliament (and a towering figure in New Zealand's short settler history) his views held some sway.

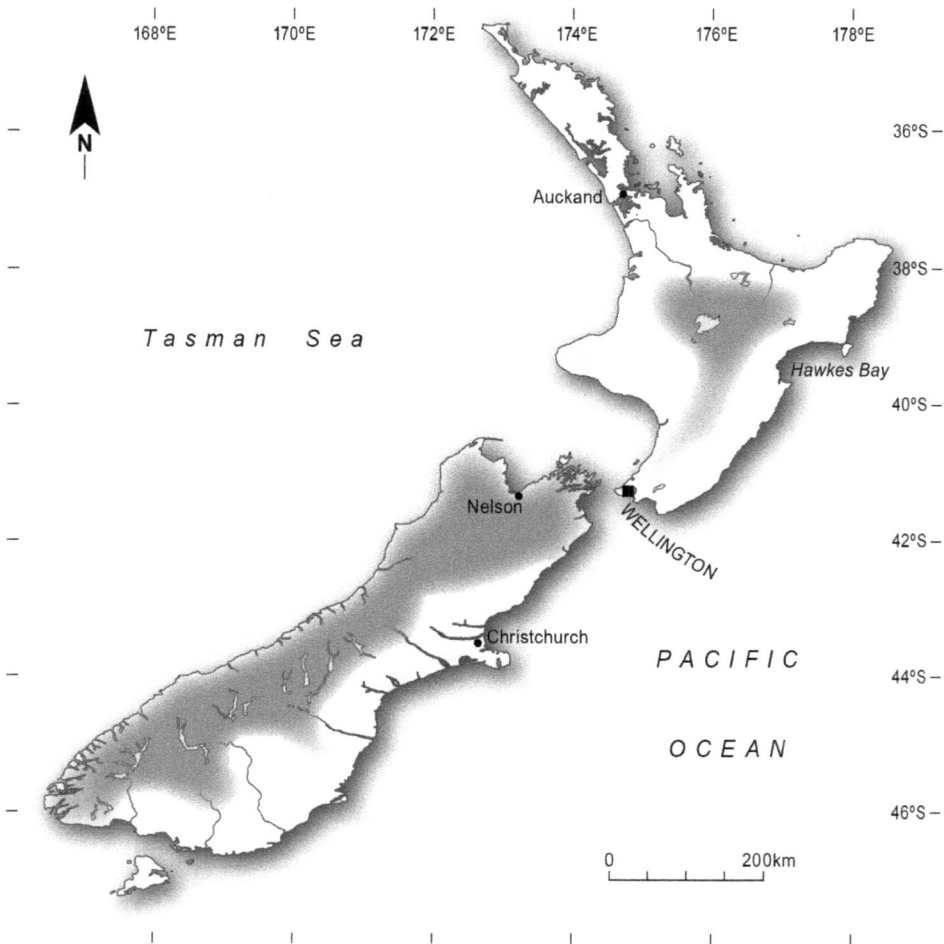

Figure 13: New Zealand.

Map by Peter Johnson.

Despite his foiled ambitions to purchase cheap freehold land, Edward Curr remained in New Zealand for over a year; he made his time profitable by importing horses from Newcastle, New South Wales, including thoroughbred mares from the stables of George Wyndham.[35] He chartered a small ship called the *Waterwitch* and imported two cargoes of 100 mares each in March and October 1855. During the first voyage stormy weather resulted in the loss of 30 horses

---

35   Report of Horse Auction, *Wellington Independent*, 15 December 1855.

and Curr lost £300 on the transaction. His luck improving, the second voyage was completed without the loss of any horses and Curr cleared £1,500. He later wrote about the eventful first voyage in one of his more entertaining literary efforts.[36] While Curr was in New Zealand, his first son, Edward Micklethwaite Vaughan Curr, was born on 10 April 1855. Less than a year later, the Currs decided to abandon their plans for a new life in New Zealand and returned to Australia in January 1856.

During his last few weeks in New Zealand, Curr wrote a series of letters to the *New Zealand Spectator* and the *Wellington Independent*, which strongly criticised the reluctance of local authorities to release the five-shilling and ten-shilling lands for freehold purchase. These letters were published as a booklet under the title *The Waste Lands of the Province of Wellington, New Zealand*.[37] The letters are among his earliest surviving writings and provide considerable insight into his views on the colonial project and, importantly, his economic justifications for his earlier squatting activities in the Port Phillip District. Unlike *Recollections of Squatting in Victoria*, these letters reveal Curr's views during the actual period he was a pastoralist.

Curr's New Zealand letters were motivated by frustration: he and his brothers had capital they wished to invest and could not understand the reluctance of the New Zealand Government to court this capital. Curr championed the role of the investor in nation building and mercilessly lampooned the apparently narrow-minded attempts of the New Zealand legislature to exclude Australian capitalists. He opened his first letter with an account of London in early 1853 (quoted above), which noted the great enthusiasm among emigrants and businesses alike for the Australian colonies. Describing the massive waves of migration in the early 1850s, Curr asked: 'How is it that New Zealand received no part of that mighty Exodus?' The answer, according to Curr, was that 'the great advantages nature has provided here have been, and are, withheld from the public'. He argued that the Wellington district had enacted legislation which 'pandered to confirm iniquitous security of Squatting tenure' despite the fact that, unlike Australia, New Zealand was wholly unsuited to a system of pastoral leases.[38]

One might, of course, propose a certain irony in the fact that Curr criticised New Zealand pastoral leaseholders for monopolising land, while simultaneously defending the squatters of Australia, whose ranks he had only recently departed. For Curr there was no inconsistency here: the very different geographical

---

36 Edward M. Curr, 'Experiences of horses afloat. By CIOS', *Economist* (Melbourne), 1, 8 and 15 October 1869.
37 Curr 1856. The original letters were published in the *New Zealand Spectator* on 28 November 1855, 22 December 1855, 16 and 30 January 1856; and in the *Wellington Independent* on 5 and 15 December 1855.
38 Edward M. Curr, 'Letter to the Editor', *New Zealand Spectator*, 28 November 1855.

conditions in New Zealand required, he argued, a different approach. To demonstrate his point, Curr trumpeted the contribution of the squatters to Australian prosperity:

> No body of men ever created so much wealth in so short a time. The squatter founded Melbourne whose history from first to last is unprecedented and unequalled in the annals of colonization. Had there been no squatter there would have been no Sydney. The overlanding squatter saved Adelaide from ruin and starvation. He has ministered largely to the Factories of England; and he has fed the thousands which England has sent forth to search for gold in his country at the Antipodes.[39]

Prosperity brought to Australia by the squatters, argued Curr, had benefited the wider settler community; not least those (like his father) who had seen the value of their town allotments grow exponentially. Curr also believed that the Squatting Age in Australia was still in its infancy and that pastoral leases remained an effective land policy for the Australian colonies:

> When New Zealand has all been traversed, sold, ploughed, where ploughing is possible, and mapped; when coasters have traced each bend of its shores, and the leadline found every shoal, – unexplored El Dorados will still be the dream of the Australian, and Rumour will whisper to Enterprise, and the spirit of Exploration still lead by the hand the unquiet, sun-burnt Squatter.[40]

Curr contended that New Zealand required an alternative land system to suit its smaller size and distinctly different terrain. He asked what signs there were that New Zealand was benefiting from the economic stimulus of settler colonial endeavour: 'Are we to look for them in your country without roads or bridges, your harbours destitute of shipping, your hills without flocks, or your plains without cultivation?' He believed that the chief reason for New Zealand's slow economic growth was the unsuitability of the pastoral lease system; the chance to acquire freehold land would, on the other hand, transform the colony. Furthermore, he argued, locking up the lands until they could fetch a higher price displayed flawed economic reasoning. In his third letter to the *New Zealand Spectator* Curr wrote:

> I maintain that people immigrate to take possession of the soil – that England has avowed the right to it by placing the management of the land in the hands of the colonists themselves, and that the only justification of ANY price being put on the land – is, to provide with the

---

39 Edward M. Curr, 'Letter to the Editor', *New Zealand Spectator*, 16 January 1856.
40 Edward M. Curr, 'Letter to the Editor', *New Zealand Spectator*, 16 January 1856.

proceeds means by which the land may be made productive, as labour, roads, &c., and to prevent the monopoly of land by those who would possess themselves of more than they have capital to make use of — or the acquisition of it by proprietors whose capital so invested is too small to be conducive to public prosperity. This is plain speaking, and will be understood even by independent electors! and the intelligence of the country! fully as well as if clothed in the subtle phraseology of Adam Smith.[41]

The principal target of Curr's impassioned treatise was the Wellington Provincial Council, which he blamed for locking up the ten-shilling lands he had hoped to purchase at Hawke's Bay. Two members of the council earned a particular rebuke: Wakefield, who was also a member of the national parliament, and the Superintendent of the Wellington Province, Dr Isaac Featherstone.[42] Regarding Wakefield, Curr observed: 'I have heard of a lately elected member of the Hutt urging in conversation the wise policy of endeavouring to exclude Australian capitalists from this country.'[43] Despite his theory of 'sufficient price', Wakefield had advocated free land grants in his own electorate, where his constituents were principally struggling farmers; he had claimed 'exceptional circumstances demanded exceptional remedies — viz. free land grants to workers'. The irony was not lost on Curr:

> The Government seems to have said, *poor* men, labourers from England are welcome here, — but not capitalists! — no enterprise! — no Australians! — we have monopolized the lands of the country and will keep them.[44]

Continuing his attack on the Wellington Provincial Council, Curr used Superintendent Featherstone as an example to expose what he saw as vested interests:

> Had I, for example, been able to purchase eight or ten thousand acres at 5s. an acre, of the least promising hills on the sheep run of his Honor the Superintendent, I should have fenced it in and improved it, and after the lapse of a few years kept on it three or four times as many sheep as his Honor now depastures on his twenty or twenty-five thousand acres. His Honor would hardly have missed this small slice off his run, and the Government chest would have closed on £2000 of my money, which

---

41 Edward M. Curr, 'Letter to the Editor', *New Zealand Spectator*, 16 January 1856.
42 See Morrell 1966. See also Foster 1966.
43 Edward M. Curr, 'Letter to the Editor', *New Zealand Spectator*, 22 December 1855.
44 Edward M. Curr, 'Letter to the Editor', *New Zealand Spectator*, 28 November 1855.

would be available for the acquisition of other lands from the Natives. In these transactions the Province would have been a gainer – but perhaps his Honor would not!⁴⁵

Curr's letters reveal him to be a man of the Scottish Enlightenment. His bush library at Tongala in the 1840s had included a copy of Adam Smith's *Wealth of Nations*, which clearly influenced his attitudes towards colonial land acquisition.⁴⁶ Although Curr did not mention John Locke specifically in his New Zealand letters, he undoubtedly believed that legitimate property rights derived from the mixing of land and labour, and that colonial land policy should reflect this. Interestingly, his economic views regarding the productive use of land, in this case employed against pastoral leaseholders and politicians in New Zealand, also provided the justification for his dispossession of Australian Indigenous landowners in the 1840s. Curr characterised the use of New Zealand land as unproductive and wasteful. His attitude to the jealous hoarders of land among New Zealand's settler elite is comparable with his attitude to Indigenous land use in the 1840s in the Port Phillip District. In Curr's mind, he was justified in usurping the land of the Bangerang and Ngooraialum because they were not using it productively; his opposition to New Zealand land policy was similarly motivated, if aimed at quite a different group.

This is not to say that Curr made more than a passing reference to Australian Aborigines in his New Zealand letters. Nevertheless, the brief recognition accorded them provides an insight into Curr's early views on colonial violence:

> The Australian squatter discovers for himself available country – marks his road with his dray wheels – fights the blacks when necessary, and makes nearly as good a use of the country he occupies as if it were his freehold property.⁴⁷

As Curr would have it, fighting the blacks was merely an inconvenient and regrettable distraction on the path towards productive land use and the creation of wealth. Decades later in *Recollections of Squatting in Victoria* Curr maintained that he was able to avoid extensive conflict with the Aborigines he dispossessed in the 1840s. When addressing his New Zealand readership in 1855 he provided an explanation for why this might have been so: specifically, he argued that the geographical and demographic conditions in Victoria and New South Wales made conflict less likely: 'These immense Provinces may be on the whole described as open, easy of access, generally not requiring made roads, and unoccupied by an aboriginal population capable of obstructing the spread of flocks and herds.'⁴⁸

---

45 Edward M. Curr, 'Letter to the Editor', *New Zealand Spectator*, 28 November 1855.
46 See Curr 1883: 359–360.
47 Edward M. Curr, 'Letter to the Editor', *New Zealand Spectator*, 16 January 1856.
48 Edward M. Curr, 'Letter to the Editor', *New Zealand Spectator*, 16 January 1856.

It is telling that, in a series of letters amounting to several thousand words, Curr said so little about the Australian Aborigines. For Curr, they did not warrant more than a brief mention in a debate about productive land use.

Droving and Drought

On 24 January 1856 Curr sailed for Sydney with his wife, young son, and various members of his wider family, proceeding then to Wide Bay north of Brisbane. He had purchased two cattle stations known as Gobongo and Toomcul, which were situated in the Burnett district about halfway between the towns of Gympie and Kingaroy. The stations were stocked with 3,200 head of cattle, for which Curr paid £2.5 per head – a total of £7,200. Arriving at the stations on 6 March 1856, he and several of his brothers began preparations for a formidable droving operation, whereby the cattle were taken overland to Melbourne in two drafts. The economic boom in Victoria ensured the cattle would be sold for a handsome profit in the southern colony. It seems that Curr took primary responsibility for the operation, while various younger brothers were employed to drive the cattle south through New South Wales. On 2 July 1856 Curr entrusted one third of the cattle to his brother Charles, who was paid £150 to see them safely to Melbourne. Curr's younger brothers Julius and Montagu also assisted with the operation, as did various stockmen employed on short-term contracts. Interestingly, both Edward M. Curr and his brother Charles recorded details of this droving trip in the same journal that Edward had used 18 years earlier when studying in France.[49]

While his brother Charles was overseeing the first stage of the droving operations, Edward M. Curr travelled to Melbourne, arriving in early August.[50] Curr probably travelled ahead of the herd in order to arrange the sale of the cattle once they arrived. In this task he received valuable assistance from his brother-in-law Hastings Cunningham, a cattle grazier who later became a prominent Melbourne wool broker.[51] In late October, after the birth of his daughter Constance, Curr left Melbourne and returned to Queensland. He wrote to Charles:

---

49 Edward M. Curr, 'A Journal' (1838), in 'Curr Family – Papers and Station Records, 1838–1937', State Library of New South Wales (SLNSW), Mitchell Library, MLMSS 2286.
50 E.M.V. Curr, 'Memoir' (1872), Murrumbogie Papers.
51 Fearon 1966: 506. Cunningham married Curr's sister Agnes in 1849. His role in the sale of the cattle in 1856 is explained in a letter Edward M. Curr wrote to his brother Charles. See Curr, 'A Journal' (1838), SLNSW, MLMSS 2286.

> I start tomorrow for Sydney being on my way to Gobongo to start off to Melbourne the remainder of the cattle, deliver up the station and bring down the ladies – I expect to be in Melbourne about the 6th of January if all goes well.[52]

Curr sold Gobongo and Toomcul without cattle for £2,000.[53] Although he did not record the price his cattle fetched in Victoria, his grandson later recorded that they were sold for between £4 and £5 per head.[54] Even taking into account the cost of employing stockmen and the loss of some cattle, it seems likely that Curr cleared several thousand pounds in only a few months.

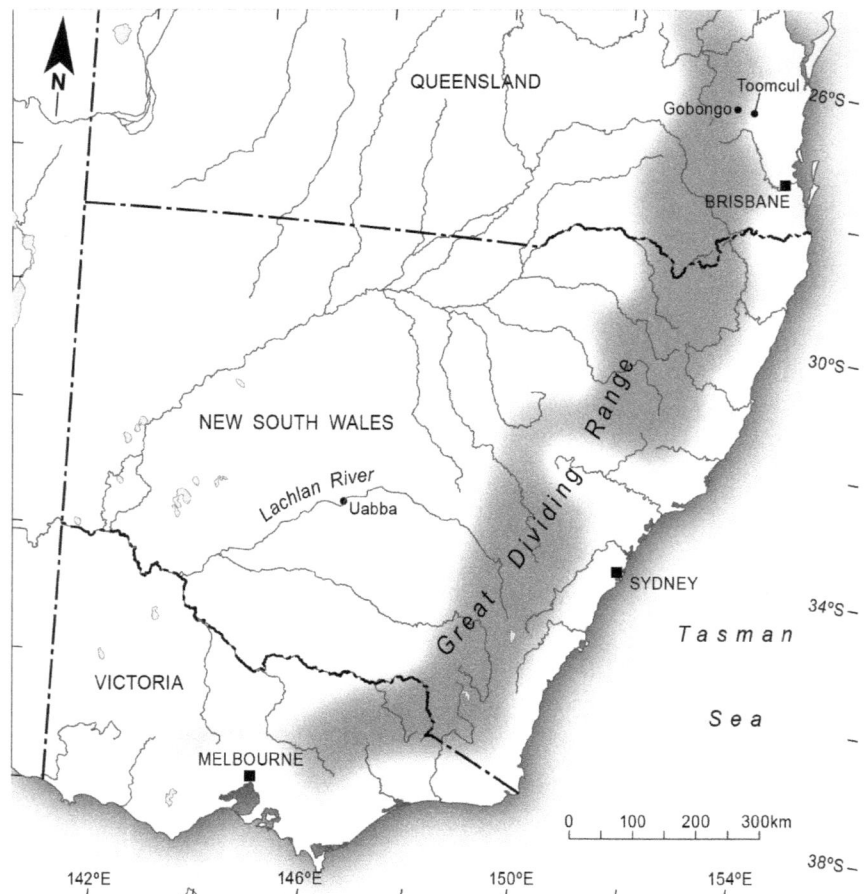

Figure 14: Eastern Australia.

Map by Peter Johnson.

---

52 Edward M. Curr to Charles Curr, 27 October 1856, see Curr, 'A Journal' (1838), SLNSW, MLMSS 2286.
53 Curr, 'Memoranda Concerning Our Family' (1877), SLV, MS 8998.
54 Curr, Edward A. 1979: 34–36.

Returning to Melbourne in January 1857, Curr made his home temporarily in St Kilda, although his young son Edward was taken to Tasmania for several months due to poor health. He spent the next year searching for another suitable pastoral investment. His family spent several months at Table Cape in north-east Tasmania, where his second son Wilfred was born in August. Meanwhile, Curr purchased a station on the Lachlan River in New South Wales called Uabba, in partnership with his brothers Richard and Julius. The station lay on the route Curr's cattle had taken from Queensland to Victoria in 1856. The Curr brothers stocked their new station with 1,000 cattle and by December 1858 Edward had brought his wife and three children to live on the Lachlan River. Richard's wife Maria also joined them. While the droving venture had been successful, Uabba would prove to be financially ruinous and destroy any chance Curr had of reclaiming the social status his family had enjoyed in the 1840s.

Curr did not record the price he paid for Uabba, nor the cost of the cattle with which he and his brothers stocked the station. It appears, however, that he committed most of his financial resources to the new venture. This proved a fateful decision: three years after purchasing Uabba, Curr and his brothers were forced to abandon the station following a severe drought. Curr's son Wilfred also died at Uabba in 1860. In his family memoir, Curr devotes very little attention to this sorry period of his life, writing simply that he was 'ruined whilst there, in consequence chiefly of the dry weather'.[55] His son Edward later recorded some more details:

> The family left Uabba Station in July 1861, after a drought, when all their cattle died and they kept their best horses alive by feeding them with kurrajong. The Lachlan River stopped running and there were only a few waterholes. They arrived in Melbourne on the 3rd September 1861 in two buggy-loads and some spare horses.[56]

Although Curr's precise financial situation is unclear, it seems likely he possessed a capital of a several thousand pounds before purchasing Uabba. In September 1861 he returned to Melbourne with '£350 in hand, and no more'.[57] It was quite a spectacular fall. In an attempt to rebuild his now modest capital, he returned briefly to horse-trading. He managed to support his family in this way for a little over a year before he began his 27-year career as a stock inspector for the Victorian Government.

---

55 Curr, 'Memoranda Concerning Our Family' (1877), SLV, MS 8998.
56 E.M.V. Curr, 'Memoir' (1872), Murrumbogie Papers.
57 Curr, 'Memoranda Concerning Our Family' (1877), SLV, MS 8998.

6. Rebuilding a Reputation

In 1850 Edward M. Curr was the head of a family pastoral empire covering 300 square miles of prime land yielding £2,000 per annum. His father was a prominent businessman and politician in Melbourne and the Curr name was well known in the newly independent Colony of Victoria. A decade later he was reduced to the necessity of accepting a salaried position with the Victorian Government to support his growing family. His subsequent career was undoubtedly a notable one and provided him with ample income; nevertheless, the painful reality of financial loss and squandered opportunities seems to have shaped his worldview. It also appears to have influenced the tone of *Recollections of Squatting in Victoria*, where it takes the form of a barely disguised nostalgia for the 1840s.

Curr regret at his financial misfortune is more explicit in a private memoir, which he dictated to his daughter Ela in 1877 and titled 'Memoranda Concerning Our Family'. A prominent theme was lost riches, as Curr outlined four occasions when circumstances conspired to deny his family a fortune. The first was his grandfather's £30,000 investment, which was squandered in 1823 by a financially illiterate French priest. The second was his father's costly dedication to the cause of Separation for Victoria. The third was the premature decision of his brother and mother to sell the family's squatting runs in 1852. Finally, Curr described the ruinous drought on the Lachlan River in 1861.

Curr's career as a stock inspector, which lasted from 1862 until his death in 1889, was the means by which he rebuilt his reputation after his failure at Uabba. It was by any measure a distinguished career, but perhaps one that Curr never anticipated. When dictating his memoir to his daughter, Curr clearly still felt pangs of regret when he remembered what might have been. His loss of socio-economic status could only be remedied by his commitment to a new career and a belief in his abilities. By the mid-1870s Curr was a senior public servant on a high salary and was able to give his children a quality education. Nevertheless, he was not a man of independent means; rather, his return to prominence after the nadir of 1861 was due to his success in the public service and his emergence as a talented writer.

Edward and Margaret Curr made their new home at 6 Chambers Terrace, Prahran, which was situated on Gardiner's Creek Road (now Toorak Road) near its intersection with Chapel Street. Mabel Curr was born in December 1861 and four more children, Ela, Justin, Hubert and Ernest, followed over the next decade. After the disastrous drought at Uabba, Curr sought a short-term solution to his financial woes: 'Having about £350 in hand, and no more, I invested £300 in horses which I took to New Zealand clearing £300 by the transaction.'[1] His expertise with horses was further evident in his literary activites over the next few years. Curr had returned to Melbourne in the aftermath of the disastrous Burke and Wills expedition. In January 1862 an extensive debate raged in the pages of the *Argus* about the future of Australian exploration and Curr was a key contributor. He supported the common view that previous explorers had been poorly qualified for the task allocated them. Importantly, for Curr, a lack of bush experience was a hindrance to most expeditions: 'Mitchell, Sturt, Burke and Grey, were soldiers and Government officers, Leichardt a foreign savant, and Gregory no bushman.'[2] Curr argued that the men best suited to exploration were the squatters, particularly those (like himself) with experience in remote areas. Australian exploration had been only modestly successful, Curr continued, because colonial administrators were inclined to appoint government officials to the task. Curr recalled his own experience as a squatter to argue his point:

> If I recollect the days of my boyhood right, I think I used now and then to sally out for three or four weeks on a hunting spree into the unoccupied country. Perhaps I took five pounds of flour with me, and with my rifle, horse, and tomahawk wandered off 150 or 200 miles. Somehow I always got back fat and well ... and yet the blacks were fierce and numerous. For the life of me I can not see what should prevent two bushmen 'to the manner born,' with two horses each, or at most three, and what they could well carry, riding to Carpentaria and back again, if they met such country as Burke passed through.

Although the 'outside squatters' were more likely to succeed in exploration, it was unlikely, Curr opined, that they would abandon their business pursuits in favour of exploration: 'in this money making land, no sufficient inducements have been held forth to tempt them to offer themselves for work'.[3]

Curr confidently continued his treatise in three more letters to the *Argus*.[4] A key argument concerned the appropriate use of horses, which he explored in considerable detail in his third letter:

> The position I take up is, that the losses in horseflesh experienced by explorers is capable of a very great reduction; that a proper selection and management of their horses would enable explorers in a journey

---

1 Edward M. Curr, 'Memoranda Concerning Our family' (1877), SLV, MS 8998. See also E.M.V. Curr, 'Memoir' (1872), Murrumbogie Papers.
2 Edward M. Curr, 'Letter to the Editor', *Argus*, 6 January 1862: 6.
3 Edward M. Curr, 'Letter to the Editor', *Argus*, 6 January 1862: 6.
4 Edward M. Curr, 'Letters to the Editor', *Argus*, 10, 16, 17 January 1862.

extending over months to perform something like double the distance usually accomplished, and that the dangers, failures, and expenses of the work would be very much lessened.[5]

His argument was in fact the prelude to a full-length book, which he likely spent much of the next year preparing. On 16 June 1863 the *Argus* announced the publication of *Pure Saddle Horses and how to breed them in Australia: together with a consideration of the history and merits of the English, Arab, Andalusian, & Australian breeds of horses*.[6] In its preliminary review of Curr's book the *Argus* immediately identified the key contention, even if it misspelt Curr's name: 'In the controversy between the Arab and the English horses, the coursers of the desert have found an able and enthusiastic champion in Mr. Edmund M. Curr.'[7]

In the 1860s there was growing concern among pundits in the horse industry that breeding practices were biased towards English thoroughbreds; as a result, reliable weight bearing horses were becoming scarce. The strong demand in India for saddle horses had elicited calls from many to introduce more Arab blood into breeding programs. Curr became a leading voice in this campaign, arguing that Australian breeders should favour Arab sires rather than English thoroughbred stallions. He contended that English thoroughbreds were bred and trained exclusively for racing and were poorly suited to general work. Furthermore, over a period of 200 years or more, the thoroughbred had been acclimatised to cool English weather, which often left it wanting in the hot Australian climate. In its review of *Pure Saddle Horses*, the *Argus* explained the key deficiency of the thoroughbred compared to its Arab competitor: 'To run two or three miles at top speed, at an early age, is the end for which the English blood-horse is destined from his birth.' In contrast, the *Argus* continued: 'The Arab horse has … been made to attain the highest perfection, as a saddle horse.'[8]

In his preface to *Pure Saddle Horses* Curr described himself as one who had 'never backed, entered, or ridden near a racer on the turf, and who yet ventures to differ in opinion with many received authorities on the subject of the horse in general'.[9] He argued that the success of the English racer and hunter had encouraged English writers 'to claim a superiority for their saddle-horses over many others, which I have no hesitation in saying exists only in their imaginations'.[10] For this reason Curr confidently announced that he intended to plead 'the cause of the Eastern horse'.[11] He was not ill-qualified to offer a treatise on this topic: in 1860 he was awarded a prize of £100 offered by the

---

5   Edward M. Curr, 'Letter to the Editor', *Argus*, 16 January 1862: 6–7.
6   Curr 1863.
7   'Book Review, Pure Saddle Horses', *Argus*, 16 June 1863: 4–5.
8   'Book Review, Pure Saddle Horses', *Argus*, 16 June 1863: 4–5.
9   Curr 1863: v.
10 Curr 1863: vi–vii.
11 Curr 1863: viii.

British Government for the best essay on the breeding of horses for India.[12] Nevertheless, Curr felt the need to justify his foray into the theory of horse breeding, insisting that his views were based on personal experience: 'They are, indeed, the results of much sweat and long journeys, weary miles, painful roads, and worn-out spurs: intimacy with many who have lived in the saddle: – and the experience of the horses of many countries.'[13]

Curr believed his breadth of experience with horses, particularly in the Australian colonies, justified his assault on the established traditions of English horse breeding. He found support from the *Argus*, which published an extensive and favourable review.[14] An spirited debate ensued, featuring both praise and ridicule for Curr's position. Among the critics, an English writer using the pseudonym 'Cobb and Co.' argued that Curr had misrepresented prevailing English views on horse breeding in order to strengthen his own argument in favour of Arab techniques.[15] Another letter attributed to 'C.H.L.' suggested that Curr's plan was impractical, to which Curr responded provocatively by accusing his critic of reading *Pure Saddle Horses* 'only cursorily'.[16] The squabble soon degenerated into tedious repetition and trivial technicalities; as Margaret Kiddle has insightfully argued of Curr, 'he loved controversy and revelled in scoring off enraged opponents'.[17]

Curr certainly anticipated that his support for Arab stallions and Eastern training techniques he would provoke the ire of those convinced of the superiority of the British in all things. Towards the end of his book he had written:

> It is of little consequence that what I have proposed is new if it be reasonable, advantageous and practicable. What if it be against the practices of England? It accords with usage still more ancient and general ... Many new things, and simple and useful, have come to us from the barbarous and the uncivilized.[18]

Curr's book asserts his status as an educated gentleman of wide experience: a pastoralist with practical knowledge, but also a traveller with an intimate understanding of exotic lands. In the full title of his book, Curr announced his intention to compare the horses of four diverse regions. The book thus served

---

12 *The Herald* (Melbourne), 22 July 1921.
13 Curr 1863: 298–299.
14 'Book Review, Pure Saddle Horses', *Argus*, 19 June 1863: 5.
15 Cobb and Co., 'Mr. Curr's strictures on English horses and authors thereon', *Argus*, 4 December 1863: 7.
16 C.H.L., 'Letter to the Editor', *Argus*, 14 July 1863: 6; Edward M. Curr, 'Letter to the Editor', *Argus*, 20 July 1863: 7.
17 Kiddle 1967: 383–384.
18 Curr 1863: 297–298.

to bolster his status as an educated travelling gentleman. His apparently open-minded attitude to the merits of techniques derived from the 'barbarous' and 'uncivilised' Arabs supported this view.

Curr's advice to Australian horse breeders was never entirely adopted, although some Arab stallions were imported to Victoria over ensuing decades. According to Kiddle, the quality of horse breeding in Victoria improved markedly after the 1860s, but not due to any significant injection of Arab blood: 'The emphasis remained on the English stud book, but more discrimination in breeding was used.'[19] Despite courting controversy (or perhaps because of it) *Pure Saddle Horses* was a modest success. It can only have added to Curr's reputation as a man of ability and contributed to his subsequent success as Victoria's Chief Inspector of Stock. It was also an early sign of his literary ability. Significantly, Curr remained an occasional *Argus* correspondent for the rest of his life. He wrote on various topics, always cultivating a persona that combined extensive bush experience with an advanced education and marked literary ability.

The Scab Act

Despite the success of *Pure Saddle Horses*, Curr was still constrained by financial reality. In November 1862 he abandoned his eight-year-long quest to re-establish himself as a colonial landholder and commenced employment as an Inspector of Sheep for the Victorian Government on a salary of £350 per annum. He was appointed Inspector of the Melbourne District, which meant he could live with his family in Prahran, although he must have travelled frequently. In his new job, Curr joined several other inspectors appointed under the recently revised 'Scab Act'.[20]

Sheep diseases such as scab and catarrh were deemed sufficiently perilous to the Australian economy that colonial governments passed various regulations attempting to control them. Early versions of the Scab Act had simply attempted to control the movement of scabby sheep, in order to minimise the spread of the disease. In 1861 the O'Shanassy Government in Victoria introduced a new bill, based largely on South Australian legislation, which attempted to tackle the disease more directly. The Legislative Assembly was told that 'a small but gradually increasing penalty would be enforced against those who would not take the trouble to see that their sheep were properly attended to, and kept clean'.[21] The new Scab Act relied strongly on the cooperation of sheep-owners

---

19 Kiddle 1967: 383–384.
20 *An Act to repeal the Act intituled "An Act for preventing the extension of the Disease called Scab in Sheep" and to substitute the provisions in lieu thereof 1862*, (Victoria).
21 Victoria, *Parliamentary Debates*, Legislative Assembly, 25 October 1861, Volume 8, 207.

and was modest compared to subsequent legislation; nevertheless, it represented a significant increase in government intervention in the pastoral industry. In 1862 some members of the Legislative Council expressed a concern that too much power would be invested in the sheep inspectors, who would need to be well paid men of high integrity in order to avoid corruption.[22] The Scab Act became law in June 1862.

Curr had substantial experience with this problematic and expensive disease. One of his first tasks as a young squatter had been 'helping to dress the sheep for scab and foot-rot'.[23] Regulations controlling the movement of scabby sheep were weak in 1841; consequently, Curr did not encounter any difficulties when he moved his father's diseased flock from Wolfscrag to Tongala in 1841: 'the country between the two places being unoccupied, I took it for granted that the "Scab Act" offered no obstacle to the removal of my flocks in the proposed direction'.[24] Scab was an ongoing problem for the pastoralists of the 1840s, and Curr's extensive experience with sheep surely recommended him to the new position he accepted in November 1862.

Curr took his role seriously and wrote regularly to the chief secretary's office with questions, reports and advice. It is clear that his enthusiasm for the job was noticed, even if his frequently verbose communiqués appeared unnecessarily detailed to the chief secretary. In January 1863 he wrote to his employer describing a common practice among stockowners in his district, which he believed was contrary to the provisions of the Scab Act. Although Curr's letter spanned several pages, the chief secretary's brief instruction to his clerk, scribbled on the back of the letter, simply stated: 'I hardly think the Inspector requires any special instructions in such cases. The law provides the remedy.'[25]

Curr's official reports reveal a confidence in his own abilities and a belief in his prospects for promotion. On 30 January 1863, for example, he wrote a long letter offering various suggestions for changes to the Scab Act. Not insignificantly, he also lobbied for higher pay; he noted that the low salaries paid to the inspectors was 'a subject of constant remark by persons connected with sheep' and further observed that the issue was 'gradually finding its way into the public papers'. Curr argued the salary did not take into account the significant expenses incurred by the travelling inspectors: 'Hence at present I do, not what is to be done, but what I can afford to do.'[26] Importantly, Curr highlighted that he had the support of many larger sheep-owners, some of whom had offered to pay his

---

22 Victoria, *Parliamentary Debates*, Volume 8, 750–751, 905.
23 Curr 1883: 45.
24 Curr 1883: 69.
25 Edward M. Curr to the Chief Secretary, 23 January 1863, PROV, VPRS 1189/P0, Unit 681.
26 Edward M. Curr to Chief Secretary, 30 January 1863, PROV, VPRS 1189/P0, Unit 681.

travel expenses to help him attend their locality. Curr soon secured an increase in his salary to £500 per annum, which would surely have been welcome after his recent financial failures.[27]

In December 1863 Curr wrote again to the chief secretary with suggestions and advice. He was motivated by a belief that momentum for change was gathering following the formation of the new McCulloch Government in June. Curr advocated more changes to the Scab Act, mostly related to stronger enforcement and increased fines; he insisted that 'the real difficulty for sheep-owners at this moment is not to effect a cure of scab, but to guard against reinfection from neighbouring flocks'. He was beginning to formulate a view that quarantine of one form or another was the primary solution to the ravages of stock diseases. On the question of scab he took a very hard line, demonstrated most clearly by his suggestion of a £200 fine for the possession of even one scabby sheep. It was an attitude that would make him unpopular among many sheep-owners, particularly those with smaller flocks, but he believed that 'one scabby sheep is like one spark of fire'.[28]

By April 1864 the political will for changes to the Scab Act had strengthened, so Curr once again offered his advice to chief secretary James McCulloch in an extensive 19-page letter. He justified his unsolicited advice in another letter the following day: 'The kindness and patience you have always shewn in listening to what I have had to say on this subject, must be my excuse for troubling you on this occasion, unasked, with my opinions.'[29] Some of Curr's recommendations were adopted in the subsequent legislation, but it would be several years before his more radical suggestions gained widespread support. In the meantime, his persistence in advocating reform won him a promotion.

In May 1864 the McCulloch Government rushed through parliament the 'Diseases in Animals Prevention Bill'. The new legislation consolidated various statues relevant to animal diseases (including the Scab Act), but also signalled a more prominent role for the sheep inspectors. The government increased their number from seven to 11 and created the new position of Chief Inspector of Sheep. Not surprisingly, Curr was appointed to this office on 17 May 1864. It appears Curr had a very positive relationship with James McCulloch, which might explain his success during McCulloch's reign as premier and chief secretary. In his new role Curr acted as an intermediary between the district inspectors and the chief secretary.[30] It was largely an administrative position, so Curr was provided with

---

27 Curr, 'Memoranda Concerning our Family' (1877), SLV, MS 8998.
28 Edward M. Curr to Chief Secretary, 4 December 1863, PROV, VPRS 1189/P0, Unit 681.
29 Edward M. Curr to Chief Secretary, 5 and 6 April 1864, PROV, VPRS 3991/P0, Unit 55.
30 Instructions to Chief Inspector of Sheep, 26 May 1864, PROV, VPRS 3991/P0, Unit 56.

office accommodation in the old treasury building in Queen Street.[31] He was given special responsibility for overseeing 'all prosecutions under the Act and all appeals arising out of them'. His salary was raised to £700 per annum, double the income he received when he began his employment 18 months earlier.

Curr soon asserted power over his subordinates. In September 1864 he recommended the dismissal of Inspector Jones (a 'confirmed drunkard') and also reported Inspector James Riley for disobedience.[32] Riley was the inspector for the Melbourne District and presumably had regular contact with his new superior officer. Curr accused him of a 'systematic refusal ... to carry out instructions' and implied that Riley resented the new power Curr had over him.[33] Curr subsequently accused Riley of 'insinuations of an insulting character' and suggested to the chief secretary that 'Mr Riley is unfitted for an Inspector of Sheep'.[34] Despite Curr's complaints, Riley retained his position as the Inspector of Sheep for the Melbourne District and later acted as chief inspector in Curr's absence.[35]

During the early period of his administration, Curr provoked the ire of a judge of the Kilmore County Court, before whom he had appeared while prosecuting a scab case in April 1864. Judge Skinner had quashed an earlier conviction, arguing the law did not require a three-shilling fine for every head of sheep enclosed on a run where scabby sheep were known to be.[36] In September, Inspector Spurling reported to Curr a subsequent outburst by the judge in Bendigo:

> His Honor Judge Skinner made the following observations. "These Scab Cases are generally got up in a very loose manner, I must say you [Inspector Spurling] have taken more trouble in this than your Chief [Curr], for he appears to be too much of a Gentleman to get off his Horse, or to dirty his hands."

Judge Skinner referred to the earlier case in Kilmore, when Curr had suggested that, if the land between Melbourne and Kilmore were unfenced, the 20,000 sheep in the area would effectively constitute one flock. Justice Skinner wryly observed: 'Mr Curr might as well say all the Geese on the swamp between Kilmore and Melbourne were one Flock and himself the greatest Goose amongst them.'[37]

---

31 Edward M. Curr to Chief Secretary, 11 June 1864, requesting his new work address be gazetted, PROV, VPRS 3991/P0, Unit 56.
32 Edward M. Curr to Chief Secretary, 7 and 26 September 1864, PROV, VPRS 3991/P0, Unit 57.
33 Edward M. Curr to Chief Secretary, 26 September 1864, PROV, VPRS 3991/P0, Unit 57.
34 Edward M. Curr to Chief Secretary, 10 October 1864, PROV, VPRS 3991/P0, Unit 57.
35 James Riley to Chief Secretary, 6 July 1868, PROV, VPRS 3991/P0, Unit 362.
36 'A scab case at Kilmore', *Argus*, 28 April 1864: 5.
37 Inspector Spurling to Edward M. Curr, 8 September 1864, PROV, VPRS 3991/P0, Unit 56.

Curr promptly complained to the chief secretary. He noted that he had not met Judge Skinner until he appeared before him six months earlier, but that he had since received 'a hostile and verbal message' from the judge. Curr was clearly outraged by the judge's remarks, but the chief secretary was reluctant to intercede: 'I cannot call a Judge to account summarily for every rude or splenetic expression which may escape him from the Bench.'[38] It is hard to say what was behind the animosity of a judge and at least one junior employee towards Curr. One might speculate that there was a sectarian motivation, fuelled by simple prejudice against Curr's Catholicism and displeasure at his rapid elevation in the public service. More likely, it would seem that Curr inherited some of the imperious manner for which his father had been renowned, which, when directed at an equally imperious judge, was bound to cause offence.

Despite all this, by 1864 Curr had established himself as the leading thinker on the problem of scab in the colony of Victoria. This was confirmed when he was awarded a £150 prize for an essay on the subject. In 1865 the Victorian Government published *An Essay on Scab in Sheep: Its Causes, Symptoms, Pathology, Best Means of Treatment, and Practical Hints for Its Avoidance and Extermination, Etc.* Curr impressed upon his reader the economic importance of the issues he addressed; namely, that scab in sheep was causing the loss of '*one seventh* of the whole revenue' of the Colony of Victoria.[39] Much of the essay outlined the accepted wisdom on treating scabby sheep, but the more controversial passages concerned the best method for eradicating the disease altogether. This was a matter that, as Curr put it, 'trenches on, and interferes with, the freedom of action of the individual sheep owner'. He explained that his solution involved 'restrictions and penalties ... surveillance and coercion'; the legislation he proposed would affect some individuals greatly, but was 'for the benefit of the entire body of sheep-owners'.[40] There is no doubt that the significant power Curr already enjoyed in his role as chief inspector provoked resentment from those who abhorred government interference in private enterprise. Yet Curr was quite willing to justify 'the interference of our legislators with our flock-owners', arguing that the economic loss made the matter one of 'national importance'. He contended that with the proper powers of legislatively backed intervention, scab could easily be eliminated throughout Victoria.[41]

In putting forward his case, Curr reviewed the limited success of the 1862 Scab Act under which he was first appointed. He remarked that while the disease might have reduced in frequency, its complete eradication had not been achieved in any district. He attributed the failure of the 1862 Act to several factors, the

---

38   Edward M. Curr to Chief Secretary, 9 September 1864, PROV, VPRS 3991/P0, Unit 56.
39   Curr 1865: 6, emphasis in the original.
40   Curr 1865: 28.
41   Curr 1865: 29.

most notable being: 'The attempt to clean the whole country at once, and to accomplish at a blow, what can only be effected by degrees.'[42] Curr advocated a staged approach, which involved the classification of sheep flocks and of scab districts as clean, scabby or *doubtful*. This third category was crucial to Curr's approach of risk management, which was made necessary by the elapse in time from sheep being infected with scab and symptoms becoming apparent.

Curr's systematic approach was to begin at the colony's northern and eastern extremities, where large areas were already free from scab. He proposed that the boundaries of these 'clean' districts might slowly be extended towards Melbourne. This would have the least detrimental effect on the income of the colony's sheep-owners, as it would not prevent those in scabby districts from taking their sheep to the market in Melbourne for sale. Clean districts, which would require restrictions on the travel of flocks and provisions for quarantine, would be less disruptive to the pastoral economy if they commenced at the periphery and slowly converged on the commercial centre in Melbourne. The 'doubtful' districts, which bordered the clean districts in the north and east, would be subject to the most intrusive aspects of Curr's proposed regime. Here the sheep inspectors would have considerable power: to fine those not cooperating with the Scab Act; to quarantine stations until they were deemed clean; and to destroy sheep 'which the owner cannot or will not cure'.[43] As logical as it sounded in theory, Curr's proposal was always going to be hard to sell. In his essay, he suggested that opposition from sheep-owners would be inevitable with 'approval only gradually growing out of fortunate results'.[44] Curr's major task as Chief Inspector of Sheep was, therefore, to build a consensus around his proposals for the eradication of scab.

An important step towards this goal was a two-day meeting of flock-owners in February 1866. Curr chaired the meeting and attempted to convince those present of the wisdom of his views. He remarked that when his *Essay on Scab in Sheep* was printed in 1865 'a large number of sheepowners were diametrically opposed to the suggestions it contained', but in subsequent conversations 'scarcely one' had disputed the validity of his arguments.[45] Curr condemned the Scab Act as 'almost useless' and said that his plan had been approved by the owners of between three and four million sheep. There was some opposition, principally from those who perceived they would be disadvantaged, but by and large Curr's ideas were endorsed.[46] Nevertheless, it would take another three years before the parliament was willing to adopt Curr's plan.

---

42 Curr 1865: 30.
43 Curr 1865: 37.
44 Curr 1865: 38.
45 Report on Meeting of Sheep Owners, 5 and 6 February 1866, 'The Scab Act', *Argus,* 7 February 1866: 5.
46 The proposals were published in the *Economist,* 16 February 1866. See also Edward M. Curr to Chief Secretary, 25 July 1866, PROV, VPRS 3991/P0, Unit 215.

Meanwhile, controversy and suspicion continued to surround the powers that Curr and the other sheep inspectors already exercised. This all came to a head in 1869 when Curr's office was charged with the illegal destruction the previous year of 7,000 sheep at a station called 'Rigby Downs'. The sheep, which were *en route* to South Australia, were alleged to be scabby, but there was some confusion as to whether the entire flock was affected, or just one straggling sheep. An order for their destruction was issued by the Attorney General and subsequently withdrawn, but the slaughter proceeded in February 1868. The controversy that embroiled Curr's department was politically charged due to the critical involvement of the Attorney General, G.P. Smith.

In August 1869 the *Argus* observed that 'the precipitancy of the Attorney-General … will cost the country something', and reported that the plaintiffs had successfully sued the Chief Inspector of Sheep for damages of £1,277 (4 shillings per head).[47] Curr challenged the ruling but was unsuccessful. Meanwhile, the local inspector, Mr McRae, was blamed for the illegal slaughter by the findings of a board of inquiry that was ratified by the Attorney General. It appeared that Curr had escaped any repercussions until Smith, who was under pressure to justify his own actions, suggested in parliament that Curr was ultimately to blame. An *Argus* correspondent wrote on 16 December 1869: 'The ex-Minister distinctly admitted that the person to blame for the ovine holocaust at Rifle Downs in March last year was the Chief Inspector and not Mr. McCrae, his subordinate.'[48] Curr defended himself in a report to parliament where he explained that he 'was necessarily guided by the very peremptory instructions he received from Mr. Smith' and that he had 'pointed out to him the unadvisability [sic] of the course he was directed to pursue'.[49] The whole episode was no doubt an unwelcome distraction in a period when Curr was lobbying for expanded powers under the Scab Act. Despite all the controversy, however, Curr's long-term quest for more intrusive legislation was soon achieved.

In 1870 the Scab Act was finally amended in line with Curr's 1865 essay. As the *Australasian* later described, the new legislation gave the chief inspector wide-ranging powers, including the ability to frame regulations without consulting the parliament: 'The act was, indeed, almost a skeleton, to be filled up and worked at the instance of the department concerned by means of regulations.' The newspaper insisted that Curr exercised these extensive powers 'for the benefit of the classes most deeply concerned'.[50] His plan was successful and the

---

47 *Argus*, 3 August 1869: 5.
48 F.H. Nixon, 'Letter to the Editor', *Argus*, 17 December 1869: 5.
49 *Argus*, 22 December 1869: 5.
50 'Obituary: Edward M. Curr', *Australasian*, 10 August 1889: 293.

Colony of Victoria was officially declared free of scab on 6 June 1876. It was an achievement of major economic importance to the colony and certainly cemented Curr's reputation as a man of considerable ability and public importance.

Chief Inspector of Stock

In June 1872 an outbreak of foot-and-mouth disease (FMD) was discovered near Werribee, in what has been described as 'the most serious incident' of its type in Australia.[51] Two separate farms were involved (belonging to Mr Bowman and Mr Cobbledick) and the disease was stamped out only after the destruction of 122 cattle, 71 pigs and 14 sheep. At the time, there was no legislative framework for dealing with diseases in cattle or pigs. Due to the serious nature of the disease, government intervention was swift and Curr played a crucial role. He first visited the affected farms on 8 June 1872 as part of an official party of three appointed by the Commissioner for Trade and Customs, William Vale. He was joined by a veterinary surgeon and a stockowner with experience of the disease; all agreed it was a case of FMD. The parliament passed temporary legislation on 11 June and established a Royal Commission on Foot and Mouth Disease.

Figure 15: E.M. Curr (1872). Thomas Foster Chuck.

Photograph. State Library of Victoria, H5056/235.

---

51 Bunn, Garner and Cannon 1998.

On 12 June 1872 Curr returned to Bowman's farm with two more veterinary surgeons, both of whom confirmed the diagnosis. Acting under instructions from the Minister, Curr immediately shot 64 cattle with the assistance of a policeman. One of Curr's subordinates, Inspector John Kerr, then proceeded to Cobbledick's farm and destroyed 58 cattle and 37 pigs. Because Curr was instructed to destroy the animals immediately, proper disposal of the animals was made extremely difficult. The carcasses at Cobbledick's farm were burned, while those at Bowman's farm were buried. Curr reported to the Royal Commission on 20 June 1872 that the disposal of the cattle he shot at Bowman's farm was only possible because of the cooler winter weather: 'In summer men could not be induced by money to work amongst cattle so long dead; it is a question with me if men could work amongst them and live.' Curr noted he was only able to enlist support 'by leading the way myself and giving them grog'.[52] The hideous task of disposing of the rotting carcasses motivated Curr to delay killing the pigs on Bowman's farm: 'I should have done so at once, but they were all in styes, and the cattle were so putrid that I didn't like to add to the stench that was there'.[53]

In its interim report, the Royal Commission recorded its thanks 'to Inspectors Curr and Kerr for their active cooperation'.[54] Curr was again commended in the final report. In fact, the FMD outbreak provided the impetus for an expansion of his role and a further increase in salary. Curr was asked during the Royal Commission if it was necessary to delegate him further powers, to which he responded: 'If I am to look after the cattle and other stock, I think it would be desirable that I should be, as inspectors in the neighbouring colonies are. At present I am in a false position altogether.'[55]

The FMD outbreak had coincided precisely with a change of government in Victoria, following a vote of no confidence against Charles Duffy's liberal administration on 10 June 1872. The first action of the new James Francis Government was the temporary legislation it passed in response to the FMD outbreak. It subsequently introduced the more comprehensive 'Diseases in Stock Bill', which consolidated government legislation relating to scab, catarrh and pleuro-pneumonia, and added new provisions for foot-and-mouth disease.[56] As a result of this legislation, in January 1873 Curr was promoted to the new position of Chief Inspector of Stock and his salary was raised to £750 per annum, which made him one of the highest paid public servants in Victoria. Curr's promotion also corresponded with the creation of Victoria's first Department of Agriculture in 1872. The closer settlement that followed the land acts of the

---

52 Royal Commission on Foot and Mouth Disease, 'Progress Report of the Commission, with Minutes of Evidence' in Victoria, *Votes and Proceedings of the Legislative Assembly*, 1872, 3 (58), 814.
53 Royal Commission on Foot and Mouth Disease, 'Progress Report', 809.
54 Royal Commission on Foot and Mouth Disease, 'Progress Report'.
55 Royal Commission on Foot and Mouth Disease, 'Progress Report', 823–825.
56 Victoria, *Parliamentary Debates*, Volume 15, 1160.

1860s justified an increase in government regulation of pastoral and agricultural matters. As the Chief Inspector of Stock, Curr held the most important position in the new Department. As late as 1884 his salary remained significantly higher than that of any other employee (the Secretary received only £516 per annum).

Curr remained Chief Inspector of Stock from 1873 until his death. Throughout his career he was a prominent voice in debates about the prevention of animal disease and the framing of quarantine laws and regulations throughout the Australian colonies. In November 1874 he attended an intercolonial conference for stock inspectors, at which the New South Wales delegate, Alexander Bruce, attempted to establish a consensus around quarantine measures for animal imports. While an uncontrolled outbreak of foot-and-mouth disease was greatly feared, Bruce was prepared to accept that complete prohibition of livestock imports was impossible. As J.R. Fisher has explained, Bruce proposed 'a system of discretionary prohibition based on information of disease status and supplemented by a lengthy quarantine period'.[57] Curr proved to be the principal barrier to an agreement; he proposed that imports from Britain be prohibited until that country was declared free of any infectious or contagious disease.[58] Fisher has argued that Curr's intransigence was partly influenced by 'tensions over intercolonial trade',[59] but Curr's record would suggest his objection was based on a more principled opposition to the compromise Bruce proposed. As Curr had already shown in relation to his program for the eradication of scab in sheep, he was willing to countenance extreme measures. For the rest of his life he consistently advocated a complete ban on the importation of livestock into Australia.

In 1877 Curr told the National Agricultural Society of Victoria that the quality of stock in Australia was so high that 'fresh importations were not needed'. According to the *Argus*, he stressed 'the difficulty of detecting disease in stock and the almost certain failure of any kind of quarantine regulations to prevent the introduction of disease'.[60] Curr was motivated to speak out on the issue by the news that New South Wales, Queensland and Western Australia were all considering lifting the ban on livestock imports from Great Britain. He mounted an argument against the superiority of English breeds that was reminiscent of *Pure Saddle Horses*, published 14 years earlier:

> Let breeders remember that there is no magic about English stock, no particular aboriginal breed of exceptional quality in Great Britain, no

---

57 Fisher 2000: 480.
58 Conference of the Chief Inspectors of Stock for the Several Australian Colonies, 'Report, Minutes of Proceedings, Resolutions, etc.', in Victoria, *Papers Presented to Parliament by Command*, Session 1875–6, Vol. 2: 4, 10.
59 Conference of the Chief Inspectors of Stock, 'Report, Minutes of Proceedings, Resolutions, etc.'
60 Edward M. Curr, 'The importation of live stock into Australia' (Paper delivered to the National Agricultural Society of Victoria, 18 September 1877), reported in the *Argus*, 19 September 1877: 5.

specially favourable circumstances of nature even ... Foreign animals are
a drawback to breeding, not needed; and if they come, they will in the
future, as in the past, bring disaster with them.[61]

Nearly a decade later Curr was still struggling to win support for prohibition over quarantine. In June 1886 he attempted to convince the Council of the National Agricultural Society to support common legislation for the whole of Australasia, which would permanently prohibit the importation of livestock from other countries.[62] Later that year he attended another Stock Conference in Sydney where he proposed a motion 'that the introduction of all bovine, ovine, equine, porcine, feline and canine animals should be prohibited, except for the purposes of zoological gardens'.[63] Curr's motion was rejected and the meeting eventually adopted a proposal to lift prohibition and introduce a rigorous quarantine program. The *Argus* was supportive of the measure and quite critical of Curr's resistance:

> The Victorian inspector of stock had the honor of leading off the discussion, a concession due to his age, his experience, and his enthusiasm. Mr. Curr was as vigorous, as eccentric, and as absurd as ever. The idea that England possesses all the excellencies in stock is described by him as 'a tradition.'[64]

Not to be cowed, Curr told the *Argus* that prohibition had only been lifted with the support of two veterinary delegates, who, Curr argued, would benefit financially from renewed stock importation and the system of quarantine that accompanied it.[65] Prominent Victorian pastoralist Thomas Shaw also jumped to Curr's defence, objecting to the sarcastic tone of the *Argus*:

> The sheep-farmers of this colony owe an eternal debt of gratitude to our chief inspector for his vigorous eradication of scab from our flocks. At first I was inclined to rebel against his clean and unclean districts, and his determined plans of removing that costly disease from our midst, but soon I saw that we were on the right track, and, thanks to the indomitable perseverance, and, if you will, 'eccentricity' and 'absurdity' of Mr. Curr, this colony was soon a clean one, and we have been a model to other colonies and countries.[66]

Curr's attitudes to stock importation, quarantine and horse breeding were certainly controversial, resisting, as they did, the common Victorian belief

---

61 Edward M. Curr, 'The importation of live stock into Australia', in *Argus*, 19 September 1877: 7.
62 *Argus*, 9 June 1886: 5.
63 *Argus*, 22 October 1886: 4.
64 *Argus*, 22 October 1886: 4.
65 Edward M. Curr, 'Letter to the Editor', *Argus*, 30 October 1886: 11.
66 Thomas Shaw, 'Letter to the Editor', *Argus*, 11 November 1886: 8.

in the superiority of all things British. He clearly believed that the validity of his arguments was obscured by prejudice. The *Argus* perhaps justifiably pointed to Curr's enthusiasm, vigour and eccentricity; his views and theories were always keenly argued, even if many were ultimately rejected. His greatest achievement as Victoria's Inspector of Stock was undoubtedly the eradication of scab. Veterinary scientist P.J. Macwhirter has described Curr's *Essay on Scab in Sheep* as a key breakthrough, which contributed to a paradigm shift in theories of contagious animal diseases in Australia.[67]

---

67   Macwhirter 1997: 515–519.

7. Recollections of Squatting

As Curr's public service career flourished, he was able to purchase a more comfortable home in St Kilda. From 1875 until his death he resided with his large family at 'Alma House' on the north-west corner of Chapel and Argyle Streets. It was an 11-room brick residence, which was valued at £2,300 in 1889. Probate records provide some insight into the nature of Curr's family life at Alma House; he owned, for example, a piano, a billiard table and a library of 500 books.[1] The financial security Curr regained in the 1860s enabled him to provide his children with a quality education. His eldest son Edward was singled out for overseas tuition by the Jesuits at Namur, Belgium, and at the college of Mondragone, near Rome. Curr did not record the nature of his daughters' education, but his three younger sons, Justin, Hubert and Ernest, attended Xavier College in Melbourne.[2]

In his 'Memoranda Concerning Our Family' Curr provided a brief but positive account of his wife Margaret: 'She has been invariably the best of wives, and on looking round I cannot help noticing how few of my friends have been as favoured as myself, in this particular'. It is predictable that Curr would speak favourably of his wife in a memoir dictated to his daughter, but there is no evidence to suggest any tensions in his marriage. He attributed his conjugal happiness to clearly defined gender roles within his marital relationship, noting that his wife was the 'supreme mistress' in his home: 'If at any time I have taken any part in our domestic concerns, it has merely been occasionally to tender my advice'.[3]

Very little evidence survives to indicate Curr's style of parenting. A notable exception is an 'agreement', which he apparently asked his three younger sons to sign in the late 1870s:

> We promise neither to throw stones nor to talk to children in the street and if one of us sees another of us break this engagement we promise to tell Papa of him, and if we are found breaking this promise we sincerely trust Papa will whip us without mercy.
>
> [Signed] Justin Curr, Hubert Curr, Ernest Curr[4]

This note, retained by the Curr family for well over a century, suggests a degree of paternal authority that was not unusual for the time. A contrast to this

---

1 Edward M. Curr, Wills and Probate: PROV, VPRS 28/P2, Units 266, 494, Item 40/072; VPRS 7951/P2, Unit 150, Item 40/072.
2 Edward M. Curr to E.M.V. Curr, 26 November 1883, 4 and 19 December 1883, Murrumbogie Papers.
3 Curr, 'Memoranda Concerning Our Family' (1877), SLV, MS 8998.
4 Justin, Hubert and Ernest Curr, Undated Agreement, Murrumbogie Papers.

stern discipline is found in a letter written by Curr to his eldest son Edward in 1883, which displays considerable pride in his younger sons' achievements. Curr reported that Justin (17) 'had four honourable mentions and got a football prize', Hubert (15) was 'well spoken of by his master', while Ernest (13) 'has given satisfaction and carried off the grand elocution prize at the Christian Bros and is lauded in the *Herald*'.[5] Curr was clearly pleased by his sons' studious ways, noting in another letter: 'It is very gratifying to find that their masters have taught them so to appreciate study'.[6]

While Curr did not neglect his other children, he certainly favoured his eldest son, whose career he carefully fostered. E.M.V. Curr was more than a decade older than his younger brothers and clearly carried the future hopes of his family. He returned from his overseas education in 1871 and worked briefly for the wool-broking firm of his uncle Hastings Cunningham. After five years at the Bank of Victoria (during which time he played football for St Kilda) he commenced a career as a pastoralist, with the strong encouragement and financial assistance of his father. Edward M.V. Curr recorded in his memoirs that in 1879 'Papa advanced me £700', which he used to establish a station in north-west Queensland called Constance Downs. In 1882 he sold this station and searched for new country around Normanton and the Gulf of Carpentaria. His uncles Marmaduke, Julius and Montagu Curr were all active in the pastoral industry of northern Queensland, which might explain his focus on this area. In 1883 E.M.V. Curr formed a partnership with Messrs Richardson and Little in the Austral Downs station, which was situated in the Northern Territory to the west of Mount Isa.[7]

It appears Edward M. Curr invested most of his available funds in his son's remote pastoral ventures and as a result had relatively little money available for his own use. He wrote to his son in 1883: 'I am still hard up and do not expect to have £100 to my credit as long as two boys are at college'.[8] In spite of this, he was content to support his son's commercial ambitions: 'It is enough that when you are able you will send me say £150'.[9] In 1885 E.M.V. Curr sold his share of Austral Downs for £3,000, a good return on his initial investment of £1,850.[10] He returned to Melbourne where he stayed for several months because his mother was ill. Margaret Curr died in April 1885 at the age of 55 and was buried in the family grave at St Kilda Cemetery. Soon after his wife's death Edward M. Curr purchased over 2,500 acres of freehold land (and several

---

5   Edward M. Curr to E.M.V. Curr, 19 December 1883, Murrumbogie Papers. Curr recorded that Ernest's success was reported in the *Herald* on 21 December 1883.
6   Edward M. Curr to E.M.V. Curr, 4 December 1883, Murrumbogie Papers.
7   E.M.V. Curr, Unpublished memoirs, Murrumbogie Papers.
8   Edward M. Curr to E.M.V. Curr, 4 December 1883, Murrumbogie Papers.
9   Edward M. Curr to E.M.V. Curr, 19 December 1883, Murrumbogie Papers.
10   Mary Margaret (Margery) Curr, 'History of the Curr Family (1798–1955)', Murrumbogie Papers.

thousand more in leasehold) near Trundle, New South Wales. The property was named 'Murrumbogie' and was adjacent to another property selected (and later purchased) by his son. The following year Curr transferred the land and leases to E.M.V. Curr. In this way, Curr was able to help establish his son on a valuable pastoral station – a task he had not managed for himself in the 1850s.

Throughout this period Curr indulged his love of literature; moreover, his stable career and generous income provided ample opportunity to develop his skills as a writer. Curr read widely and was a regular contributor to newspaper columns on diverse topics. He appears to have derived considerable pleasure from writing at its most basic level; whether addressing technical matters or exploring topics of more general interest, his prose was rich and descriptive. Curr's inclination to be an author had first emerged at Stonyhurst College, where he filled his leisure time writing reviews of books and novels. There was no shortage of literary inspiration from within his own family: his grandfather, father, and paternal uncles were all published authors. Curr pursued this literary interest during his final year of schooling in France, keeping the journal that is the earliest surviving example of his work. If he wrote anything substantial during his busy squatting years it has not survived, although he and his brothers assembled an impressive 'Bush Library' at Tongala, which featured at least 150 volumes.[11]

By the mid-1850s Curr's boyish fascination for literature and creative writing had matured into a marked ability to write competently, lucidly and argumentatively.

The four letters he wrote to newspapers in New Zealand, attacking what he viewed as the land monopolising policies of the colony's legislature, are considerably more accomplished than his earlier writings. In his final letter to the *New Zealand Spectator* he explained that he was soon to leave the colony but would leave a significant legacy: 'I have in writing these letters forged a good weapon, which may be taken in the hand of any future assailant of these agrarian injustices'.[12] Curr's parting shot at New Zealand's legislators displays a firm belief in the power of the written word. His self-confidence was affirmed when the *New Zealand Spectator* republished his letters in booklet form shortly after he left the colony.[13] The weapon imagery alludes to the well-known proverb 'the pen is mightier than the sword', suggesting Curr was already very confident of the power of his prose.

Over subsequent years, Curr applied his abilities with considerable self-assurance to a variety of topics. Writing principally in the pages of the *Argus*, he addressed many practical matters, including exploration, horse breeding, and stock disease. His letters were typically longer than necessary: it appears

---

11   Curr 1883: 359–360.
12   Edward M. Curr, 'Letter to the Editor', *New Zealand Spectator*, 30 January 1856.
13   Curr 1856.

he wished not only to convince his readers of a particular point of view, but equally he hoped to display his accomplished ability to write descriptively and creatively. These were not quickly written letters to a newspaper editor; they were confidently argued essays of literary merit, conveying as much about Curr's enjoyment of writing as they did about the many topics he treated. This commitment to quality in writing regardless of topic is best illustrated by Curr's *Essay on Scab in Sheep* (1865). While addressing a seemingly practical matter, Curr clearly intended that the essay would be one of literary worth:

> It is curious to remember that the little parasite of which I speak ... should have attracted the attention of Celsus and of Aristotle, and that his ravages, which were sung by Virgil, should be under the ban of the Legislature of Old England, as well as of Young Australia.[14]

As Curr saw it, he was not merely contributing a technical essay on a sheep disease: he was engaging in an age-long discussion that linked him with the scientific and literary pursuits of ancient Greece and Rome.

As has been noted, Curr's first full-length book, *Pure Saddle Horses*, was published in 1863. The literary style evident in this book exhibits many of the characteristics of his later writings. To the modern reader the authorial voice often appears overtly modest and apologetic, as the following passage from the preface demonstrates:

> In offering this work to the public, none can feel better than the Author the necessity for asking some indulgence for entering on a theme which has already been treated of by so many. This becomes, apparently at least, the more needed by one to whom the subject is not professional ... and who yet ventures to differ in opinion with many received authorities on the subject of the horse in general, and to call in question doings and customs which have been considered beyond the reach of contradiction.[15]

It was most likely passages like this one that prompted a reviewer to note the 'classical and nervous language' with which Curr put his case about horse breeding.[16]

Another writer of a more specifically literary bent later satirised a somewhat verbose passage from *Pure Saddle Horses* for comic effect. In his classic Australian novel *Such is Life* (1903), Joseph Furphy (alias Tom Collins) quoted *Pure Saddle Horses* during an extended discussion of the enigmatic Australian bushman's

---

14 Curr 1865: 5.
15 Curr 1863: v.
16 C.H.L., 'Letter to the Editor', *Argus*, 14 July 1863: 6.

ability to stay astride a difficult horse. Furphy's ironic contention was that the perfect horseman was chiefly defined by his ignorance ('the less brains he has, the better') and he found a useful demonstration of his theory in Curr's pages:

> Edward M. Curr knew as much of the Australian horse and his rider as any man did; and this is what he says of the back country natives:-
>
> 'They are taciturn, shy, ignorant, and incurious; undemonstrative but orderly; hospitable, courageous, cool and sensible. These men ride like centaurs,' etc., etc.
>
> Yes, yes - but why? Looking back along that string of well selected adjectives doesn't your own inductive faculty at once place its finger on Ignorance as the key to the enigma. Notice, too, how Curr, being a bit of a sticker himself, is thereby disqualified from knowing that the centaurs were better constructed for firing other people over their heads than straddling their own backs.[17]

Furphy was a democratically minded chronicler, who was inclined to ridicule all his principal characters in equal measure. Consequently, his light-hearted jibe at Curr's apparent ignorance of the anatomy of a centaur should not be taken too seriously. Nevertheless, Furphy's insight was to note Curr's overly elaborate use of language, which is often characterised by a 'string of well selected adjectives'.

Much of the evidence Curr presented in *Pure Saddle Horses* derived from his own experiences in Australia and overseas. In time, he would direct his literary efforts increasingly towards the task of relating his own varied life experiences. A significant yet now largely forgotten example was a series of three letters he wrote to Melbourne's *Economist* in 1869. They were titled 'Experiences of Horses Afloat' and ostensibly offered advice on how horses might profitably be exported to India. Curr did not intend, however, to confine his contributions purely to practical advice: such an approach would not have justified an entire broadsheet page of text spanning three issues of the newspaper. Curr wrote his letters under the alias 'CIOS' (Chief Inspector of Sheep) and began by suggesting 'the great majority of shippers' did not possess the necessary knowledge to transport horses at sea: 'Previous, however, to considering the arrangements on which success depends, I have a mind to offer the reader some of my experiences of the matter'.[18] Curr's entertaining account of his horse-trading exploits occupies the first two parts of his lengthy account; only in part three does he turn to practical advice. His primary aim was to entertain his reader.

---

17 Furphy 1903: 279.
18 Edward M. Curr, 'Experiences of horses afloat. No. I. By CIOS', *Economist* (Melbourne), 1 October 1869: 3.

The subject matter for 'Experiences of Horses Afloat' was Curr's first foray into horse-trading in 1855, when he exported two equine cargoes to New Zealand. Curr explained that he had sought the advice of an experienced horse-trader named Mr S— before he departed Newcastle with his first load of 100 mares. Mr S— suggested that Curr was giving his horses too much water (ten gallons per day instead of four) and insisted such a course 'must be injurious on board ship'. Curr's interlocutor further explained that he usually expected to lose at least one horse per day once they were loaded. Curr's departure for New Zealand was delayed for eight days due to unfavourable winds, during which time he ignored his friend's advice and continued to 'overwater' his horses. Despite hot weather, he did not lose a single animal.

> My friend S—, I was told, was very much perplexed at what he heard and saw about my doings, and their success, which were, I believe, pretty freely commented on by persons interested in the shipment of stock, but he evidently to the last considered my ten gallons a horse to be a foolish and wicked innovation, coupled with an unaccountable obstinacy and vicious determination not to die (as they should have done), on the part of my horses. Frankly, an uneasy and disturbed manner on S—'s part led me to surmise that in some way or other, the even tenor of my friend's truly philosophic mind had been disturbed, and his really kind spirit galled by the failure of his theory. He talked of allowing his nags, next trip, only two gallons a day. Really I should not have been sorry if one or two horses had died to keep him on good terms with his opinion. When one experienced pronounces oracularly against the doings of a novice, it is so provoking when things do not turn out as they should![19]

In the early part of his narrative, Curr had established himself as a competent man who, while a horse-trading novice, was clearly in tune with the needs of his animals. When the winds changed and Curr finally departed, his voyage to New Zealand took 24 days instead of the usual twelve. Water became scarce, but Curr supplemented his supply by adding two quarts of seawater to every two gallons of fresh water: 'I lost no horses from either hunger or thirst, whatever I may have done from other causes'.

Curr was deliberately talking up his innate horse wrangling ability for narrative effect; while he had proven Mr S— wrong on the issue of water, his inexperience of horse transportation remained. The narrative arc in the second instalment of Curr's account reflects the adage that 'pride comes before a fall'. Continuing with his rich description Curr explained:

---

19   Edward M. Curr, 'Experiences of horses afloat. No. I. By CIOS', *Economist* (Melbourne), 1 October 1869: 3.

> It was I think about nine o'clock in the evening of our eighth day out that I was reclining in the cuddy sky-light smoking my pipe. The skipper sat opposite on a hen-coop. The breeze was strong and gusty … For myself, though our voyage had sped but slowly, I was altogether in a pleasant mood. The air was cool and exhilarating, and though a bank of clouds was slowly rising to windward, the stars shone brightly overhead. From the hour, too, it may have been, but the smoothing charms of a glass of rum had lulled my spirit. My horses were all strong; I had lost none of them. Disquietude concerning them had ceased. Indeed, I had almost begun to doubt whether horses ever died at sea; at all events without gross mismanagement.[20]

Curr asked his Captain how it was that so many horses died while on board ships. The skipper replied that it was probably due to mismanagement and commended Curr for his seemingly effective innovation. He did, however, issue a warning: 'before the end of the trip you'll have your eyes opened, I know'. Curr continued:

> I do not like to have my eyes opened. Constitutionally I am averse to the operation. I have always found it disagreeable. The very expression is uncongenial; it seems to imply the gaining of knowledge, doubtless, but in a sinister way: it impresses me somehow with the idea that the opening, will be (on the part of the eyes) to something disagreeable. However, I am digressing.

Curr's recognition of his tendency to digress did not bring him to the point; in fact, he appeared actively to avoid it. He continued with an elegant but tangential description of the ship he had chartered – a retired naval vessel called the *Waterwitch*:

> It was, as I have said, about nine o'clock; the labours of the day were over. We were just laying our course. The wind had increased. The old gun-brig was rolling and wallowing about between the seas as frolicsomely as a young lady porpoise in her most flirtsome mood, before the cares of a family have occurred to repress her buoyancy; much on the same style, I presume as of yore, in the days of her trim youth, when, freighted with jolly tars and blithe middies, her ensign flying at her gaff, and sporting some half-dozen long guns, she chased slavers off the coast of Guinea; or insisted on impertinent inquiries of suspicious looking craft along the Spanish main.

Eventually Curr came to the point and explained that the ship tossed so much in the rough wind that one third of his horses were seriously injured:

---

20   Edward M. Curr, 'Experiences of horses afloat. No. II. By CIOS', *Economist* (Melbourne), 8 October 1869: 3.

Inexorable confusion!– the dead, the dying, the injured, and the sound, all heaped together. As for myself, I presumed that I was just going through the process of having my eyes opened![21]

Thirty horses died before the *Waterwitch* reached Wellington – 'the ocean levied a heavy toll'. Curr's entertaining description of the voyage thus served as an extended prelude to the practical advice he offered in his third and final contribution to the *Economist*.[22] Although it was published 14 years before *Recollections of Squatting in Victoria*, Curr's 'Experiences of Horses Afloat' is similar in style to the later work; through its rich description, tangential observations, prominent use of irony and autobiographical foundation, 'Experiences of Horses Afloat' is in many ways a prototype for Curr's most famous work.

A Bilingual Poet

At around the same time that Curr was writing his humorous prose account of horse-trading, he was also applying his leisure time to the production of a volume of verse. He called it *Des Bétises = Frivolities* and it consisted of poems written in both French and English. Curr penned a version of each poem in both languages, with the corresponding verses appearing on either side of each page opening. His lengthiest poem was titled 'Delphine' and was inspired by the French Romantic novel of the same name, written by Madame de Staël in 1802.[23] De Staël was exiled by Napoleon after the release of her novel, which offered a critique on the limitations of women's freedom in an aristocratic society. Curr attempted to capture in verse the doomed romance of Alphonso and Delphine; the following two stanzas are representative of his bilingual creation:

Que le jeune Alphonse de Lautrec	That, in a castle's garden,
Dans le jardin d'un chateau,	Beneath a pomegranate's shade,
'A l'ombre d'un grenadier	By where a silvery brook
Sur les bords d'un ruisseau	Its soothing murmur made,
Tout seul chantait les louanges	Young Alphonso de Lautrec
De son espiègle cousine	Sung of Provençal belles the queen,
Jolie, jeune, svelte et brunette,	His cousin – charming and brunette,
Sa bien-aimée Delphine.	The light of his eyes – Delphine!*

* Curr 1868: 10.

---

21 Edward M. Curr, 'Experiences of horses afloat. No. II. By CIOS', *Economist* (Melbourne), 8 October 1869: 3.
22 Edward M. Curr, 'On the shipment of horses to India. No. III. By CIOS', *Economist* (Melbourne), 15 October 1869: 3.
23 de Staël 1995.

Des Bêtises = Frivolities was printed in Melbourne by Henry Dwight, a successful bookseller who had published verse by more prominent poets such as George McCrae and Richard Horne.[24] Curr's booklet appeared with two front covers, reflecting the bilingual nature of his project. The fifth page included a prominent disclaimer, warning the reader of his limited experience in French: '*Lis si tu veux, mais je te dis d'avance; Je n'ai passé, que dix-huit mois en France*'.[25] Curr dedicated the collection of poems to his sister Florence, who had joined the Catholic order the Sisters of Mercy. He was vaguely apologetic for inflicting his homespun verse upon his sister:

> You'll think, dear Finny, that it were enough
> To write, and not to print, such sapless stuff;
> Just hinting in your kindest, gentlest, way,
> How much you deem I've led myself astray;
> That if the woes of 'Delphine' must be sung,
> Why should I venture on a foreign tongue?
> …
> Well then, dear sister, let me, *entre nous*,
> In two words say the object I'd in view:
> 'Twas about this trash, so quizzed my wife and daughter,
> That I thought I'd make you partner in our laughter.
> Remember, too, if it will spare vexation,
> Printing, darling, is not publication.[26]

As further justification, Curr suggested to his sister that mirth should not be the exclusive domain of youth ('is't not well sometimes to play the fool?') and concluded by describing the joy his poetry writing had brought both him and his family.

> So in the ev'ning, whilst my little Mabel
> With Ela danced as well as she was able,
> And Constance played from her new music-book,
> Or the three gathering round, would sing 'Malbrouck;'
> Justin the while climbing behind my chair,
> Amusing himself shouting in my ear;
> I'd at my table laughing pass my time,
> In ill-known tongue scribbling the puerile rhyme.[27]

---

24   McLaren 1972: 121–122.
25   Curr 1868: 5. Roughly translated, Curr's disclaimer explains: 'Read if you wish, but I say in advance; I passed only eighteen months in France'.
26   Curr 1868: 7.
27   Curr 1868: 9.

Des Bêtises = Frivolities is hardly a major contribution to either French or English verse; it is illustrative, however, of Curr's flair for language and love of poetry. Later, when writing his most famous work, he regularly employed phrases in foreign languages to enliven his text. Moreover, as we shall see below, he frequently quoted great English poets, including Shakespeare and Byron. *Des Bêtises* provides, therefore, a useful insight into the literary tastes of the author of *Recollections of Squatting in Victoria*.

Curr's four major written works of the 1860s exhibit all the essential characteristics that came to fruition in his 1883 masterpiece. In *Pure Saddle Horses* he displayed his detailed understanding of the life and requirements of the Australian squatter; he also proved his ability to write a full-length book. His *Essay on Scab in Sheep* showed a determination to write with flair, even on technical matters. In both of these works he also revealed his capacity to tackle controversial subjects with confidence and authority. 'Experiences of Horses Afloat' displays Curr's considerable talent for descriptive writing; it is also a prime example of his skill at story telling and his ability to use irony and humour when recounting his own experiences. Finally, *Des Bêtises* reveals Curr's aptitude for foreign languages and his broader interest in literature. Curr was able to combine all of these elements when he wrote *Recollections of Squatting in Victoria*. It might fairly be argued, therefore, that his best-known work was published as much for its literary accomplishment as it was for its value as an historical record of the 1840s.

Curr's Literary Inspiration

Recollections of Squatting in Victoria is greatly enhanced by its regular allusions to English literature. Such allusions were, of course, common in the literary culture of the period, but Curr's particular enthusiasm for this approach played a key role in his literary success. His memoir is also notable for its frequent use of words and phrases in French. Taking his description of early Melbourne as an example, we read that during his first visit in 1839 he stayed at the cottage of a friend, 'who resided *en garçon* on the Yarra ... his family not having yet arrived to join him'. A few pages later Curr explains the apparent folly of auctioning town allotments without the provision of champagne and lavish refreshments – 'the *mise en scène* would have been critically wrong'. Describing the arrival of a new servant woman at Wolfscrag, Curr relates that she 'seized at once on my not very extensive *batterie de cuisine*, and transported it in a trice to the kitchen'. Subsequently, when recalling the spearing of 70 sheep by Aborigines on the

Murray River, Curr describes the resultant feast as a 'rather costly *déjeuner à la fourchette*, in which my father had compulsorily played the part of absentee host'.[28]

Curr's linguistic experimentation extended to other foreign languages. From Portuguese, a language his father spoke fluently, Curr borrows *entre rios* to describe the principal portion of his squatting run between the Murray and Goulburn Rivers.[29] Curr's text also features regular phrases from classical languages: when recalling the enthusiasm of the early Melbourne residents for separation from New South Wales, he suggests that Sydney officials 'must have groaned from every pigeon-hole (*ab immo pectore*)'; later, he conveys the remoteness of Tongala by dubbing it 'a sort of *ultima thule*'.[30] The regular use of foreign language phrases heightens the sense of literary accomplishment in Curr's work and increases its appeal to the educated audience for which Curr was primarily writing.

Recollections of Squatting in Victoria is littered with literary references, some more identifiable than others. Not surprisingly, Shakespeare features regularly; for example, Curr borrows a phrase from *Henry IV, Part 2*, when marvelling at the ability of the Wongatpan tribe to sleep in their canoes among mosquito-infested reeds. Such a course was employed as a defence against hostile tribes, but it troubled Curr nonetheless:

> it would be hard to imagine anything more miserable than a family passing a night in a damp canoe in the foetid atmosphere of a reed-bed – not, as the poet says,
>
> 'Hushed with buzzing night-flies to their slumbers,'
>
> but stung to madness by villainous mosquitoes, which generally abounded in the locality.[31]

Various other poets were worthy of inclusion in Curr's work. In Chapter 11, 'A Ride to Muddy Creek', Curr recounts the amusing story of a well-mannered Scottish inn-owner, who was tersely ordered by his senior partner to eject a drunken and penniless patron: 'On this mild reproof, Mr. Nichol Forbes, like one of Ossian's heroes, "On his hill of storm arose in wrath."'[32] Curr alludes to the works of controversial Scottish poet James Macpherson (1736–96), who

---

28 Curr 1883: 3, 11, 61, 195. *En garçon* – as a boy (bachelor); *mise en scène* – setting of the scene; *batterie de cuisine* – kitchen utensils; *déjeuner à la fourchette* – lunch on the fork.
29 Curr 1883: 217.
30 Curr 1883: 4, 127. *Ab immo pectore* – from the bottom of my heart; *ultima thule* – in medieval geography, a distant place located beyond the borders of the known world.
31 Curr 1883: 242. Curr adapts a phrase from Shakespeare's *Henry IV, Part 2* (Act 3 Scene 1), which appears in the original as 'hushed with buzzing night-flies to thy slumber'.
32 Curr 1883: 111.

apparently produced English 'translations' of ancient Scottish-Gaelic epic poems narrated by 'Ossian'.[33] Another Scottish poet, Thomas Campbell (1777–1844), provided inspiration for Curr's description of 'The Deserted Camp' of the Wongatpan, where he found only a mangy dingo that broke into 'the dreary howl common to his kind':

> Again and again beginning at his lowest and ascending to his highest note, Pokka gave out his melancholy cry, reminding me of Campbell's melodious line–
>
> 'The wolf's long howl from Oonalaska's shore.'
>
> I did not wait for him to finish his solo. A shot from my gun rolled him over in the midst of his melody … terminating at once misery and mange, as well as some danger to my flocks.[34]

Curr was very familiar with the English poets. In Chapter 15 of *Recollections of Squatting in Victoria* he describes a moonlit night in 1842, when his brother Charles surmised he saw a ghost:

> In the bright starlight nothing unusual met my eyes. The lamp in the shepherd's hut I could see was out, and my kangaroo dogs were not there, but everything seemed quiet. Above the lamp of heaven was
>
> 'Riding near the highest noon,'
>
> and around everything was as cold and crisp as might be, so I paced backwards and forwards for a while, thinking of my brother, and perhaps, as I looked up to the sky, recalling Shelley's verses—
>
> 'Tell me, Moon, thou pale and gray
> Pilgrim of Heaven's homeless way,
> In what depth of night or day
> Seekest thou repose now?'
>
> After a few moments passed in this way, I returned to the hut and resumed my seat at the fire.[35]

In recalling the night, Curr borrows from three famous English poets in quick succession. First, he employs the metaphor of the 'lamp of heaven', which appears in Byron's early collection of verse, *Hours of Idleness* (1807).[36] 'Riding

---

33 Dafydd Moore, 'Ossian', *The Literary Encyclopedia*, 6 October 2004 (The Literary Dictionary Company), <http://www.litencyc.com/php/stopics.php?rec=true&UID=1287> (Accessed 15 March 2008).
34 Curr 1883: 150. Curr's quote is from Campbell's 'The Pleasures of Hope' (1799).
35 Curr 1883: 158.
36 'How sweetly shines, through azure skies, The lamp of Heaven on Lora's shore'. George Gordon (Lord) Byron, 'Oscar of Alva', in *Hours of Idleness* (1807).

near the highest noon' derives from Milton's 'Il Penseroso' (1631), while the verse from Shelley is from his poem 'The World's Wanderers' (1820). The use of such rapid poetic allusion when describing an event long past is a clear indication of Curr's central motive: his book is primarily a collection of creatively crafted and nostalgic recollections – not a dispassionate and accurate record of historical events. Curr's suggestion that he 'perhaps' recalled Shelley's verses implies, of course, that on the moonlit night in 1842 he did nothing of the sort. Curr thinks of Shelley when he *recalls* the moonlight: his book is a memoir, not a diary – a literary product of the 1880s not a disinterested and contemporary chronicle of the 1840s.

Of all the English poets, Curr's major influence appears to have been Lord Byron, who features prominently and regularly throughout *Recollections of Squatting in Victoria*. For Curr, the allure of Byron's poetry derived, at least in part, from Byron's interest in Spanish subjects. Hence, when describing the grace and dignity of movement among the men of the Ngooraialum tribe, who were occasional visitors at Tongala, Curr refers to Byron's *Don Juan* for a useful comparison:

> Byron proposes, as typical of this sort of thing—
>
> 'The Andalusian dame from mass returning,'
>
> but though I have had, perhaps, more opportunities than his lordship of seeing and admiring the stately Andaluza, I can hardly give her the preference, in the point of erect and graceful bearing, over the Ngooraialum stalking forth from his camp wrapped in his opossum-rug.[37]

Later, when describing the hunting parties that met and caroused at 'The Punt' (Moama) in the late 1840s, Curr again quotes from *Don Juan*: 'There's nought, no doubt, so much the spirit calms; As rum and true religion'.[38] Curr's fondness for Byron is best indicated by the final passage of *Recollections of Squatting in Victoria*, where he reflects on the years he spent on the Goulburn River with his younger brothers:

> Of the little circle who used to be merry at Tongala five-and-thirty years ago – alas!
>
> 'Kaled, Lara, Ezzelin are gone,'

---

37 Curr 1883: 134. Curr quotes Byron's *Don Juan*, Canto XII, LXXV: 'She cannot step as does an Arab barb, Or Andalusian girl from mass returning'.
38 Byron, *Don Juan*, Canto II, XXXIV. See Curr 1883: 385.

and the two who remain are old; and the writer, in lieu of the stirring pleasures of youth, has learnt to content himself with a book and an easy chair.[39]

Curr's nostalgic conclusion is typical of the overall tone of his book; he employed Byron's verse to convey the sense of loss and regret he felt when he recalled his youth. The quote is from Byron's *Lara*, an epic tale of a haunted and doomed hero written in 1814. When read in context, Byron's verse hints at Curr's broader implication: 'And Kaled — Lara — Ezzelin, are gone, Alike without their monumental stone!'[40] The lack of recognition for Byron's fallen heroes suggests a parallel with the diminishing significance of the Curr family, as its achievements in the 1840s faded from memory. On the penultimate page of *Recollections of Squatting in Victoria*, Curr had related his story of the 'tall, burly, good-tempered looking Scotchman', who in 1854 had inveighed against the 'new chums' who swarmed to Melbourne during the gold rush, lamenting their ignorance of the Port Phillip pioneers: 'I'll give this gentleman [Curr] a week to find a man who ever heard of his father, or of separation either'.[41] By closing the book with a quote from Byron's *Lara*, Curr implied (at least to those familiar with the poem) that he regretted the poor recognition accorded the pioneering squatters; particularly those, like the Currs, who had largely passed from general knowledge: 'Alike without their monumental stone!'

'A most entertaining volume'

George Robertson published *Recollections of Squatting in Victoria* in June 1883. Very little is known regarding the circumstances of its production: it was likely the result of several years of leisurely work, penned in stolen moments at Curr's city office or at home in Prahran or St Kilda. No correspondence survives to establish how or when Curr wrote it, or if the text underwent substantial redrafting prior to publication. Curr most likely wrote the book for his own enjoyment, as he had earlier shown an enthusiasm for writing and a fondness for entertaining reminiscences. It was probably not a highly profitable hobby, although Curr wrote to his son in December 1883 that he hoped to receive 'a few pounds ... from the sale of my book'.[42] Nevertheless, it was a significant achievement for Curr to have the book accepted by Robertson, one of the most successful publishers of the period, whose prominent authors included Marcus Clarke and Rolf Boldrewood.[43]

39 Curr 1883: 452.
40 Byron, *Lara*, Canto II, XXV.
41 Curr 1883: 451.
42 Edward M. Curr to E.M.V. Curr, 19 December 1883, Murrumbogie Papers.
43 Holroyd 1976: 37–38.

Figure 16: Edward M. Curr.

Painting. Edward M. Curr, 1965, *Recollections of Squatting in Victoria*, edited by Harley W. Forster. Abridged (Carlton, Vic.: Melbourne University Press).

During Curr's own lifetime, *Recollections of Squatting in Victoria* received favourable reviews. The *Argus* described it as 'a most entertaining volume' and noted that 'his narrative gives one an excellent idea of the pastoral life of the period, with its hardships, its difficulties, and its vicissitudes'.[44] The *Brisbane Courier* exclaimed that 'one cannot lay it aside without a feeling of regret the narrative is restricted to a period of only ten years of the life experiences of such a facile writer'.[45] The *Argus* focussed on two important chapters of Curr's book,

---

44 Book Review, 'Squatting in Victoria', *Argus*, 20 June 1883: 9.
45 *Brisbane Courier*, 13 June 1883: 5.

which have certainly contributed to its enduring value: 'Changes in Connection with Flora and Fauna' and 'The Bangerang'. Since its publication *Recollections of Squatting in Victoria* has been increasingly recognised as an important early reflection on the environmental effects of European pastoralism; Curr's account of the impact of livestock on soil structure and of the role of fire in Australian ecology have been particularly valued.[46] The *Argus* reviewer anticipated this historiographical development:

> In the seventeenth chapter [Curr] skims the surface of a subject deserving of more serious and scientific treatment. We refer to the changes which have been and are being brought about in the flora and fauna of Australia, in consequence of the occupation and cultivation of its territory by Europeans.[47]

The *Argus* also presaged the enduring influence of Curr's descriptions of Aborigines, identifying *Recollections of Squatting in Victoria* as a prelude to his major ethnological work: 'One of the best chapters in the book is that which devotes to the Bangerang tribe of aborigines'.[48] The *Argus* described Curr's ethnography of the Bangerang as 'an acceptable contribution to our stock of knowledge', which presumably lent weight to the campaign to publish Curr's more serious ethnological work, *The Australian Race*.

The final conclusion of the conservative *Argus* was that the squatters deserved their fortune, principally because of the unsavoury characters they were forced to employ on their stations:

> to be compelled to associate from day to day, for years together, with 'horse stealers, machine-breakers, homicides, disorderly soldiers, drunken marines, house breakers, petty thieves, and so on,' as a good many of the squatters were, was rather a high price to pay for subsequent ... affluence.[49]

Perhaps unconsciously, the *Argus* reviewer recognised a centrally important function of Curr's *Recollections of Squatting in Victoria*: in his book Curr constructed for himself a position of social superiority over his convict shepherds and, of course, over the Indigenous people whose land he occupied.

It should be noted, however, that Curr never intended to write a dispassionate, and objective account of the 1840s; it is others who have wrongly assumed his book to be as much. The very title of Curr's work is an explicit recognition of its subjective viewpoint. Furthermore, Curr wrote in his preface that his account

---

46 Pyne 1991: 103–104, 199, 216; see also Shaw 1996: 109.
47 Book Review, 'Squatting in Victoria', *Argus*, 20 June 1883: 9.
48 Book Review, 'Squatting in Victoria', *Argus*, 20 June 1883: 9.
49 Book Review, 'Squatting in Victoria', *Argus*, 20 June 1883: 9. The reviewer is quoting Curr 1883: 443.

of Victoria's early colonial life was 'seen through the medium of individual experiences, possibly of not a very representative sort'. Nevertheless, Curr trusted that his reminiscences would be appealing to a wider readership: 'An excuse for the publication of mere personal matters will, it is hoped, be found in the contrast their relation exhibits between the past and the present state of things in Victoria'.[50] It is clear that Curr understood the value of his observations to posterity. He realised that the pace of change in Victoria all but guaranteed that a well-written memoir would find an enthusiastic audience. The steadily growing status of Curr's book in twentieth-century Australian historiography demonstrates that he was correct.

---

50   Curr 1883: v.

8. 'The native is a child'

Through his notable career as a senior public servant, Edward M. Curr recovered some of the social status he had lost following the disastrous drought at Uabba. Importantly, his career successes highlight his commitment to the settler colonial project in Australia; his working life was dedicated to ensuring the productive and profitable use of land by the pastoral industry. In the 1870s Curr also became deeply interested in the Aboriginal people whose lands had been appropriated to sustain the pastoral industry. His alternative career as an Aboriginal administrator and ethnologist sits uncomfortably alongside his principal life purpose, which was to profit from the pastoral opportunities accorded by British Imperialism in Australia. Significantly, Curr's career in Aboriginal administration has been largely overlooked until quite recently. In this context, the problematic nature of Curr's account of traditional Yorta Yorta or Bangerang custom becomes starkly apparent.

For Curr, it was his long experience of Australian bush life, and particularly his status as a pioneering squatter of the 1840s, which underlined his claim to authoritative knowledge and justified his emergence as an expert on 'the Blacks'. In 1881 he asserted his credentials as an Aboriginal administrator when he told a parliamentary inquiry: 'They are an easy people to manage. I managed four times as many as there are at Coranderrk when I was nineteen years old.'[1] Furthermore, Curr regularly asserted his 'wide experience' to bolster his ethnological credibility in his major work *The Australian Race* (1886).

In 1875 Curr had joined the Colony of Victoria's Board for the Protection of the Aborigines (BPA). He was one of three new members appointed during a board shake-up probably orchestrated by the vice chairman, R. Brough Smyth, who, like Curr, was a senior public servant with an interest in ethnology.[2] Curr served on the BPA during a period of great controversy regarding the future of the Coranderrk Aboriginal station, near Healesville. Coranderrk lay within the traditional territory of the Kulin nation. The troubles at Coranderrk were sparked by the dismissal of the general inspector John Green in 1874. Green had managed Victoria's six Aboriginal reserves since the re-establishment of the protectorate system in 1861 and had taken a particular interest in Coranderrk. He was a sympathetic manager, as he explained to the board in 1863: 'My method

---

1   Victoria. Coranderrk Aboriginal Station. 'Report of the Board appointed to enquire into, and report upon, the present condition and management of the Coranderrk Aboriginal Station, together with the minutes of evidence', in Parliament of Victoria, *Papers Presented to Parliament by Command*, Session 1882–3, Vol 3 [henceforth Coranderrk Inquiry (1881)], 120. Curr gave evidence to the Inquiry on 8 December 1881.
2   Barwick 1998: 111.

of managing the blacks is to allow them to rule themselves as much as possible.'[3] He also rejected the view that Aborigines were 'incapable of instruction' and argued that 'blacks' and 'half-castes' were equally quick to learn.[4] Green had the support of the board until 1872 and his work at Coranderrk was widely praised.

Figure 17: The Aboriginal Settlement at Coranderrk (1865). Charles Walter.

Engraving. State Library of Victoria, H4082.

In the 1870s the economic potential of the Coranderrk land began to influence the decision making of the BPA. Initially the board resolved to make Coranderrk profitable by growing hops under the direction of agriculturalist Frederick Search. In 1874, however, changes in legislation dictated that any profit from the farm at Coranderrk should be returned to the government's consolidated revenue; the under-funded BPA thus lost a financial incentive to persevere with Coranderrk. Meanwhile, Aboriginal residents protested against the hiring of European labour on the hops farm. John Green increasingly supported the Coranderrk residents and soon found himself at odds with Frederick Search. Consequently, the board dismissed Green in 1874, prompting the Coranderrk residents to submit a petition in protest.

---

3   John Green to Central Board Appointed to Watch over the Interests of the Aborigines, 28 July 1863, quoted in Barwick 1998: 67.
4   Barwick 1998: 79.

8. 'The Native is a Child'

MR. JOHN GREEN—[FROM A PHOTOGRAPH BY CHARLES WALTER].

Figure 18: Mr John Green (1865). Charles Walter.

Engraving. State Library of Victoria, IAN25/08/65/13.

R. Brough Smyth, vice chairman of the BPA, was a key figure in the campaign against John Green. Other members of the board, who had known of Green's work for more than a decade, were concerned he had been mistreated. In 1875 Smyth consolidated his power by the appointment of three new members sympathetic to his views on Coranderrk; they were Edward M. Curr, Albert Le Souëf and Frederick Godfrey. Le Souëf had an early connection with Aboriginal administration (his father had managed the Goulburn River protectorate station in the early 1840s) and had spent many years on pastoral stations in northeast Victoria. He was later associated with the development of the Melbourne

Zoological Gardens, where he was secretary and then director from 1870 to 1902.[5] Like Curr, Le Souëf displayed a nostalgic interest in Aboriginal culture; for the Melbourne Intercolonial Exhibition of 1866 he and his wife Caroline had produced 'The Le Souëf Box', a collection of miniaturised Aboriginal weapons contained in a wooden box, which was decorated with idyllic pre-contact scenes in the life of the Taungurong people.[6] Godfrey was a squatter, businessman and member of the Legislative Assembly; he apparently used his parliamentary connections to solicit membership for himself, Curr and Le Souëf. The three men had strong personal connections dating back to their time as pastoralists in the 1840s. Le Souëf and Godfrey were also closely linked through the Zoological and Acclimatisation Society. Victoria's chief secretary was the *ex officio* chairman of the BPA but rarely (if ever) attended meetings; so leadership of the board essentially resided with the vice chairman, and Godfrey, Curr and Le Souëf all occupied this position over subsequent years.

Figure 19: Albert Le Souëf (1872). Thomas Foster Chuck.

Photograph. State Library of Victoria, H5056/567.

---

5   McEvey 1975: 80–81.
6   Edmonds 2006: 117–139.

At Curr's first BPA meeting on 7 July 1875 an unprecedented deputation of Kulin men arrived to register their protests regarding the situation at Coranderrk. These Indigenous men were soon encouraged, however, to ignore the largely intransigent board, preferring to lobby parliamentarians, journalists and other sympathetic Victorians. Poor attendance at BPA meetings in this period essentially enabled Smyth and his three new colleagues to determine board policy. On 4 August 1875 Curr, Godfrey and Le Souëf formed a subcommittee to examine the future management of Coranderrk and visited it three days later.[7] Curr later described his first visit to the troubled station:

> We all thought the place exceedingly undesirable; that it was impossible to do any good there. We reported that to the Board, and recommended that the station should be removed. We did this on the very first visit. We were all accustomed to blacks; we had no doubt about what we recommended. I knew nothing about the antecedents of the place or even the name of the manager.[8]

Curr believed that because he was 'accustomed to blacks' he was qualified to judge the situation at Coranderrk after only one visit and from a position of ignorance regarding its history. He and the other board newcomers stressed health concerns as a key motivation for their decision, but they were certainly also concerned about the potential for political agitation, as Coranderrk was only 67 kilometres from Melbourne.

Curr, in particular, believed that the problems at Coranderrk were essentially a matter of discipline, which was undermined by contact between the Indigenous residents and white sympathisers. His concerns about 'outside interference' were highlighted by the actions of Moravian missionary Brother Johann Stähle, who had been appointed acting manager of Coranderrk after John Green's suspension. Like his predecessor, Stähle showed considerable sympathy towards the Coranderrk residents. On the very day Curr and his companions visited Coranderrk, Victoria's newly elected premier and chief secretary, Graham Berry, received a letter from Stähle, who, on behalf of the Coranderrk residents, requested the dismissal of the hops farm master Robert Burgess. Stähle sent the letter by registered mail to the chief secretary because earlier complaints sent to Smyth had been ignored. Smyth and Curr were both furious that a subordinate public servant had bypassed the authority of the board, while Godfrey was embarrassed at having to provide an explanation to Berry, his political adversary.[9]

---

7 Central Board for the Protection of the Aborigines [BPA], 'Minutes of meetings', National Archives of Australia [NAA], Series B314, 4 August 1875.
8 Coranderrk Inquiry (1881), 120.
9 Barwick 1998: 113.

On 25 August 1875 the BPA voted to abandon the Coranderrk station. The board hoped to convince the chief secretary that proceeds from the sale of the Coranderrk land would be more than adequate to meet the cost of setting up a new station. At the same meeting the BPA resolved to employ for two months a pastoral station manager, Christian Ogilvie, who was instructed to inspect all six Aboriginal stations in company with Curr.[10] Only three weeks later, Curr successfully proposed a motion to dismiss Stähle and permanently appoint Ogilvie.[11] Momentum for change continued and on 21 September 1875 the board voted to send Ogilvie and Curr to search for a new remote location for Coranderrk on the Murray River.[12] The two men subsequently became key proponents in the campaign to close down Coranderrk. Curr later described Ogilvie as 'one of the few friends I had'.[13] Moreover, Ogilvie was a very close friend of Le Souëf; the pair had managed pastoral stations together in the early 1850s and Ogilvie had served as best man at Le Souëf's wedding.[14]

In December Curr successfully proposed that Christian Ogilvie be appointed general superintendent of Victoria's six Aboriginal stations. Curr's motion, which was seconded by Le Souëf, gave considerable power to Ogilvie, even over those stations run by missionaries.[15] In January 1876 the board also received Curr and Ogilvie's report, which recommended closing Coranderrk and moving its Indigenous residents to a new station at Kulkyne, which was situated hundreds of miles away on the Murray River.[16] Curr was quite honest about the advantages of the proposed location, which he later described as 'a strip of country which is never likely to be thickly settled, which has good climate, plenty of fish, and is removed from disturbing causes'.[17] Yet Curr and Ogilvie's plans were stalled by a parallel controversy that embroiled R. Brough Smyth. In 1876 a parliamentary inquiry upheld complaints against Smyth of 'tyrannical and overbearing conduct' towards his subordinates in the Mines Department; he resigned from all his public offices in May.[18] The BPA had been transformed by the appointment of Curr, Le Souëf and Godfrey in 1875, so the closure of Coranderrk remained official policy even after the resignation of Smyth. Nevertheless, the sensational case of 'the half-mad Bureaucrat' drew attention to the situation at Coranderrk.

---

10 BPA, 'Minutes of meetings', NAA, Series B314, 25 August 1875.
11 BPA, 'Minutes of meetings', NAA, Series B314, 14 September 1875.
12 BPA, 'Minutes of meetings', NAA, Series B314, 21 September 1875.
13 Edward M. Curr to E.M.V. Curr, 19 December 1883, Murrumbogie Papers.
14 A.A.C. Le Souëf, 'Personal Recollections of Early Victoria' (c.1895), Typescript, South Australian Museum, 40, 42, 75.
15 BPA, 'Minutes of meetings', NAA, Series B314, 14 December 1875.
16 BPA, 'Minutes of meetings', NAA, Series B314, 12 January 1876.
17 Coranderrk Inquiry (1881), 120, emphasis added.
18 Hoare 1976: 161–163.

In the midst of the inquiry into Smyth's conduct, pro-Coranderrk articles appeared in the *Age* and *Leader* newspapers, one of which was titled 'Coranderrk Hop Farm: Mr Green and Mr R. Brough Smyth'.[19] They were written by agricultural editor John Lamont Dow, a radical liberal with ambitions to enter the Victorian Parliament.[20] Dow praised the efforts of Green and the residents of Coranderrk and criticised the board's expenditure on European labour for the hops farm. The flames of controversy were fanned by the concurrent frenzy surrounding Smyth; Dow's articles connected the two controversies in the public imagination. David Syme was the proprietor of both newspapers and his brother George edited the *Leader*. Crucially, George Syme had recently resigned his membership of the BPA in protest against Green's dismissal and the plans to close Coranderrk. Both the *Age* and the *Leader* newspapers, whose readership far exceeded that of the conservative *Argus*, lent considerable support to the Coranderrk cause over subsequent years.[21]

Meanwhile, attendance at BPA meetings improved as long-serving members became concerned about the situation at Coranderrk. The free rein enjoyed by Curr, Le Souëf and Godfrey was tightened and the board became more cautious. In January 1876 a former board vice chairman and parliamentarian, James MacBain, attempted to limit the substantial powers recently granted to Christian Ogilvie. Although MacBain's motion was unsuccessful, it represented a clear challenge to the authority of Curr, who had championed Ogilvie's rapid elevation. On 17 February 1876 the board reached a compromise and resolved to reappoint John Green to a subordinate role under Christian Ogilvie, but Green declined the offer.[22] Curr was the sole member of the board who opposed the reappointment of Green on any terms; he was surely motivated by Green's opposition to the planned closure of Coranderrk. The board met again the next day and three long serving members (led by MacBain) proposed an unconditional offer of re-employment to Green; they were voted down by Curr, Le Souëf, Godfrey and new member Sherbourne Sheppard, a former squatter and old acquaintance of both Curr and Le Souëf. Sheppard had owned the Tallygaroopna run, located on the Goulburn River not far from Curr's Tongala, and had invited his friend Le Souëf into partnership there in the 1850s.[23] Several months later MacBain complained in parliament about the influence of Curr and his companions: 'they formed a little family as it were' and appointed a new inspector (Oglivie) 'for doing what he did not know'.[24]

---

19 John Lamont Dow, 'Coranderrk Hop Farm: Mr Green and Mr R. Brough Smyth', *Age*, 19 February 1876. See also Barwick 1998: 125.
20 Dow 1972: 93–95.
21 Barwick 1998: 114.
22 BPA, 'Minutes of meetings', NAA, Series B314, 12 January 1876, 16–17 February 1876.
23 A.A.C. Le Souëf, 'Personal Recollections of Early Victoria' (c.1895), Typescript, South Australian Museum, 86.
24 Victoria, *Parliamentary Debates*, Session 1876, Volume 25, 984.

The Coranderrk issue had emerged as a key point of divergence in BPA policy, but the division at board level was only one obstacle that stood in the way of Curr's plans. In Victoria the late 1870s was a politically tumultuous period, when the radical liberal politician Graham Berry vied for power with his conservative opponents. Coranderrk became one of many issues that characterised the political landscape. John Lamont Dow, a protégé of Berry, took up the Coranderrk cause in the pages of the *Age*; the Aboriginal residents also received considerable support from the philanthropist Ann Bon. The BPA spread counter-propaganda through the *Argus*, but even this newspaper was not uncritical of the board's management of Coranderrk.[25]

The Coranderrk Rebellion

For almost the entire period of Curr's membership of the BPA (1875–1883), the future of the Coranderrk station dominated public debate over Aboriginal policy. Diane Barwick's *Rebellion at Coranderrk* traces in detail the many attempts of the BPA to undermine the increasingly politically mobilised residents of Coranderrk. Barwick justifies her title by referring to the contemporary record: 'Dismayed officials frequently used the term rebellion to describe Aboriginal tactics in openly resisting and defying lawful authority.'[26] The rebellion was directed chiefly at members of the BPA, specifically those like Curr who were stubbornly committed to the closure of Coranderrk. The Indigenous people of Coranderrk played a shrewd political game, using petitions, letters and deputations to government ministers to win support for their cause. In particular, younger Aborigines educated at protectorate and mission schools used the literacy skills they had acquired to advocate for their people. Both Robert Wandin and Thomas Dunolly were authorised to speak on behalf of their leader William Barak and exerted considerable influence through their command of written language.

Michael Christie has noted the irony that a protectorate education was designed to further the assimilation of Aboriginal people, not empower them politically.[27] The BPA had previously carried out its duties with very little scrutiny, but the politically mobilised Coranderrk residents ensured this would no longer be the case. Nevertheless, the increased public criticism of the BPA only seemed to strengthen its determination to close Coranderrk. Barwick has shown clearly that through 'ignorance and profound paternalism' the newer board members (Curr, Godfrey and Le Souëf) dismissed the idea that the Kulin had adapted their traditional culture to accommodate 'a new kind of political expertise'.[28]

---

25 Barwick 1998: 115, 178.
26 Barwick 1998: 1.
27 Christie 1990: 118.
28 Barwick 1998: 114–115.

The board was so convinced that various letters and petitions were the result of outside interference that it twice hired detectives to analyse the handwriting on petitions from Coranderrk.[29] The detectives found that Barak's spokesman Thomas Dunolly had written the relevant documents, which represented the genuinely held views of the Aboriginal signatories.

Figure 20: William Barak (1876).

Photograph. National Archives of Australia, A1200, L22062.

---

29   Van Toorn 1999: 335; see also Van Toorn 2006: 123–151.

The BPA was unable to contain the Coranderrk Rebellion. In 1877 the former board member and *Leader* editor George Syme encouraged Graham Berry (now on the opposition benches) to push for a Royal Commission on the Aborigines, which commenced its hearings in April.[30] Curr was the only board member to give evidence, although Godfrey was one of the commissioners. As a principal architect of the plan to close Coranderrk, Curr's credibility was significantly challenged during the hearings. When he gave evidence on 1 June 1877, he argued that removal was necessary for reasons of both health and discipline. He explained that the climate at Coranderrk was unsuitable and stressed that even the original owners of the area had only visited it in summer. Curr argued that Coranderrk was not the traditional country of its residents and therefore removal to the Murray River was perfectly justifiable. He had little sympathy for the views of William Barak, who had said in 1876: 'The Yarra ... is my father's country. There's no mountains for me on the Murray.'[31]

Curr's concern about the health of Coranderrk residents was genuine, but he was clearly also motivated by his belief that 'outside interference' was undermining the discipline of a 'childlike' race. He told the commissioners:

> Members of the Board, casual visitors, cricketers, and Members of Parliament have probably little idea of how their visits interfere with discipline. The native is a child, and very little unsettles him and even makes him fractious, and probably the height of pleasure to him would be to get a Member of Parliament to listen to his grievances. To him no doubt the casual suggestion of an alteration even seems like a condemnation of his ordinary superior, and is no doubt very pleasant to him. Hence this influx of visitors to Coranderrk does not seem desirable.[32]

When Curr was later asked by the commissioners to make any final suggestions in writing, he committed himself once more to the closure of Coranderrk: 'With the proceeds of the sale of Coranderrk a fitting station might be set on foot, stocked, and possibly made self-supporting.'[33] The commissioners asked if Aborigines should be forced to reside at the proposed new reserve against their wishes, to which Curr responded: 'the black should, when necessary, be coerced just as we coerce children and lunatics who cannot take care of themselves. If they are not coerced, they cannot be preserved from extinction.'[34]

---

30 Barwick 1998: 114.
31 *Leader*, 19 February 1876; quoted in Christie 1990: 118.
32 Victoria. Royal Commission on the Aborigines (1877). 'Report of the Commissioners ... together with Minutes of Evidence', in Parliament of Victoria, *Papers Presented to Parliament by Command*, Session 1877–78, Vol 3, 77.
33 Royal Commission on the Aborigines (1877), 79.
34 Royal Commission on the Aborigines (1877), 78.

Although the Royal Commission did not recommend the closure of Coranderrk, the BPA's commitment to that course remained firm. In the wake of the inquiry, Curr's colleagues elected him vice chairman of the board, so his determination to close Coranderrk continued to shape board policy. By July 1878, however, the board had become concerned by Curr's intransigence on the issue and elected Henry Jennings as the new vice chairman. Meanwhile, Graham Berry had taken power in Victoria once again after winning the 1877 election. Berry owed much to his protégé John Lamont Dow, who had galvanised support for Berry's reform agenda and had won a seat of his own in the new parliament. In 1878 Dow submitted a report to Berry on the Coranderrk issue, which recommended John Green be reappointed and the BPA disbanded. Berry cautiously stayed his hand, but it was clear at least that the closure of Coranderrk was not on the new government's agenda.[35]

By the end of the decade the influence of the trio of BPA members who had reshaped policy in 1875 was waning. Godfrey resigned in March 1879 before travelling overseas. Meanwhile, Curr and Le Souëf began to disagree on significant issues, notably the treatment of 'half-castes' residing on the government reserves. The Royal Commission had not recommended sending 'half-castes' out to work, but Le Souëf proposed as much in December 1878. Curr was strongly opposed to such views and became isolated as assimilationist ideology took hold. Curr once again pushed for the abandonment of Coranderrk in May 1879 and was partially supported by Le Souëf, but he was fighting a losing battle.[36]

The political situation remained volatile, particularly after Graham Berry narrowly lost the March 1880 election. Berry returned to power a few months later at the head of a shaky coalition, but his policy regarding Coranderrk was far from certain. There were ongoing protests from Coranderrk residents in 1880, mostly against the manager Rev. Frederick Strickland. During this period Curr was acting vice chairman of the BPA and he was unsympathetic to the protests. In October Strickland reported that 'not a man on the station' would do anything when ordered.[37]

---

35   Barwick 1998: 162–163.
36   Barwick 1998: 167.
37   Barwick 1998: 174.

Figure 21: General view of Aboriginal Mission Station, Coranderrk (1880). Fred Kruger.

Photograph. State Library of Victoria, H2006.123/9.

In March 1881 Coranderrk leader William Barak once again walked the 67 kilometres to Melbourne and led a deputation to the premier. He requested the BPA be abolished and that his people be allowed to manage Coranderrk themselves under John Green's guidance. The philanthropist Ann Bon, who had been lobbying on behalf of the Coranderrk residents, joined Barak for his meeting with Berry. Le Souëf subsequently told members of the BPA that Bon's role would convince Berry that the abandonment of Coranderrk was unavoidable because of 'continual interference'.[38] In fact, Berry assured Barak that he would not be removed from Coranderrk and promised a parliamentary inquiry.

Political instability continued when Bryan O'Loghlen deposed Graham Berry in July 1881. The BPA once again lobbied for the closure of Coranderrk; meanwhile, John Lamont Dow called for board reform through the pages of the *Age*.[39] The new chief secretary, J.M. Grant, honoured Berry's promise of a parliamentary inquiry, to which he appointed the local member for Healesville E.H. Cameron as chairman. Despite attempts by the BPA to influence the membership of the inquiry, Grant also adopted the recommendations Berry had received on this issue from a young Alfred Deakin. Crucially, Deakin had suggested the

---

38 BPA, 'Minutes of meetings', NAA, Series B314, 6 April 1881; see also Barwick 1998: 178–179.
39 *Age*, 14 July 1881; see Barwick 1998: 183.

appointment of Ann Bon and former BPA member Dr Thomas Embling.[40] Grant also appointed two local landholders recommended by the BPA, but this did not satisfy board members, who protested against the Deakin-inspired appointments in September.[41] Grant then added two further members to the inquiry after it began collecting evidence; one was a BPA recommendation but the other was John Lamont Dow, whose presence tipped the balance of opinion against the BPA.

The transcript of Curr's evidence to the 1881 Parliamentary Inquiry into Coranderrk displays quite clearly his views regarding the management of Aboriginal people. It also reveals the pressure he was under to justify both his and the board's policies. On 8 December Curr was asked if he thought it desirable to relocate the Coranderrk residents against their will:

> Anyone who knows the blacks knows their will is nothing, that they might have a serious objection now which they would not remember three months afterwards. I would suggest that they should be moved for their own benefit ... If I saw my child playing on the brink of a well I should remove the child even if he cried. I should remove the blacks from Coranderrk whether they liked it or not. I do not believe they have any strong objection.[42]

Curr's evidence provides a valuable insight into his thinking regarding Aboriginal people at precisely the time he was writing his two major written works, which have so influenced historians and native title judges alike. The common twentieth century view that Curr was atypically sympathetic towards Aboriginal people must be carefully qualified by reference to this evidence, which shows that his sympathy was of a repressively paternalistic kind. A further passage from his evidence to the 1881 inquiry displays the internal contradictions of his paternalistic attitude:

> 4833. Has not the Board persistently for years endeavoured to get the people removed from Coranderrk? – Certainly not.
>
> 4834. Are you sure that yourself and Mr. Jennings and others have not written letters recommending their removal? – We did, but that is not the question you asked.
>
> 4835. Did you ever consult the blacks about the question? – No.
>
> 4836. Do you think that is fair? – Most decidedly for their good.

---

40 Barwick 1998: 183–184.
41 BPA, 'Minutes of meetings', NAA, Series B314, 7 September 1881.
42 Coranderrk Inquiry (1881), 120.

> 4837. Are they children? — They are.
>
> 4838. Are they not men? — No, they are children. They have no more self-reliance than children.
>
> 4839. If they offend against the law are they punished like children? — No, like men.
>
> 4840. Is that just? — I did not make the laws.
>
> 4841. Should they be judged in our courts of justice as men, and punished as men, if you say they are children? — They are children in some respects; but when they steal they know they are doing wrong.[43]

Curr maintained his view that the problems at Coranderrk were due to outside interference and he singled out John Green: 'It has been the impression of the Board that Mr. Green has kept Coranderrk in a state of hot water for the last seven years.'[44]

The nine-member inquiry divided into two factions and was unable to agree on all issues when presenting the final report to parliament. Nevertheless, the members unanimously concluded that Coranderrk should not be closed. They also agreed that the station was 'not so well managed as could be desired'.[45] The key difference of opinion between the two factions related to the role the BPA had played in the Coranderrk controversy. A majority of five members (including Bon, Embling and Dow) signed 'Addendum A', which contained the following damning indictment of the board:

> The natives appear to have been chiefly stirred into a state of active discontent by the pertinacity of the Central Board in pressing upon successive Governments the gratuitous advice that the Blacks should be removed from Coranderrk. The natives also bitterly complained of the removal of Mr. Green, who appears to have won their confidence and respect. On these points the evidence is very full.[46]

The signatories of Addendum A also noted that charges of 'immorality and untruthfulness' against the natives had not been proven and suggested that the Board 'should be relieved of the management of Coranderrk'. The other four inquiry members, including the chairman E.H. Cameron, issued their own 'Addendum B', which argued that the problems at Coranderrk 'cannot be so easily laid to the charge of the Central Board'. They drew attention to the board's

---

43 Coranderrk Inquiry (1881), 121.
44 Coranderrk Inquiry (1881), 120.
45 Coranderrk Inquiry (1881), iii–iv.
46 Coranderrk Inquiry (1881), vi.

apparently successful management of the five other Victorian Aboriginal stations and gave some credence to the board's suggestion of outside interference by noting the access of Coranderrk residents to 'credulous sympathizers'.[47]

The O'Loghlen Government did not formally respond to the Coranderrk Inquiry; it did, however, appoint four new members to the BPA in June 1882. One of these was Alfred Deakin, although he resigned soon afterwards in protest against the government's inadequate response.[48] For Curr, the findings of the inquiry represented a major repudiation of the policies he had championed as a member of the BPA. He was associated more than any other board member with the campaign to close down the Coranderrk reserve; he was also firmly committed to a paternalistic policy of strict discipline and rejected the emerging assimilationist doctrine of the period.

Protection or Assimilation?

Curr's membership of the BPA corresponded with a period of significant change in Aboriginal policy, as earlier policies of containment on reserves gave way to a commitment to gradual absorption into the white community. This shift culminated in the *Aborigines Protection Act* of 1886, which drew an official distinction between 'full-bloods' and 'half-castes'. It was largely framed in response to the Coranderrk Rebellion and it had the direct effect of undermining Indigenous protest, as 'half-caste' residents (many of them centrally involved in political activism) were forced to leave the reserve. Penny Van Toorn, who has written extensively on the role of literacy in the Coranderrk rebellion, suggests that the 1886 Act separated the 'speaking generation from the writing generation, thus cutting a vital line of communication between Aboriginal communities and white government authorities'.[49]

Edward M. Curr was, however, opposed to this new approach. In fact, he was the only significant voice on the BPA to resist a distinction between 'full-blood' and 'half-caste'.[50] He believed that all Aborigines at Coranderrk should be removed to a remote station on the Murray River and he gave little credence to ideas of assimilation or absorption. Curr's policy was, of course, no less disruptive to Indigenous culture; he placed little value on Kulin attachment to country, nor the desire of William Barak and others to remain at Coranderrk. In a period

---

47 Coranderrk Inquiry (1881), vii.
48 Barwick 1998: 248.
49 Van Toorn 1999: 341.
50 For a similar argument, see Stephens 2003: 237, 243.

when Aboriginal policy was in a state of flux, he remained committed to the *status quo* – a repressively paternalistic approach of incarceration, which was grounded in an explicit ideology of racial superiority.

Unlike the more liberal-minded politicians and activists of the 1880s, Curr believed that Aboriginal decline was inevitable and absorption or assimilation was not a realistic possibility. He subscribed to the popular theory that Australian Aborigines were a dying race. In explaining as much to the 1877 Royal Commission he demonstrated an uncomfortable irony surrounding the Chief Inspector of Stock being involved in Aboriginal administration:

> That they must die out is, I think, a foregone conclusion. Were they as valuable commercially as short-horned cattle, or merino sheep, there would be no fear of their dying out. The fact is we have pretended but never really wished to save them from extermination.[51]

Importantly, Curr's belief that Aborigines would die out was grounded in his frankly expressed view that Aborigines were inferior to the white invaders:

> The Anglo-Saxon in Australia, as elsewhere, does not foster weakly races. He wants their lands. He is thinking of riches. He tramples them under feet without thinking what he does.[52]

In this way, Curr clearly belongs to an earlier era of Aboriginal policy, which focussed on incarceration rather than assimilation. Although he certainly hoped to slow the gradual process of extinction, he was relatively untroubled by the imminent demise of the Aborigines, which he saw as inevitable. For Curr, the role of the BPA was to protect the Aborigines from eradication at the hands of a superior white race for as long as possible. In a very real sense, Curr viewed the role of the board as the preservation of an ancient and inferior race of people, in the interests of scientific inquiry if nothing else. He saw, no doubt, a similarity between the work of the BPA and the efforts of his board colleague Albert Le Souëf, who was the Director of Melbourne's Zoological Gardens.[53]

During the 1877 Royal Commission, Curr was questioned about the absorption of the Aboriginal population into the settler community. In particular, the commissioners sought his views on a proposal to board out Aboriginal children. Curr responded sceptically:

> Persons who advocate boarding out do so, I believe, with a view to that measure aiding in the absorption by the whites of this colony of

---

51 Royal Commission on the Aborigines (1877), 77.
52 Royal Commission on the Aborigines (1877), 77.
53 Marguerita Stephens argues that Le Souëf 'looked to the colony's natives with the same scientific eye that he directed towards its curious fauna'; see Stephens 2003: 203.

the remnant of our black population. This absorption to my mind is a mistake — there is no absorption in the case and I think never can be; substitute eradication for absorption, and I think you will be correct. The history of other similar races points to this conclusion. Where are the fifty thousand blacks who inhabited this country forty years ago? Have they been absorbed? Have the Red Indians in America been absorbed? You cannot make the blacks like us. A black can never become one of us; his color will not alter nor his propensities.[54]

Curr believed that removing 'half-castes' from reserves to bring about their absorption was a mistake. He was not entirely convinced that assimilation was impossible, but rather believed it would take a very long time. In explaining as much to the commissioners, he once again drew an analogy with the livestock he routinely encountered in his day-to-day work: 'To begin, we should remember that as a mob of wild cattle cannot be tamed in a single generation, so we cannot at once civilize these people.'[55] For Curr, the assimilation of the Aborigines would be a very gradual process, which would take many generations if it were to be achieved at all. He viewed the world according to a racial hierarchy, which placed his own English heritage at the pinnacle. He illustrated this view with reference to his fellow British colonists, arguing that 'neither the Irishman, the Scot, nor the Welshman has as yet developed into an Englishman, though they have gradually adopted our language'.[56] For Curr, of course, Aborigines faced a far greater challenge if they were to 'develop into an Englishman'. This ideology underpinned Curr's firm resistance to a policy of absorption.

Given Curr's evidence to the 1877 Royal Commission, it is unsurprising that he rejected the distinction between 'half-caste' and 'full-blood' when it emerged in the late 1870s. John Lamont Dow, who was so critical of Curr's plans to abandon Coranderrk, was a key advocate of such a distinction. In 1878 he suggested to his mentor Graham Berry that the troubles at Coranderrk derived partly from tensions between 'full-blood' and 'half-caste'. Barwick has argued that Dow misinterpreted the factionalism at Coranderrk when he drew this distinction.[57] Thus, it was radical liberals like Dow who influenced the emergence of a truly assimilationist policy. Dow's views were soon mirrored in official BPA policy, particularly after new members were appointed in 1882. Curr became increasingly isolated and resigned his position on the board in April 1883. Only a few months earlier his colleagues had voted to retain Coranderrk and secured funds from parliament to develop the station. In this context, it was probably clear to him that it was time to move on.

---

54 Royal Commission on the Aborigines (1877), 77.
55 Royal Commission on the Aborigines (1877), 77.
56 Royal Commission on the Aborigines (1877), 77.
57 Barwick 1998: 162–163.

In 1877 the commissioners had asked Curr if he thought patriarchal rule must remain for several generations; he responded, 'Yes, I do most decidedly.'[58] Just as he had advocated extensive powers for the Inspectors of Sheep in the 1860s, Curr urged that the BPA should have unfettered control over Aborigines: the government, he argued, 'should invest the board with almost entire authority for all time'.[59] The board would need to appoint a 'General Manager', whose essential qualities Curr described in a final written submission he made to the commissioners:

> He should, I think, be a first-class man, as very early experience convinced me that the blacks (even in their savage state) both clearly discriminated between the educated gentleman and others less fortunate, and that to the former they yielded readily an obedience and confidence (most beneficial to themselves) which the latter never succeeded in obtaining. On the proper choice of a general manager hangs, in my opinion, the fate of the remnant of our black population.[60]

When noting his 'very early experience' Curr clearly referred to his youthful years as an 'educated gentleman' who encountered 'savage' Aborigines on the Goulburn and Murray rivers. His superior and authoritative tone is also prevalent in *Recollections of Squatting in Victoria*, where he describes more fully his early experiences. These views, combined with his conviction that Aborigines were akin to 'children' or 'lunatics', raise legitimate questions as to why Curr later acquired a reputation among historians of sympathy towards Aboriginal people. A pervasive historiographical ignorance regarding Curr's role in Aboriginal administration seems the only plausible explanation. Although certain passages in *Recollections of Squatting in Victoria* might imply a degree of sympathy towards Curr's Indigenous neighbours, his controversial membership of the Board for the Protection of Aborigines provides a strong counter narrative, which must be acknowledged when weighing his credibility as an observer of Aboriginal custom.

---

58 Royal Commission on the Aborigines (1877), 78.
59 Royal Commission on the Aborigines (1877), 79.
60 Royal Commission on the Aborigines (1877), 90.

9. The Australian Race

In 1873, two years before he joined the Board for the Protection of Aborigines, Edward M. Curr made a startling discovery regarding Aboriginal languages. While conversing with 'a Blackfellow of the Swan Hill neighbourhood' he noticed the man using a word in common with the Ngooraialum people, whose territory lay more than 200 kilometres to the south-east. This was particularly surprising to Curr, as he knew that the Bangerang people, who traditionally occupied the intervening territory, did not use this word. He subsequently observed that the Bangerang 'were encircled by a number of tribes, which spoke related languages, which differed materially from theirs'. This circumstance caused Curr to ponder what might be discovered about the migration of Aboriginal peoples by a comparative analysis of their vocabularies. His interest in ethnology derived, therefore, from an interest in the languages of the tribes he had encountered while squatting in the 1840s.[1]

Curr had earlier declined an invitation to join a group assembling vocabularies of Victorian Aboriginal languages, but his linguistic discovery in 1873 triggered a new curiosity. He began collecting vocabularies using a circulated list of 'a few common English words' for translation. Sending his wordlist to 'stock-owners here and there', Curr soon observed 'some order in what had heretofore appeared a mere jumble of related tongues'. Inspired by his early findings he expanded his word list to over 100 words and sought the assistance of colonial governments and the press.[2] In this way, Curr recruited a wider range of informants, including missionaries, government officials as well as pastoralists and stockmen. The project was also a family affair: Curr's youngest brother Montagu and his eldest son Edward, who were both pastoralists in the far north of Queensland, each contributed several vocabularies, while Curr himself assembled vocabularies for 27 Victorian languages. The wordlist included native flora and fauna, basic relationship terms, body parts, weapons, numbers and a range of other words. Describing his project to the *Argus* in 1883, Curr wrote: 'My collection comprises vocabularies of about 200 of our languages, drawn up for comparison on a uniform plan, many of them in duplicate and triplicate.' He further stressed that the approximately 300 contributors were 'residents in the bush'.[3]

---

1   Curr 1886, vol 1: xiii–xiv.
2   See, for example: *Queenslander*, 20 May 1876: 22; *South Australian Advertiser*, 17 May 1876: 3.
3   Edward M. Curr, 'Letter to the Editor', *Argus*, 9 January 1883: 10.

No. 96.—KAMILAROI.

By Montagu Curr, Esq.

Kangaroo	- ngulanoo.	Hand	-	- mala-roo.
Opossum	- ka-goo-in.	2 Blacks	-	-
Tame dog	- yambe.	3 Blacks	-	-
Wild dog	-	One	-	- goreen.
Emu	- d-pingo-burri.	Two	-	- bulla.
Black duck	- bin-dur-ra.	Three	-	- bulla-go-go-run.
Wood duck	- wool-ad-dthoo.	Four	-	- in-ca-moo.
Pelican	-	Father	-	- mudjo.
Laughing jackass	d'char-run-gul.	Mother	-	- yag-e-roo.
Native companion	d'tharwo-booga.	Sister–Elder	-	- kool-a-moo.
White cockatoo	- koolera.	,, Younger	-	
Crow	- d'thong-oo-boore.	Brother–Elder	-	
Swan	-	,, Younger	nga-boor.	
Egg	- d'thandoo.	A young man	-	- yab-bi-ree.
Track of a foot	- d'janna.	An old man	-	- mo-a.
Fish	- bulbi.	An old woman	-	- wom-me-ra.
Lobster	-	A baby	-	- good-a-dthoo.
Crayfish	- jin-ju.	A White man	-	- mud-dtha.
Mosquito	- ong-go-in.	Children	-	-
Fly	- melg-na.	Head	-	- nganggul.
Snake	-	Eye	-	- mille.
The Blacks	-	Ear	-	- kun-dtha.
A Blackfellow	- bungil.			
A Black woman	- bunya.			
Nose	- goonyeen.			

Figure 22: Extract from a vocabulary of the Kamilaroi, Leichardt River, supplied by Montagu Curr.

Edward M. Curr, 1886, *The Australian Race* (Melbourne: John Ferres, Govt. Printer), vol II, 320.

For Curr's collection to be valuable for purposes of comparison, a systematic approach to transcription was desirable, but with such a large number of contributors this goal was elusive. Curr himself recognised the difficulty, explaining that 'it is often difficult to decide whether certain sounds should be expressed by b or p, others by d or t, and others by k or g'.[4] He addressed this problematic issue by attempting to impose a uniform system of spelling on the vocabularies he received, but this process must have been fraught with difficulty.[5] Although he originally aimed to make a study of Aboriginal languages, he was increasingly drawn to a more general ethnographic approach. Accordingly, he asked many of his correspondents to return a questionnaire on tribal customs and manners to supplement the standard vocabulary. The questionnaire consisted of 83 items that the Australian anthropologist A.P. Elkin later described as being 'in the range of what could be called physical and cultural anthropology'.[6] Curr was interested in such issues as territorial range, demography, physical characteristics, clothing and ornamentation, weapons, wars, marriage and disease. For the most part, however, Curr's study revolved around language.

Curr initially had no intention to publish his collection due to a mistaken belief that his Aboriginal protection board colleague R. Brough Smyth had long been engaged on the subject. He gradually was convinced, however, that his work was important. This was particularly the case following the publication in 1878 of Smyth's *Aborigines of Victoria* – Curr was unimpressed and later wrote an extended critique of Smyth's work.[7] As Curr's project of collection grew in scale, he began to ponder how he might interpret the data he had obtained. Although he later expressed suspicion of the scientific fashions that he believed had influenced other prominent scholars, he found his own inspiration in the work of the English philologist Hyde Clarke, who was then vice president of the Anthropological Institute of Great Britain and Ireland. In November 1879 the Royal Society of Victoria heard a paper by Clarke, which (as Curr put it) 'drew attention to certain affinities between the Mozambique and Australian Languages'.[8] Clarke took a vocabulary of the 'Yarra tribe' from Smyth's *Aborigines of Victoria* and compared it with a family of languages from Portuguese Africa contained in Koelle's *Polyglotta Africana* (1854). He concluded: 'There is, therefore no mistake that the language of the Melbourne tribes is of common origin with those of Mozambique.'[9] Ironically, Clarke relied on a vocabulary compiled by John Green, the former manager of the Coranderrk Aboriginal

---

4   Curr 1886, vol 1: 4.
5   Curr 1886, vol 1: 247.
6   Elkin 1975: 12.
7   Curr 1886, vol 1: 237–244.
8   Curr 1886, vol 1: xv.
9   Clarke 1879: 170–176.

reserve and a major antagonist of Curr's during the Coranderrk Rebellion.[10] This might help explain why Curr was initially sceptical of Clarke's conclusion: 'To me the position seemed doubtful, as I knew many of the words on which it was based were accidental, and not prevalent in our languages'. Nevertheless, Curr investigated Clarke's hypothesis more thoroughly and ultimately concurred: 'The evidence I have on this subject seems indisputable.'[11]

Inspired by Clarke, Curr was drawn into a wider debate about racial origins, which transformed his project from one of compiling vocabularies to a fully-fledged ethnological work. Importantly, Clarke provided not only theoretical inspiration, but also encouragement and support, as Curr explained: 'the writer is under no small obligation to that gentlemen for the kindly interest he has evinced in this undertaking'.[12] Clarke's encouragement probably galvanised Curr's resolve to pursue a project he initially thought beyond his expertise. Driven by a belief that the Aboriginal race was dying, he found himself 'on the threshold of an ethnological work ... without any previous preparation'. After more than a decade or labour, his project culminated in a four-volume work with the prosaic title *The Australian Race: Its Origin, Languages, Customs, Place of Landing in Australia, and the Routes by Which It Spread Itself Over That Continent*. In the introduction, Curr explained the prime motive behind his research:

> As *raison d'être* for this publication then, it may be pointed out that when the author drifted into his undertaking, many tribes were passing away, leaving no record behind them, and no one seemed likely to step in and do what was necessary for ethnology.[13]

In compiling his work, Curr received considerable support from government officials around Australia. Consequently, his list of acknowledgments reads almost like a *Who's Who* of Australian colonial politics in the 1880s. He thanked colonial secretaries from all the mainland Australian colonies, numerous under-secretaries, the Governor of Western Australia Sir Frederick A. Weld, who had been a contemporary of Curr's at Stonyhurst College, and the former Governor of South Australia, New Zealand and the Cape Colony, Sir George Grey. The involvement of all these prominent men certainly lent weight to Curr's project and probably contributed to the Victorian Government's decision to publish *The Australian Race*. Curr certainly had excellent political connections, deriving from his father's role in securing independence for Victoria and from his own senior public service position. By the 1880s his key political ally was

---

10 Smyth 1878: 99–117.
11 Edward M. Curr, 'Letter to the Editor', *Argus*, 9 January 1883: 10. See also Edward M. Curr, 'Letter to Hyde Clarke', 8 September 1880, State Library of New South Wales, MLDOC 2095.
12 Curr 1886, vol 1: xv.
13 Curr 1886, vol 1: xiv–xv.

Jonas Felix Levien, who as minister for mines and agriculture was responsible for Curr's department. Curr dedicated *The Australian Race* to Levien, 'through whose influence it was published by the Government of Victoria'.

Before recommending the work be published, Levien had arranged for a copy to be sent to the Agent General in London, who submitted Curr's drafts to the president of the Anthropological Institute, W.H. Flower. The *Argus* reported Flower's favourable opinion in November 1884: 'The linguistic portion of the work … seems most valuable, and contains much new and important information, collected at great labour, and well worth publishing.'[14] Although Flower recommended publication, his review appears somewhat equivocal; by noting the particular value of 'the linguistic portion of the work' he almost seems to damn Curr's wider ethnography with faint praise. This might have been due to Curr's conclusions regarding the racial origins of the Aborigines, which did not agree with Flower's own. Whatever the case, an endorsement from the president of the Anthropological Institute was sufficient reason for Levien to push for publication.

Curr submitted the first part of his manuscript to the government printer in February 1885.[15] The first volume was published in March 1886 and was distributed at the Colonial and Indian Exhibition in London that year.[16] Publication of all four volumes was slow, however, and was not completed until September 1887. In a surviving personal copy of the work, Curr recorded his frustration at the slow rate of publication, noting that it had been printed months earlier but that Victoria's premier, Duncan Gillies, 'would not direct its publication'. No money was spent on advertising, leaving Curr to distribute a few copies to the colonial press. Curr concluded: 'Altogether the work appeared under very disadvantageous circumstances.'[17]

The first three volumes of *The Australian Race* were divided into 23 sections or 'Books', while the large-format volume 4 featured a comparative vocabulary and a map showing the locations of each tribe referred to in the work. The 244-page 'Book the First' occupied most of the first volume and featured Curr's general account of the languages, manners and customs of the Australian Aborigines and his arguments about their origins and routes of migration across the continent. The remainder of the first volume and all of volumes two and three contained Curr's vast collection of vocabularies, divided into 22 books according to geographic location and linguistic affinity. Each book included

---

14   *Argus*, 3 November 1884: 5.
15   Edward M. Curr, Note regarding publication of *The Australian Race*, 20 September 1887, Murrumbogie Papers.
16   *Argus*, 19 March 1886: 5.
17   See Dixon 1980: 13; Curr's annotated edition is held by the Menzies Library at The Australian National University.

an introductory preface, which usually featured a short regional ethnography written by Curr based on the questionnaires he had received. In some cases, however, Curr republished in full the ethnographic accounts of other trusted writers. Reviewing the work in Melbourne, the *Argus* noted the sheer scale of Curr's undertaking: 'The four volumes before us represent the work of a lifetime – work not done only for pecuniary gain, but as a labour of love.'[18]

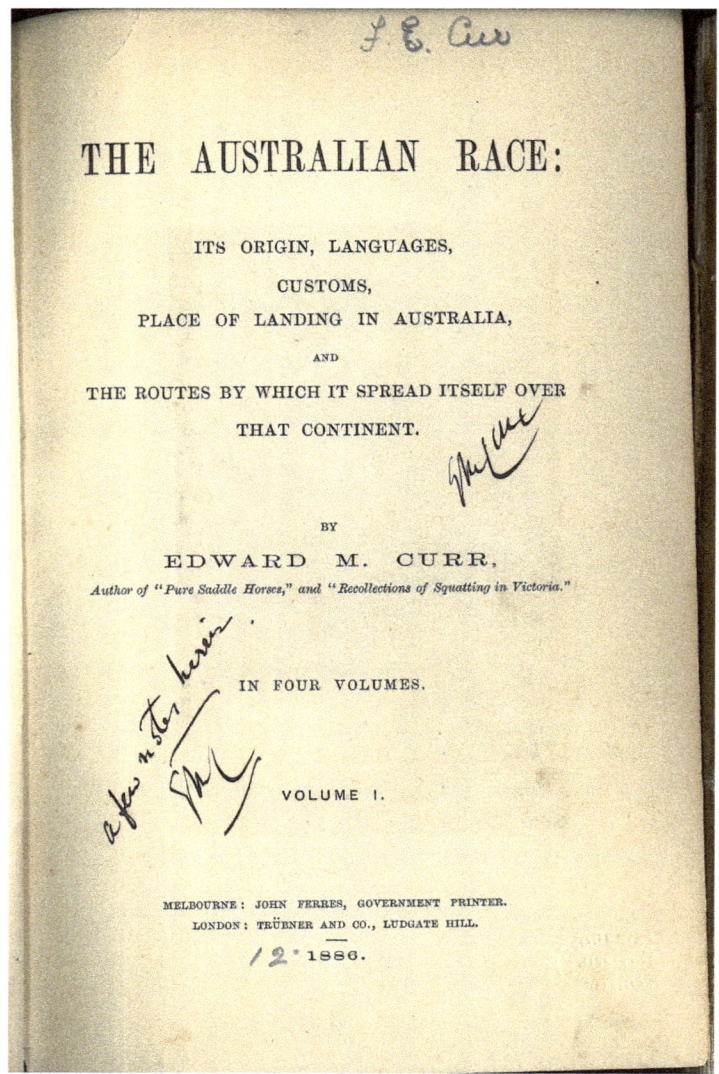

Figure 23: Title Page of *The Australian Race* signed by Edward M. Curr.

Menzies Library, The Australian National University.

---

18   Book Review, 'The Australian Race', *Argus*, 24 September 1887: 4.

Comparative Philology and Racial Origins

Although Curr was overtly self-conscious and aware of his lack of ethnological training, he made tentative steps into the broader field of anthropology. In the period when he embarked on his project, British anthropology was emerging from a tumultuous and divisive period. During the 1860s members of the Ethnological Society of London had resigned to form the rival Anthropological Society of London, the complicated split involving intellectual disputes as well as social and political differences. The 'anthropologicals' tended towards polygenism and exhibited a more starkly racialist conception of human diversity. The 'ethnologicals' were more accommodating of Darwinist thinking, which (for some) provided a new scientific basis for the unity of all humanity. Nevertheless, the two societies represented substantially overlapping intellectual fields: they met in the same building on different nights and many were members of both societies.[19] In 1871 they merged to form the Anthropological Institute of Great Britain and Ireland, but the disciplinary boundaries of anthropology remained fluid. Although Curr was an enthusiastic student of the languages, customs and manners of the Australian Aborigines, he did not take a strong position on many of the major theoretical questions of anthropology in the period. The loss of Curr's correspondence certainly hinders a study of his intellectual engagement, but an analysis of *The Australian Race* suggests he was broadly distrustful of anthropological theory. It is possible, however, to identify Curr's principal theoretical influences and the key to this is his great interest in language.

Curr viewed language as a valuable lens on the prehistory of an ancient race and the key to determining racial origins. In taking this approach he followed an earlier ethnological orthodoxy epitomised by the work of James Cowles Prichard (1786–1848). Reaching its peak in the mid-nineteenth century, Prichard's approach built on a biblical understanding of human history, which assumed all the 'races of man' were descended from the sons of Noah and that linguistic diversity derived from the 'scattering of tongues' at the Tower of Babel. As George Stocking has explained, the task of Prichard and his fellow ethnologists was to 'to establish connections between the races of men on the basis of similarities of physical type, religion, political institutions, customs, and above all, language'.[20] The diffusion of the various races around the planet, it was assumed, had occurred within the relatively short timeframe of human existence implied by scripture. Given the relative youth of the human family, it was conceivable that linguistic analysis might enable ethnologists to trace its family tree back to the Ark. In Prichard's time, therefore, comparative philology and ethnology were closely related disciplines.

---

19 Stocking 1987: 248–257.
20 Stocking 1987: 51–52.

Prichardian ethnology could not, however, survive intact the 'revolution in human time' that occurred in the 1850s. The discovery in 1858 of a cave in Brixham containing 'numerous human artefacts *in situ* with extinct animals' was the catalyst for a fundamental reassessment of the span of human existence.[21] The publication of Darwin's *On the Origin of Species* the following year compounded this effect; in particular, the evolutionary paradigm undermined the primacy of language, which could no longer be used to map the entire span of human existence. Comparative philology had emerged as a discipline in Germany and a key proponent in Britain was the émigré Max Müller, who had studied in Berlin before moving to Oxford in 1851. Müller was strongly antievolutionary and responded to the Darwinian challenge by declaring 'language is our Rubicon, and no brute will dare to cross it'.[22] Müller's staunch resistance was not, however, sufficient to maintain the place of comparative philology at the centre of ethnological inquiry. Comparative anatomy, for example, attracted many scholars (such as Darwin's champion T.H. Huxley) who were searching for a more naturalistic anthropology. Furthermore, the diffusionist approach of Prichardian ethnology, which presupposed that all humans were descended from a single family, increasingly gave way to a developmentalist interpretation of human history.

Given Curr's limited theoretical engagement, it is difficult to say with certainty why he adhered to an earlier model of ethnological inquiry when writing *The Australian Race*. He might have had a religious motivation, as a biblical timescale is clearly implied by several statements in *The Australian Race*: he speculated, for example, as to when 'the descendants of Adam developed the Negro type'; similarly, he suggested that the Aboriginal arrival in Australia was 'probably prior to the dawn of history' and their occupation of the continent had been completed only 'some centuries back'. Alternatively, Curr's predominantly linguistic approach might have derived more simply from his own love of language, rather than a strongly held religious or theoretical stance. He did not make plain his views on Darwin's theory, but he did suggest that 'sporadic variation' was an implausible explanation for physical differences between Aborigines and Africans. In his assessment of human diversity Curr leaned towards monogenism, which was an article of faith among earlier ethnologists. He noted, for example, the striking similarity between Aboriginal class-marriage and other such systems in Asia, Africa and America – 'a circumstance which should go far to uphold the doctrine of the unity of the human race'. Given all these indications of his intellectual influences, it is probably significant that Curr opted not to define his field of inquiry as 'anthropology', preferring to use the older term 'ethnology'.[23]

---

21 Stocking 1987: 73.
22 Stocking 1987: 57–61.
23 Curr 1886, vol 1: 152, 204–207, 182, 111.

Curr's commitment to comparative philology as a theoretical approach was evident in his response to an *Argus* report in 1882, which stressed the need for 'a sufficient record of our native languages whilst there is yet time' and urged the Government to employ 'some competent gentleman' for the task. The newspaper described Curr's work-in-progress as 'admirable as far as it goes', but suggested that something more than the compilation of vocabularies was required: 'Mere isolated words can teach the classifying philologist nothing more than the connexion of one tribe with another.'[24] Curr clearly needed to defend his undertaking, which by that time was well known to the wider community. In his response he noted the work of R.G. Latham, 'an authority in such matters', whose *Elements of Comparative Philology* (1862) was based 'almost entirely on vocabularies'. Latham was a former vice-president of the Ethnological Society of London and in 1852 had been appointed the director of the ethnological department at the Crystal Palace.[25] An intellectual heir of Prichard, he was a standard bearer for philology as the bedrock of ethnological research. In addition to citing Latham, Curr also recalled a letter to a newspaper from Max Müller, which 'strongly urged the great utility to science of such compilations'. Anxious to assert the value of his project, Curr described Müller as 'the highest authority on philology'. Nevertheless, Curr was quite aware of his own lack of experience: 'I am no philologist, and I cannot pretend to say what might be the value to science of the material I have got together.'[26]

Reflecting his theoretical approach, Curr began *The Australian Race* with a chapter on language, in which he explained: 'Generally, the only reliable records of the early history of a savage race are its languages, customs, and physical characteristics, but particularly its languages.'[27] A reviewer in Melbourne's *Argus* suggested that dealing with language before racial origins was 'an inversion of the natural order of things' – in so doing the reviewer either missed the point of Curr's theoretical approach or deliberately chose to question it.[28] Curr estimated that the number of Aboriginal languages prior to white invasion was about 500, of which over 200 were covered in his book.[29] He concluded that, while distinct, these languages were closely related: 'we find that the whole of the Australian languages are pretty nearly as intimately connected as Spanish and Portuguese'.[30] Curr qualified this view by suggesting some 'linguistic disturbance' in the languages of the north coast of Australia; nevertheless, he offered various 'proofs' through a comparative study of vocabularies to suggest that 'the whole of the languages proceed from one'. Extending his study to a

---

24   'A plea for the Australian language', *Argus*, 18 November 1882: 6.
25   Ridler 2004.
26   Edward M. Curr, 'Letter to the Editor', *Argus*, 9 January 1883: 10.
27   Curr 1886, vol 1: 3.
28   Book Review, 'The Australian Race', *Argus*, 24 September 1887: 4.
29   Curr 1886, vol 1: 13.
30   Curr 1886, vol 1: 5.

grammatical analysis Curr found fewer but striking examples.³¹ He supported his linguistic argument with related theories based on physical appearance, arguing that similar variations of physical characteristics within tribes around Australia suggested that the Australian tribes were descended from a common progenitor, which was itself the result of a racial cross.³² It is important to note, however, that Curr employed comparative anatomy to provide *supporting* evidence for his predominantly linguistic argument – an approach in line with the Prichardian model of ethnology.

In his commitment to comparative philology Curr was greatly influenced by his mentor Hyde Clarke, who played a significant role in the emergence of the discipline of anthropology, institutionally if not intellectually. Clarke had earlier been a member of both the Ethnological Society and the Anthropological Society, but fell out with the council of the latter after he publicly questioned its finances.³³ After the two societies reunited Clarke was a prominent figure at the Anthropological Institute, serving as a council member or vice-president for most of its first two decades. In various publications Clarke had employed philology to explore racial affinity.³⁴ His prominence at the Anthropological Institute demonstrates the fact that while comparative philology's status had declined it was not entirely undermined. In the paper that so influenced Curr, Clarke had disputed the view of 'some distinguished anthropologists' that Australia was 'a centre of the human race, from which India and Africa were peopled'. He suggested the linguistic evidence was proof of the contrary and proclaimed Africa 'the great centre of languages, of mythology, and of civilization'.³⁵

In supporting Clarke's theory, Curr took a different view from many contemporary scholars. Huxley had earlier noted a similarity between Aborigines and Dravidians, a Caucasian branch from India. R. Brough Smyth implied the Aborigines might be Caucasian in origin, as did Alfred Russel Wallace. In 1891, Flower and Lyddeker argued that Melanesians originally peopled Australia but were later displaced by 'a low form of Caucasian melanchroi'. A.W. Howitt subsequently concluded this theory was the most credible.³⁶ The principal conclusion of Curr's comparative philology – that 'the Australian is by descent a Negro, crossed by some other race'³⁷ – was, therefore, an unpopular view; not that this would have discouraged Curr, who was supremely confident and contrary by nature.

---

31 Curr 1886, vol 1: 10.
32 Curr 1886, vol 1: 36.
33 Rainger 1978: 68.
34 See, for example, Clarke 1878: 44–65.
35 Clarke 1879: 174–175.
36 Anderson 2002: 190; McGregor 1997: 36.
37 Curr 1886, vol 1: 152.

In addition to proposing a common origin for Africans and Australian Aborigines, Curr used his comparative vocabulary (and to a lesser extent some observations on custom) to develop a theory for the process by which the Aborigines occupied the Australian continent. He conjectured that the original Australians had arrived in the Kimberley region of north-west Australia, 'probably within a hundred miles, on one side or the other, of Camden Harbour'.[38] A more accurate prediction was not possible, Curr explained, due to the lack of vocabularies from that area. From the northwest, this original population spread out over the continent in three distinct waves of migration. Curr's predictions were inferences based on divisions he observed within the languages and customs of the Aborigines. In proposing three main tribal divisions – Western, Central and Eastern – Curr pointed to linguistic affinities within each group, but also to the presence or absence of certain cultural elements. According to Curr's scheme, the Eastern division was distinguished by the use of the negative adverb for tribal names; the Central division was peculiar for the prevalence of circumcision, sub-incision, or both; while the Western division evinced neither of these features.[39] He depicted these divisions in a large map contained in volume 4 of *The Australian Race*.

In speaking of sub-incision Curr coined the term 'the Terrible Rite' and in the interests of decency he could only explain the practice using a Latin note: '*funditur usque ad uretheram à parte infera penis*'.[40] In a letter to his son written in about 1883 he was more specific: 'It has become a matter of interest to me, of great interest, to ascertain what portion of this continent is, and what portion is not, occupied by what you call the Whistle-Cock-Blacks (those who split the penis.)'[41] Initiation rites became a defining characteristic of Curr's Central division and thus a key basis for his arguments about routes of migration. His argument relied, however, on some problematic assumptions, as A.P. Elkin later observed: 'Curr ... associated diffusion of cultural elements, particularly initiation rites, with the migration of tribal groups, not realising that such rites and other cultural elements and social divisions, spread from tribe to tribe through contact.' Elkin still saw value in Curr's three divisions, but rather than interpreting them as routes of migration, he defined them more broadly as 'corridors of communication'.[42]

Although Curr's prime focus on language linked him to a Prichardian ethnological approach, he was not entirely oblivious to more recent developments in anthropology. He was able, for example, to accommodate elements of an evolutionary or developmentalist approach within what was the broadly

---

38 Curr 1886, vol 1: 202.
39 Curr 1886, vol 1: 197.
40 Curr 1886, vol 1: 74.
41 Edward M. Curr to E.M.V. Curr, undated [c.1883], Murrumbogie Papers.
42 Elkin 1975: 14; see also Elkin 1970: 707.

diffusionist assumptions of comparative philology. This tension at the heart of Curr's work was not unusual; indeed anthropology was struggling to cope with the various intellectual crosscurrents that defined the discipline in this period. Curr's receptiveness to aspects of the evolutionary paradigm is evident in a final observation regarding the origins and migrations of Aboriginal people:

> I am led to conclude that the Australian race is of vast antiquity, and that, owing to the remarkable isolation to which it has been subjected, it has preserved more of the customs, linguistic peculiarities, and ways of thought of the Black races of antiquity than any other people now existing on the globe; and that hence, if we would realise what the earliest Black savages were like, we must study the Australian before he passes away.[43]

A staunch social evolutionist could easily have drawn such a conclusion, but it sits more uncomfortably alongside a strictly biblical anthropology, which assumes that the 'lower' races were 'the degenerate descendants of far superior ancestors'.[44] Curr did not address the question as to the origins of 'the earliest Black savages', perhaps leaving it to the reader to decide whether they evolved from ape-like ancestors or degenerated from a more advanced biblical ancestral family. Nevertheless, a degenerationist approach is implicit elsewhere in Curr's work, such as his suggestion that apparently sophisticated elements in Aboriginal languages probably derived from the languages of more advanced ancestors.[45] It is also evident in his deference to Max Müller, who resisted evolutionism and remained faithful to a biblical view of human diversity.[46] This theoretical inconsistency is unsurprising given Curr's limited engagement with the social evolutionary model of anthropology. He did not cite Darwin's *Descent of Man*, nor did he discuss pioneering works of the evolutionist perspective in anthropology, such as T.H. Huxley's *Man's Place in Nature* (1863) or E.B. Tylor's *Primitive Culture* (1871). He briefly addressed John Lubbock's *The Origin of Civilisation* (1870), but principally to identify what he saw as factual inaccuracies.[47] Curr's fundamental interest was the Australian Aborigines, the study of which he approached more from the perspective of an antiquarian than a theoretically inclined scholar.

---

43   Curr 1886, vol 1: 207.
44   Stocking 1987: 154.
45   Curr 1886, vol 1: 19.
46   Stocking 1996: 18.
47   Curr 1886, vol 1: 236.

10. Ethnographic Rivalries

The Australian Race was the last of four significant ethnographic works to be published in Melbourne in less than a decade. The first was R. Brough Smyth's *Aborigines of Victoria* (1878), which like Curr's work was published by the Victorian Government. In subsequent years the Melbourne-based bookseller George Robertson published Lorimer Fison and A.W. Howitt's seminal *Kamilaroi and Kurnai* (1880) and James Dawson's study of Aborigines in western Victoria titled *Australian Aborigines* (1881). Robertson also published Curr's *Recollections of Squatting in Victoria* in 1883. In *The Australian Race* Curr took the opportunity to assert the superiority of his own ethnographic work. In several passages he was highly critical of both Smyth and Fison, while Dawson and Howitt did not escape unscathed.[1]

Curr also compiled a recommended reading list for works on the Australian Aborigines, the vast majority of which were published before 1850. His primary concern was to promote the accounts of those who had early contact with Aborigines and whose observations he thought reliable. This list of 'the most trustworthy writers on our Blacks' included early government officials (Phillip, Hunter and Collins), explorers (Mitchell, Grey and Eyre) and missionaries (Threlkeld, Ridley and Taplin). Of the more recent works of his rivals, he recommended only Dawson's *Australian Aborigines*.[2] His omission of Fison and Howitt was particularly telling, as *Kamilaroi and Kurnai* had already earned a positive international reputation as a pioneering work of social anthropology. Curr, however, was not significantly engaged with anthropological discourse, only reading more recent theoretical works if they touched on the Australian Aborigines. He stressed personal experience over theoretical approaches and eschewed the intellectual debate that surrounded his endeavour. It is not surprising that he chiefly valued written works that were produced by explorers and early government officials, whose experiences were similar to his own.

Curr believed the integrity of his evidence derived from his own personal experience of bush life. Moreover, he stressed that his collaborators were often men with a similar background to his own, as he had sent his *pro forma* questionnaires to 'stock-owners here and there'.[3] These were men with actual bush experience, not armchair anthropologists with a surfeit of education but a deficit of personal experience among 'the Blacks'. When assessing the evidence of other writers, Curr regularly assumed the ultimate authority of the bushman. Typical statements by Curr included: 'I have never witnessed nor

---

1   Dawson 1881; Fison and Howitt 1880; Smyth 1878.
2   Curr 1886, vol 1: 235.
3   Curr 1886, vol 1: xiv.

heard any bushman mention such a state of things'; or, 'this passage will, I think, be looked on by bushmen as sheer extravagance'.⁴ Curr's 'stock-owners here and there' might indeed have been well placed to observe Aborigines first hand, but the involvement of so many of his informants in the pastoral industry certainly casts doubt on the impartiality of their statements. Many collaborators had a clear motive to portray Aborigines as hopelessly primitive, as such a view justified (in their own minds) colonial land acquisition.

Curr's emphasis on bush experience is readily apparent in his concerted attack on the work of his colleague R. Brough Smyth:

> Mr. Smyth as we know is no bushman and has no acquaintance with our Blacks in their savage state; and he furnishes another instance of the fact that book lore never compensates in such matters for the want of knowledge which comes of personal intercourse alone.⁵

Figure 24: R. Brough Smyth (c.1880). George Gordon McCrae.

Drawing. National Library of Australia, nla.pic-an6312205.

---

4   Curr 1886, vol 1: 126, 132.
5   Curr 1886, vol 1: 238; see also a similar comment on page 52: 'we know that Mr Smyth has no personal knowledge of the Blacks'.

Curr devoted several pages of *The Australian Race* to correcting the numerous errors that he had identified in Smyth's book.[6] He offered qualified praise for Smyth's descriptions of Aboriginal weapons, but noted 'they are not entirely free from even important errors'.[7] He also refuted Smyth's elaborate description of the typical Aboriginal approach to setting up a new camp, insisting that '[the] operation is got over very quietly, and is soon completed; all of which is very different from Mr. Smyth's fancy picture'.[8] Curr derived much mirth from Smyth's interpretation of an artefact that Curr had obtained in the Burdekin area, which was apparently used to cure illness through sorcery:

> One of these … I formerly lent to Mr. R. Brough Smyth, not knowing at the time what was its use, and he has depicted in his *Aborigines of Victoria*, and described it as probably a fish-hook! I have since had full information concerning it. That a fish with a mouth sufficiently capacious to take in an object of such length would be too heavy to be held by so fragile a hook, as I pointed out, failed to convince him of his mistake. But how often does one meet with similar such haphazard statements in the accounts of savages![9]

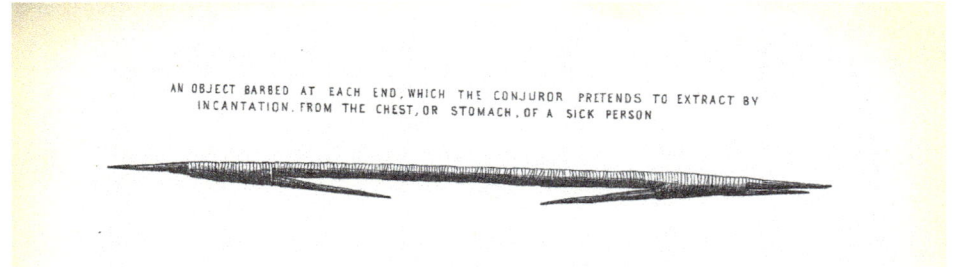

Figure 25: R. Brough Smyth's 'fish-hook'.

Edward M. Curr, 1886, *The Australian Race* (Melbourne: John Ferres, Govt. Printer), vol I, 146-147.

Curr's extended critique of Smyth's volumes focussed principally on the section devoted to language. He noted there were many inconsistencies in Smyth's collection of vocabularies and singled out a contribution from John Green, the former manager of the Coranderrk Aboriginal Station. As noted, it was Green's vocabulary that had earlier influenced Curr's mentor Hyde Clarke to suggest a link between Aboriginal languages and those of Portuguese Africa. Curr declared that Green had 'evidently no knowledge of Aboriginal languages, or of any language but his own'. He argued that Green had asked 'some Black' for a translation of an English phrase, then 'treat[ed] the corresponding

---

6   Curr 1886, vol 1: 237–244.
7   Curr 1886, vol 1: 143.
8   Curr 1886, vol 1: 243.
9   Curr 1886, vol 1: 49.

phrase as a word for word rendering'. With barely concealed contempt Curr concluded: 'Of the different construction of the two languages he has evidently little idea.'[10] Smyth and Curr had been allies against John Green during the Coranderrk protests, but by the 1880s Curr was dismissive of both. He argued that Smyth should have contented himself with 'compilation' and with 'pictorial representations of weapons and implements'. By attempting to present 'a succinct narrative' investigating 'even the *nuances* of savage life in Victoria', Smyth too often fell into error: 'in some cases it would be easier to rewrite a chapter than to expose half of its shortcomings'.[11]

Although Smyth was a principal target, Curr did not shirk from identifying errors in previous works, even those written by people he broadly admired. For example, in volume 3 he included an extended account of the customs of the Kabi (Gubbi Gubbi) people written by the young Presbyterian minister and aspiring anthropologist John Mathew. While Curr's decision publish Mathew's account was certainly a compliment, he was careful to direct the reader to its shortcomings:

> From that gentleman I learn that some years back he spent a short time in the country of the *Kabi*, and I attribute the fullness of his description of the tribe rather to his love of ethnological studies, which has led him to observe and remember what came under his notice, than to that ripe knowledge which results from long experience.

Curr further stressed that Mathew had lived among the Kabi in a period when contact with white settlers had altered traditional custom. To underline his own authority, Curr noted his own experience among the Kabi in 1856 (eight years before Mathew) when he had owned the cattle station Gobongo.[12]

James Dawson's *Australian Aborigines* (1881) attracted mild but significant criticism: Curr explained that it contained 'several glaring errors' balanced by 'a good deal of trustworthy and minute information'.[13] Curr and Dawson's first point of divergence was Aboriginal numeracy, on which point Curr insisted: 'No Australian Black in his wild state can, I believe, practically count as high as seven.'[14] In disputing Dawson's alternative view, Curr noted: 'In fact, in a number of his statements that writer stands alone.' His principal disagreement with Dawson related to 'the existence of government among the Blacks'.[15] Based on his experience in western Victoria, Dawson had proposed a complex system of tribal government, characterised by the existence of chiefs: 'Every tribe has

---

10   Curr 1886, vol 1: 243–244.
11   Curr 1886, vol 1: 237–238.
12   Curr 1886, vol 3: 120–121, 152–195.
13   Curr 1886, vol 1: 55.
14   Curr 1886, vol 1: 32.
15   Curr 1886, vol 1: 55.

its chief, who is looked upon in the light of a father, and whose authority is supreme.'[16] He outlined the various rights enjoyed by these chiefs, including multiple wives and personal servants; he also described intertribal relationships and argued there existed a semi-democratic method for appointing new tribal chiefs. Curr was bewildered:

> How comes it that all this authority and state could have existed unperceived by the early squatters, Commissioners of Crown Lands, and Protectors of the Aborigines, none of whom ever mentioned it in their conversations or reports? How was it that the chiefs who are said to have habitually treated with neighbouring chiefs never made themselves known to the Whites?[17]

Figure 26: James Dawson (1892). Johnstone, O'Shannessy & Co.

Photograph. State Library of Victoria, H2998/84.

---

16 Dawson 1881: 5–6.
17 Curr 1886, vol 1: 56.

Curr scepticism regarding the extent of Aboriginal government was a common theme in *The Australian Race*. He questioned, for example, the view of the missionary George Taplin that a chief called 'Rapulli' governed each of the 18 clans of the Narrinyeri people in South Australia. Curr observed that Taplin took charge of the Aboriginal station near the mouth of the Murray River in 1859 and authored various accounts of the Narrinyeri between 1863 and 1879. Noting that Taplin's observations regarding tribal government did not appear in his writings until 1874, Curr downplayed the significance of a form of government that took 'a diligent inquirer' so many years to discern.[18]

The question of tribal government provided a further reason for Curr to criticise Smyth, who had suggested the Victorian tribes were 'governed by regular councils of old men'. In refuting Smyth's claim, Curr outlined his own views on the subject:

> Mr. Smyth has failed to recognize that, outside of the family, the power which enforces custom in our tribes is for the most part an impersonal one, and that the delegation of authority to chief or council belongs notoriously to a stage of progress which the Australian race has not reached.[19]

In disputing the claims of Dawson, Taplin and Smyth, Curr pointed to the ethnographic work of Edward John Eyre in his *Journals of Expeditions of Discovery into Central Australia* (1845). A pastoralist, explorer, and later the controversial Governor of Jamaica during the Morant Bay rebellion, Eyre had been a protector of Aborigines on the Murray River in South Australia from 1841. He included in his *Journals* 'an account of the manners and customs of the Aborigines', in which he asserted 'there can hardly be said to be any form of government existing among a people who recognize no authority'. Curr explained 'I entirely concur' and quoted a large slab of Eyre's text.[20]

The existence or otherwise of tribal government became a prominent issue after the Melbourne *Argus* reviewed *The Australian Race* in 1887. James Dawson quickly wrote to defend his position and somewhat tersely remarked: 'I would not have taken any notice of these reviews had I not, amongst other absurdities, been struck by Mr. Curr refuting the existence of chiefs.' Dawson had arrived in the Port Phillip District a year before Curr and had extensive pastoral experience. On this basis, he was entitled to defend himself against Curr's criticism: 'when I wrote my book *Australian Aborigines* I did so from an intimate knowledge of the habits and customs of the blacks'.[21] Crucially, Dawson claimed the same

---

18 Curr 1886, vol 1: 59.
19 Curr 1886, vol 1: 52.
20 Eyre 1845, vol 2: 315; Curr 1886, vol 1: 59–60.
21 James Dawson, 'Mr. Curr's work on the Australian race' (Letter to the Editor), *Argus*, 21 October 1887.

authority upon which Curr relied, which might explain why Curr tended to be milder in his criticisms of Dawson compared to his other rivals. It might also explain why, in this case, Curr chose to stress the potential for ethnographic corruption when Aborigines had come into contact with white settlers. Good ethnography, he suggested, required not only extensive bush experience, but also a healthy scepticism of Aboriginal informants; while Dawson had 'taken great pains to secure accuracy in his statements' he had 'allowed the Blacks, now well versed in our ways, to impose on him as aboriginal a number of ideas which have resulted from their connection with the Whites'.[22]

James Dawson found support, however, from A.W. Howitt, who wrote to the *Argus* claiming he had both personal knowledge and evidence from reliable correspondents to contradict Curr's claim. Howitt noted there were other matters on which he disagreed with Curr and promised an extended critique would follow.[23] A few weeks later Dawson wrote to F.W. Chesson, the secretary of the Aborigines Protection Society in London, expressing concern that Curr's 'ponderous work' would be viewed as authoritative and arguing that Curr's 'extraordinary assertion' brought into question the accuracy of his work more generally. He explained that he had the support of Howitt and of 'every intelligent person acquainted with the Aborigines in the early days of the Colony'. Crucially, Dawson added a final request that Chesson might forward his letter to the Anthropological Institute. Chesson obliged, sending the letter to none other than Curr's erstwhile mentor Hyde Clarke.[24] Meanwhile, Howitt prepared two papers – one for the Royal Society of Victoria and one for the Anthropological Institute – in which he refuted several of Curr's key claims.

Lorimer Fison and Communal Marriage

Howitt had good reason to question the accuracy of Curr's work: his friend and collaborator Lorimer Fison had been the subject of a sustained attack in *The Australian Race*. Fison's contribution to *Kamilaroi and Kurnai* (1880) attracted Curr's derision for its assertions about marriage custom and Howitt was inevitably drawn into the debate. The rivalry between Curr, Fison and Howitt extended back many years. In 1880 Fison had written to the eminent American anthropologist Lewis H. Morgan explaining his decision to seek immediate publication of *Kamilaroi and Kurnai* in Melbourne, rather than wait up to two years for publication by the Smithsonian Institution in Washington. He and Howitt were both wary regarding the work George Taplin and Curr were doing

---

22   Curr 1886, vol 1: 55–56.
23   A.W. Howitt, 'Letter to the Editor', *Argus*, 28 October 1887.
24   James Dawson to F.W. Chesson, Secretary of the Society for the Protection of Aborigines, 11 November 1887, State Library of New South Wales, MLDOC 1747.

in the same field of inquiry. According to Fison, Taplin had incorporated into his work whole sections of letters from Fison and Howitt, without attributing them to their authors. Curr's research was similarly a source of concern, as Fison explained:

> Another man called Curr is in the field and he is in possession of several of our facts. Moreover, our printed circulars long ago set him on the track. He wrote to Howitt claiming our territory. As Howitt said in his letter to me thereupon: 'If we don't make haste we shall be accused of ploughing with the Taplin and Curr heifers.'[25]

Fison and Howitt got their work published in Melbourne, but certainly would have preferred the imprint of the Smithsonian Institution, which had published Morgan's influential *Systems of Consanguinity and Affinity of the Human Family* in 1871. Morgan had become a friend and mentor to both Fison and Howitt. A circular letter from Morgan, received by Fison in Fiji in 1869, sparked his interest in kinship systems and Morgan guided his subsequent research in Australia. Fison was among the first converts to Morgan's social evolutionary model for the history of human marriage and he loyally defended Morgan against his critics.

Morgan had expounded a theory for the evolution of human marriage, which suggested that from an initial state of 'promiscuous intercourse' human sexual relationship had evolved through various stages, designated the communal family, the barbarian family, the patriarchal family and the civilised family. Linked to these stages were a series of systems for kinship terminology described by Morgan as 'systems of consanguinity'. Fison and Howitt sought to defend and expand Morgan's classificatory system through an analysis of Australian data. In the early chapters of *Kamilaroi and Kurnai*, Fison described the system of class divisions among the Kamilaroi, which he argued was prevalent (with minor variations) throughout the Australian continent. He then explained the laws for marriage between classes, which he described as 'theoretically communal'; in other words, 'based upon the marriage of all the males in one division of a tribe to all of the females of the same generation in another division'. By *'theoretically communal'* Fison meant that there was linguistic evidence of communal marriage as a past practice, even if it were no longer prevalent.[26] In making this inference Fison built on E.B. Tylor's theory of cultural survivals, which he later elaborated in a presidential address for the Australian Association for the Advancement of Science: 'Our own modern civilisation, too, is full of fossilised anomalies, which by the aid of savage custom can be traced back to a time when they were full of life.'[27] In the second half of the book Howitt contributed a chapter

---

25   Stern 1930: 425.
26   Stocking 1996: 18–19, 24, 28; Fison and Howitt 1880: 50–51.
27   McGregor 1997: 27, 35.

titled 'The Kurnai: Their Customs in Peace and War', which included detailed observations on marriage custom. To this Fison responded with a 'Theory of the Kurnai System'. Broadly speaking, Howitt and Fison argued that the Kurnai were at a later stage in the evolution of marriage, but vestiges of communal or group marriage remained, particularly in the laws surrounding 'marriage by elopement'.

Fison and Howitt had adopted with enthusiasm a social evolutionary model for anthropology. As a Wesleyan missionary, Fison faced some personal anguish in doing so, but Howitt reputedly kept a picture of Darwin above his bed.[28] In contrast Curr showed little interest in the pioneering works of evolutionary anthropology. Moreover, he was clearly concerned by the degree of scholarly credibility that surrounded *Kamilaroi and Kurnai*. He observed that while Fison's work exhibited 'many appearances of thoroughness', in many respects it was 'quite at variance with fact'.[29] Curr questioned Fison's argument that apparently obsolete Kamilaroi relationship terms were vestigial evidence of a past system of communal marriage. Furthermore, Curr argued that Fison's account was confused, and its lack of clarity had led to a misleading conclusion that group marriage *still existed* in some cases. He argued there was evidence of this falsely drawn conclusion both in reviews of Fison's work and in the preface by Morgan.

A key issue here was Curr's suspicion regarding an overtly theoretical approach to ethnographic writing. He believed that Fison was lured by scientific fashion: 'it seems to me that, when a statement has been pronounced important in scientific circles, there are not wanting educated White men who will support it on very insufficient grounds'. Curr boldly suggested that Fison's object had been 'to demonstrate, right or wrong, a foregone conclusion' and that he had 'not hesitated to keep from his readers facts which tell strongly against his arguments'.[30] If a charge of deceptive presentation of evidence were not enough, Curr suggested Fison was blindly devoted to his theories to the point of gullibility. He argued, for example, that care was required when dealing with the evidence of unreliable Aboriginal informants:

> Every one acquainted with the Blacks will, I think, bear me out when I say that the greatest care is necessary in taking their statements; for their desire to please and their disregard of truth are such that, if a White man making inquiries allows his views or wishes to be known, he is almost certain to find the Aboriginal agreeing with him in every particular.[31]

---

28 Stocking 1996: 19–20.
29 Curr 1886, vol 1: 119.
30 Curr 1886, vol 1: 132.
31 Curr 1886, vol 1: 131.

James Dawson had earlier registered a similar concern, when he explained that in his research with Aborigines in western Victoria 'suggestive or leading questions have been avoided as much as possible'.[32] Fison, Curr believed, did not show the same level of care in his inquiries about marriage custom; moreover, his commitment to certain 'doctrines or systems' had caused him to ignore 'what I and thousands of bushmen know to be facts'.[33]

Curr's dismissal of a theory of communal marriage revealed his reluctance to entertain alternative explanations for sexual practices that he viewed simply as prostitution.[34] Moreover, his criticisms of Fison derive from a strong belief that ethnographic endeavour was the proper domain of the first hand observer:

> I cannot help remark how strange it would have been had a law of compulsory prostitution existed, and its discovery been left to Mr. Fison, who has no personal knowledge of our tribes, and been overlooked by persons who lived amongst them, were well acquainted with their customs, and published detailed accounts of what they had learnt…[35]

For most of his life as an ethnologist Fison lived in Fiji and his research was largely conducted by correspondence through intermediaries. For Curr, he was not a first hand observer and therefore easily dismissed. Howitt, on the other hand, was a true bushman: he famously led the rescue party for the disastrous Burke and Wills expedition in 1861; furthermore, in his work as a police magistrate in Gippsland he had travelled extensively on horseback and interacted with the Kurnai people over a sustained period. Curr apparently had some admiration for Howitt's ability and experience, which is perhaps why he concentrated his attack on Fison. He did, however, chastise Howitt for allowing the inclusion of Morgan's preface, which clearly suggested that communal marriage was a prevalent and contemporary custom:

> That Mr. Howitt, who has lived in the bush, sanctioned the publication of this passage I cannot believe, as I should think he is aware that women in our tribes have never been found living with one man one day and with another the next, *but that the reverse is a matter of notoriety.*[36]

Curr simply could not fathom a theory of Aboriginal kinship that differed from his own observations that the Aboriginal husband 'is the absolute owner of his wife (or wives)' and that 'the man was despotic in his own mia-mia or hut'.[37]

---

32 Dawson 1881: iii.
33 Curr 1886, vol 1: 119.
34 Curr 1886, vol 1: 120–122.
35 Curr 1886, vol 1: 128.
36 Curr 1886, vol 1: 126, emphasis in original.
37 Curr 1886, vol 1: 109; Curr 1883: 247.

Although Curr did not hold back in his strong criticisms of Fison, his dispute with Howitt played out in more subtle ways. He denied Aboriginal women any role in the selection of a husband, 'unless Mr. Howitt's account of the *Kurnai* be correct, which I doubt'.[38] In the third volume of *The Australian Race* Curr included several vocabularies of the 'Gippsland language', including one provided by Howitt and one he penned himself. Importantly, he used his prefatory remarks to question the accuracy of Howitt's writings on the Kurnai. While noting Howitt's 'interesting account' he explained that it 'differs in some important particulars' from information he had obtained from John Bulmer, a missionary in charge of the Lake Tyers Aboriginal reserve in East Gippsland. Accordingly, Curr wrote his own account of the Gippsland tribes based on Bulmer's material. Curr explained: 'As I think Mr. Bulmer an excellent authority, I shall lay before the reader the statements which I have received from him.'[39] It was a subtle rebuke that was no doubt noticed by Howitt. For the most part, however, Howitt was shocked by Curr's attack on Fison; he proceeded to defend his friend's reputation and expose Curr's errors (as his biographer suggests) 'with scorn and conviction'.[40]

Figure 27: A.W. Howitt (1895). Johnstone, O'Shannessy & Co.

Photograph. State Library of Victoria, IAN01/08/95/4.

---

38 Curr 1886, vol 1: 108.
39 Curr 1886, vol 3: 539.
40 Walker 1971: 297.

In December 1889 Howitt delivered a paper to the Royal Society of Victoria, in which he diplomatically described *The Australian Race* as 'the outcome of the labour of years', also noting that it bore 'the authoritative stamp of publication by the Government of Victoria'. In disputing many of Curr's conclusions, Howitt explained it would be necessary to draw on material he had previously published in the journals of the Anthropological Institute in London and the Anthropological Society of Washington. This juxtaposition of publication by a settler government with publication by learned international societies was surely not accidental; he further remarked that his and Fison's theories had been 'very generally accepted by anthropologists'.[41] Although Howitt moderated his criticisms due to the death of Curr only a few months earlier, he argued forcefully that Curr was mistaken in his denial of both Aboriginal government and of group marriage. Providing numerous examples he stressed that group marriage was 'in actual existence' in large parts of central Australia. His prime example was the 'Pirauru' practice among the Dieri people of South Australia, first described by the police trooper Samuel Gason in 1874.[42] Howitt disputed Curr's interpretation that there was 'occasional prostitution' in Aboriginal tribes: 'The Pirauru practice is not "prostitution," but a well recognised and lawful "group marriage," and to its laws, as Mr. Gason has shown, all the people of the tribe give obedience.' He also defended Fison's inference of the past practice of group marriage based on relationship terms. Howitt explained that Curr had failed to understand both the principle of group marriage and the nature of Aboriginal relationship terms: 'the late Mr. Curr did not study the subject with that analytical care which was necessary in order to place himself in a position to speak with certainty'.[43]

Howitt subsequently pitched his rebuttal to an international audience in an article for the *Journal of the Anthropological Institute,* titled 'The Dieri and Other Kindred Tribes of Central Australia'. He noted Curr's incorrect assumption that Aboriginal languages featured substantive collective terms ('uncle, aunt, nephew, niece, cousin, and so on'), which were equivalent to English usage. Through a detailed analysis he argued that Curr had misunderstood the nature of the kinship terminology he was attempting to translate. He then noted a passage in Curr's work 'which cannot be passed over in silence'. He referred to Curr's charge that Fison had deliberately withheld evidence contrary to his argument, to which Howitt responded:

> Had he devoted that attention to the question which the nature of the subject requires, he could not have fallen into the error which he has committed, nor would he have so recklessly levelled such a serious charge

---

41 Howitt 1889: 96–97, 114.
42 Gason's spelling was 'Pirraooroo', which he translated 'paramour'; see Wood 1879: 260–261, 277, 302.
43 Howitt 1889: 128, 133.

of literary dishonesty against a fellow-worker in the anthropological field. When he comes to see the nature of his own error, it is to be hoped that he will deeply regret the rash and unwarranted assertion which I have quoted.[44]

Although Howitt's article on the Dieyeri was published in 1891 it was apparently written before Curr died, which might explain why he was more forthright in his criticisms than he was in the paper he gave to the Royal Society of Victoria. As we shall see in chapter 11, Howitt continued his critique of Curr in *The Native Tribes of South-East Australia* (1904).

Curr was never afraid to argue a controversial point and all his written works display an assured confidence and argumentative style. Moreover, while many of his criticisms of other ethnologists appear self-serving, some are certainly close to the mark. It is true, for example, that the influence of theoretical paradigms on Fison and Howitt was significant.[45] W.E.H. Stanner has observed that *Kamilaroi and Kurnai* 'was rightly acclaimed a landmark in anthropology', even if the subsequent collapse of the evolutionist perspective 'obscured the merit of this pioneer work'.[46] Curr's distaste for Fison and Howitt's theoretical inclinations might thus be seen as prescient. Nevertheless, his lack of engagement with theoretical questions and preference for 'facts' undermined the impact of *The Australian Race* in scholarly circles. Certainly, as the discipline of anthropology emerged, Curr's name faded from prominence, while Howitt became a key player in the development of a nascent science.[47]

Ethnography and Aboriginal policy

In addition to asserting his authority over ethnological rivals, Curr used *The Australian Race* to promote his views regarding the likely destiny of Aboriginal people. In this way, *The Australian Race* provides an important insight into Curr's political and ideological preoccupations and fits neatly with the views he expressed while serving on the Board for the Protection of Aborigines. His ethnological views supported, reflected and complemented his stubborn commitment to a repressively paternalistic policy of protection and his staunch resistance to the emerging ideology of assimilation. The most obvious example of this is Curr's rejection of any meaningful form of Aboriginal government. Significantly, Curr's close ally on the Board for Protection of Aborigines, Albert le Souëf, had also refuted the existence of chiefs in his short contribution to

---

44 Howitt 1891: 52–53.
45 McGregor 1997: 34, note 27.
46 Stanner 1972a: 175–176; Stanner 1972b: 432–435; see also Griffiths 1996: 53–54.
47 Marguerita Stephens argues that Howitt's prominence frustrated Curr. See Stephens 2003: 273.

Smyth's *Aborigines of Victoria*.[48] Their denial of a complex system of authority within Aboriginal tribes certainly illuminates their response to the Coranderrk Rebellion: the chiefly authority of William Barak could not derive from traditional Kulin culture, but must be the result of contact with the whites – that is, John Green's 'outside interference'.

Curr's view of Aborigines as childlike, voiced so prominently at the 1877 Royal Commission on Aborigines and the 1881 Coranderrk Inquiry, was just as pronounced in *The Australian Race*. In assessing the mental characteristics of the Aborigine, Curr described him as quick of mind, observant and self-reliant, but 'less steady, persevering, and calculating' than the English peasant: 'His mind in many respects is that of a child.' This observation led Curr to the conclusion that while the education of Aborigines had shown some positive results, meaningful change would be a gradual process. He suggested that the experience in 'our Aboriginal schools' had been that early progress in reading, writing, and arithmetic was not sustained into adulthood: 'instead of advancing, it is doubtful whether he will fully maintain through middle age what he learned in his youth'. On this basis Curr concluded that '*the savage cannot be raised to the level of our civilization in a single generation*'.[49] It was this pessimistic view of Aboriginal advancement that led Curr to advocate supreme power over Aboriginal people for several generations to come.

A nostalgic admiration for the Aborigine in his 'wild state' also led Curr to conclude that Aboriginal education schemes had been a mixed blessing: 'many of us agreed that the schooled generation was not an improvement'.[50] This sceptical view further illuminates Curr's attitude to both the Coranderrk protests and the broader question of how to manage the 'half-caste'. He viewed the educated half-caste as a threat to the settler-colonial order: 'a considerable experience of them, at the Government Aboriginal stations, shows that they have more brains than the full-blooded Blacks and are more difficult to manage'.[51] This observation surely derives from his experiences regarding Coranderrk – perhaps he had in mind Robert Wandin or Thomas Dunolly who used their literacy skills so effectively to oppose the policies of the protection board. While others in the 1870s and 1880s were inclined to emphasise the greater potential for assimilation of 'half-castes', for Curr their apparently greater intelligence was simply a challenge to proper discipline on the Aboriginal reserves.

There is some irony in the fact that the Victorian Government published *The Australian Race* in the same year that the parliament revised the *Aborigines Protection Act* to enable the exclusion of 'half-castes' from the Aboriginal reserves

---

48 Smyth 1878, vol 2: 295.
49 Curr 1886, vol 1: 42, emphasis in original.
50 Curr 1886, vol 1: 43.
51 Curr 1886, vol 1: 42.

in the interests of assimilation. Curr's dubious attitude towards Aboriginal advancement was evident most obviously in his resistance to assimilationist discourse. While his opposition to proposals to remove half castes from the reserves derived partly from concerns over their welfare (particularly that of young girls), it was equally based on a rigid belief that Aborigines were almost irredeemably primitive: 'I am convinced that, were they once more returned to their forests and cut off from communication with the Whites, they would in a single lifetime become again exactly what we originally found them.' For Curr, high rates of Aboriginal mortality combined with the apparent failure of attempts to educate or civilise those who survived led to only one conclusion, expressed at the 1877 Royal Commission and reiterated in *The Australian Race*: 'The White race seems destined, not to absorb, but to exterminate the Blacks of Australia.'[52] Given this, it is hardly surprising that Curr advocated the relocation of all Aboriginal people to a remote reserve, by force if necessary.

When refuting Lorimer Fison's claims about communal marriage, Curr stressed that his alternative evidence originated from 'the time when Aboriginal laws and manners were as yet undisturbed by the advent of our settlers'.[53] He made a similar argument against Dawson's 'chiefs', which he insisted did not exist in pre-contact Indigenous culture. Curr implied that only an educated gentleman with early experience of the Aborigines 'in their savage state' was qualified to undertake a major work of ethnography. He thought, no doubt, that similar qualifications were advisable in the realm of Aboriginal policy. Among Curr's key rivals, only Dawson had experienced the Port Phillip District in the 1840s. Smyth, Howitt and Fison were all about a decade younger than Curr and had arrived in Victoria during the Gold Rush – they were the 'new chums' who had so irritated Curr when he returned to Melbourne in 1854.[54] Diane Barwick has argued that both Curr and his friend Le Souëf 'despised the liberal views of 1850s immigrants like Smyth and Howitt'.[55] Howitt had sat on the 1877 Royal Commission that rejected Curr's plan to close Coranderrk.[56] Curr and Smyth were briefly aligned as members of the protection board, but Curr later blamed Smyth (among others) for the embarrassment he experienced over Coranderrk.[57] Dawson was clearly no 'new chum', but he too had a different vision for Aboriginal destiny in his capacity as a local Guardian of Aborigines, as evidenced in his submissions to the Royal Commission. In this context, it is important to note that Curr's scholarly rivalries were mirrored in the realm of Aboriginal administration.[58] *The Australian Race* provided Curr with a platform to assert his own credentials and to promote his own contentious views on the destiny of Australia's Indigenous people.

---

52   Curr 1886, vol 1: 105.
53   Curr 1886, vol 1: 126.
54   Curr 1883: 450–451.
55   Barwick 1984: 103.
56   Royal Commission on the Aborigines (1877).
57   Barwick 1984: 103.
58   Corris 1972: 35–36.

11. 'My sable neighbours'

Curr's ethnological endeavours had been triggered by his interest in the language of the Bangerang people, whose lands he had occupied while squatting in the 1840s. He waited, however, until the final section of *The Australian Race* (Volume 3, 'Book the Twenty-Third') to advance his theory as to why the Bangerang language differed so markedly from those of surrounding tribes. He suggested that the circumstance was 'both unusual and worthy of notice, and could not fail to have been the result of something uncommon in the past history of the population of those parts'.[1] Curr argued that the Bangerang people and their neighbours belonged to separate waves of Aboriginal migration. To help his reader visualise this process, he highlighted Bangerang territory in red on his map in volume 4. His more detailed explanation of Bangerang origins built on a similar argument that he had mounted in volume 2 regarding the origins of the so-called 'Darling Tribes', which is worth outlining briefly. Curr related a foundation narrative prevalent among the tribes of the lower Darling River, which had been recorded by a Commissioner of Crown Lands, C.G.N. Lockhart, in about 1852:

> It is to the effect that in the far past a Blackfellow, whose name I have not learnt, arrived on the banks of the Darling, which was then uninhabited. He had with him two wives, named Keelpara and Mookwara. These two Eves of the Darling Adam, as Mr. Lockhart calls him, bore their lord children, and in due time the sons of Mookwara took as wives the daughters of Keelpara, and their children inherited Keelpara as their class-name; and the sons of Keelpara married the daughters of Mookwara, and their children bore Mookwara as their class-name.

Curr observed that Lockhart's report agreed with the evidence of language and custom that he had collated: 'Of the correctness of these traditions I feel no doubt'.[2] As to the reasons for the foundational journey of the 'Darling Adam' and his two wives, Curr guessed that he had probably committed a crime punishable by death in his tribe of origin (perhaps the theft of his two wives) and had therefore escaped to remote and unoccupied territory.

Curr's elaborate but compelling explanation for the origins of the 'Darling Tribes' was supported by both Aboriginal tradition and his own comparative analysis of language and custom. It provided a useful model for a more speculative solution to the puzzle of Bangerang origins. Unlike the Darling example, however, Curr did not build on Bangerang oral tradition, but relied solely on a linguistic

---

1 Curr 1886, vol 3: 568.
2 Curr 1886, vol 2: 165–166.

argument. He noticed several similarities between the Bangerang language and a language spoken more than 1,000 kilometres away at 'Mungalella Creek' in south-west Queensland:

> From these circumstances and a general knowledge of the ways of the race, I am led to conjecture that, as in the case of the Darling tribes, [see Vol II, p 166] the progenitors of the Bangerang were a party of young men, who, finding themselves without wives, absconded (possibly from Mungalella Creek) with some of the young women whom the old men had monopolized. That, in order to evade pursuit, the young people travelled on over many a mile of unknown country until they reached that expansion of the Murray called Moira, where they located themselves, and where we found their descendants living. That long (perhaps a century or two) after they had settled in that locality and spread to the Goulburn, and increased and broken up into several tribes, which spoke distinct dialects, they were overtaken by the general wave of population, which for ages had been evermore rolling south across the whole width of the continent; that the newcomers, as they advanced, occupied the country on every side of the Bangerang, hemmed them in, and peopled all the lands they found untenanted, and at last completed the occupation of the continent.[3]

The theories Curr mounted regarding the origins of both the Darling and Bangerang tribes reveal his confidence in the explanatory power of comparative philology. Given what we now know, however, about the great antiquity of Aboriginal society in Australia, it is hard to view Curr's arguments as more than speculation. Inferences based on linguistic affinity, while conceivable within a biblical timescale, are difficult to sustain over a history of tens of thousands of years. Curr's paradigm also assumes a linear, orderly and fixed process of migration, where once a tribe is established in a particular location it remains there, only spreading due to overcrowding or young males absconding with wives. Moreover, Curr's scheme does not allow for the influence on culture and language of trade and communication between tribes in the long period after occupation of the continent was complete.

Aside from his conjecturing about the origins of the Bangerang people, Curr's account of their manners and customs in *The Australian Race* is relatively short. He offers a good explanation for this brevity: 'having described their manners in a former work, it will be unnecessary to go into the subject here'.[4] The former work was, of course, *Recollections of Squatting in Victoria*, published a few years earlier. In his memoir Curr had stressed his extensive early knowledge of the Bangerang, while also recognising that his scientific interest developed at a much later period:

---

3   Curr 1886, vol 3: 569; a similar explanation can be found in Curr 1883: 305.
4   Curr 1886, vol 3: 568.

> I knew well every member of the tribe, besides something of their language, wars, alliances, and ways of thinking on most subjects, but still it is a matter of regret with me now that I did not, when I had the opportunity, make myself acquainted with several matters concerning which science of late years has become interested.[5]

Short descriptions of Bangerang custom appear at appropriate points in the general narrative of *Recollections of Squatting in Victoria*, but Curr also included a 77-page chapter titled 'The Bangerang Tribe'; it is more akin to a standard ethnography, although the predominantly light-hearted and entertaining tone of the book still prevails. For this reason, it is important to draw a distinction between Curr's two principal written works. Curr conceived *The Australian Race* as a scientific project, even if he recognised his limited experience in ethnology. While his methodology might be questioned and his ideological preoccupations exposed, *The Australian Race* remains, nonetheless, a scholarly work. In contrast, *Recollections of Squatting in Victoria* is more often ironic, playful or irreverent than it is scholarly and serious. It is first and foremost a diverting memoir, which frames its descriptions of Aboriginal people in a predominantly nostalgic tone.

All of the passages from Curr that were quoted by Justice Olney in his *Yorta Yorta* judgement are found in *Recollections of Squatting in Victoria*. This was the principal yardstick against which legitimate Yorta Yorta tradition was measured. A detailed critique of the ethnographic content of his memoir is therefore essential, if Curr's role in the *Yorta Yorta* case is to be properly understood. Deborah Bird Rose, an anthropologist who assisted the Yorta Yorta in their claim, suggested shortly after the case that Curr 'contextualised his observations within the imperial genre of the gentlemanly account of the native'.[6] She did not condemn Curr's account of the Bangerang as wholly inaccurate; rather, she advocated a nuanced and critical reading of his text, which recognised the genre in which Curr was writing. In his memoir, Curr positioned himself as a product of civilised British bourgeois culture, in contrast to his 'savage' neighbours who are routinely classified according to the standard tropes of colonial observation: the lazy native, the feckless native, the instinctive native, the wasteful native, the superstitious native, the brutal native, the patriarchal native or the ungoverned native. It is worth considering some examples of how these tropes play out in Curr's text.

In a statement that anticipated a key theme in *The Australian Race*, Curr recalled that he did not observe 'anything resembling government' among the Bangerang. Despite this assertion, Curr proceeded to describe a formal system of

---

5   Curr 1883: 230–231.
6   Rose 2002: 44.

hearing grievances at a tribal level and the application of a 'penalty sanctioned by custom'. Later, when he described the Bangerang custom of discussing 'public affairs' during or after the evening meal, Curr noted:

> As regards such discussions, writers *who have not lived in the bush*, and acquired a personal knowledge of the Blacks and their manners, frequently describe in a circumstantial way, and as a thing well known, a council of old men, somewhat on the *Patres conscripti* pattern, who deliberate in company, and indeed govern the tribe. As a fact, however, as far as I could learn, nothing of the sort existed amongst the Bangerang. Usually, when matters of general interest were pending, it was the custom for anyone who chose, to harangue the camp.[7]

So, while Curr recognised structures of social organisation among the Bangerang, he resisted likening them to 'government' as he understood the term. On the question of traditional laws he gave some ground: 'though there was no government, there were certain important practices among the Bangerang which deserve to be called laws'.[8]

The Bangerang, according to Curr, lacked another crucial marker of a civilised society: 'Religious worship the Bangerang had none'. Curr observed that the Bangerang believed in a 'powerful spiritual being' characterised by its malevolence, which Curr believed had wrongly been equated with the Devil of Christian belief. He added that the Bangerang believed firmly in the existence of ghosts and that their spiritual world was characterised by superstitions such as a 'dread of being caught in a whirlwind, and other fancies of the sort'.[9] Curiously, although Curr was inclined to belittle the spiritual beliefs of the Bangerang, elsewhere in his book he describes in detail his brother Charles' apparent encounter with a ghost: 'My brother, to the day of his death, continued to believe firmly that what he saw that night was a ghost – in which I am inclined to agree with him'. Curr anticipated scepticism from his reader and invited him 'to smile if he likes', but he concluded by suggesting that 'a belief in the supernatural is as constant in the human mind as the instinct of self-preservation'.[10]

Another important trope that is evident in Curr's account of the Bangerang is his assertion of a rigid patriarchy. He focussed on the apparent brutality of the Bangerang marital union and the supremacy of the male in all matters: 'In domestic life the man was despotic in his own mia-mia or hut; that is, over his wife, or wives, and such of his children as had not relinquished parental protection'.[11] Characterising Indigenous gender relations in this way served

---

7 Curr 1883: 257, emphasis in the original.
8 Curr 1883: 244–245.
9 Curr 1883: 274–275.
10 Curr 1883: 160–161.
11 Curr 1883: 247–248.

to justify dispossession. And yet, Curr also recognised the sexually aggressive role of the former convicts who staffed the pastoral stations: 'we know that [Aborigines] had constantly very serious charges to advance against shepherds, in connection with their conduct towards the females of the tribe.'[12] Curr offered this as a general observation and did not relate it to his own experience, but the diary of George Augustus Robinson suggests that Curr's shepherds were no exception to the rule: 'Mr. Curr said the Pinejerines [Bangerang] never had venereal until one of his men brought it and gave it to seven women and they gave it to the rest'.[13]

Curr characterised gender relations on the frontier in such a way that asserted his own civilised identity. In contrast to the 'savage' Bangerang, and indeed his ex-convict shepherds, Curr appears, as Rose puts it, like 'a knight in shining armour who will rescue native women from the hardships of life with native men'.[14] We might compare Curr's account of the apparently subservient Bangerang wife to the brief mention he makes of his own wife in a family memoir:

> Finding in my experience, that interference on the part of the husband in little domestic concerns, frequently leads to discontent on the part of the wife, I made it my rule from the beginning that my wife should be supreme mistress in my house.[15]

The contrast Curr draws between gender roles in British and Bangerang society is surprisingly rigid and raises questions as to underlying cultural motivations. Rose argues that Curr and others like him were principally concerned with constructing their own gentility: 'they are writing about themselves first and foremost, and their audience, first and foremost, is a set of like minded gentlemen.'[16] The implications of this bias are significant, as Clare Land has recognised: 'Curr appears blind to Koori women's cultural and political power, consistently focussing on men's culture, work, skills and authority while denigrating those of women'.[17]

Curr's account of the Bangerang was regularly expressed in a negative relation to the genteel white society with which he identified. Thus, when describing Bangerang forms of greeting and personal intimacy, Curr explained: 'Neither kissing, shaking hands, nor any other salutation of the kind was in use amongst the tribe, though frequently men of different tribes made exchanges of arms or articles of dress in token of goodwill'.[18] Curr was not unobservant, and was

---

12 Curr 1883: 120.
13 G.A. Robinson, Sunday 26 March 1843, in Clark 2000, vol 3.
14 Rose 2002: 41–44.
15 Edward M. Curr, 'Memoranda Concerning Our Family' (1877), SLV, MS 8998.
16 Rose 2002: 40.
17 Land 2002: 7.
18 Curr 1883: 268.

able to apprehend the meaning of behaviours not present in his own culture; nevertheless, he frequently defined Bangerang custom in opposition to his own culture, which was always implicitly (and often explicitly) marked as superior. Moreover, Curr's account of the Bangerang conveys a prevailing mood of curiosity; a fundamental aim was to describe exotic, inexplicable and peculiar elements of Bangerang culture.

In the concluding pages of his account of the Bangerang, Curr offered praise for many attributes he credited to his former neighbours: a 'tenacious' memory; a 'personal courage … decidedly above par'; a 'remarkable' ability to navigate in the bush; and a cheerful temperament — 'Fun is a ready passport to his goodwill'.[19] Curr stressed, however, that admirable Aboriginal skills were innate and instinctive, rather than reasoned or logical. The ability to 'find his way about the bush' was, wrote Curr, 'more akin to instinct than to reason' and comparable to a similar ability in cattle. Because Curr could not perceive the methods of Bangerang navigation, he assumed that the ability was 'born with him in embryo'; he was unable to attribute it to cultural knowledge passed from one generation to the next. Similarly, he concluded: 'As regards courage … the white man has more resolution, and the black-fellow better nerve'. While Curr attributed many positive traits to an instinctive nature, he stressed that the Bangerang man was inferior to his 'civilized brother' in 'cultivation, morality, generosity, gratitude, truthfulness, steadfastness, perseverance, industry, and the power of long-continued labour.'[20]

Despite the racial differences Curr perceived, he regularly described himself as a friend of the Bangerang. He recounted a reunion with several young men, years after he had left Tongala: 'they received me with the most enthusiastic expressions of goodwill … in fact, there was nothing they would not do for me'.[21] In the absence of contemporary Bangerang accounts, which might serve to corroborate Curr's view, it is worth considering Curr's strong motivation to portray his relationships with the Bangerang in this way. Obviously, Curr's apparently strong friendship with the Bangerang immediately implies their dispossession was not resented and was therefore justifiable. Furthermore, the appearance of friendship serves to establish Curr's authority as an Aboriginal administrator. Crucially, Curr wrote his account during a period when his policies as an Aboriginal administrator were strongly criticised and eventually rejected. Curr's constant references to his 'sooty friends' or his 'sable companions' also served to bolster his authority as an ethnologist. Finally, Curr's account of his relationship with the Bangerang is symptomatic of a shallow nostalgia that permeates his book.

---

19 Curr 1883: 294–298.
20 Curr 1883: 296, 298.
21 Curr 1883: 269–270.

Imperialist Nostalgia

Recollections of Squatting in Victoria is a good example of what Renato Rosaldo has dubbed 'Imperialist Nostalgia'.[22] On the one hand, Curr's narrative displays a clear understanding of the ways in which the pastoral economy destroyed the way of life of Aboriginal people. On the other hand, his book includes passages that lament the loss of Bangerang culture and the passing of his 'sooty friends'. Curr, like so many colonists, attributed the decline of Aboriginal people to the expansion of British 'civilisation', which he viewed as an inexorable process. Certainly, Curr recognised his principal reason for occupying Bangerang lands, noting that for most of the 1840s 'money-making went on swimmingly';[23] and yet, by employing a racialised discourse he was able to deflect any sense of wrongdoing on his part. Consequently, his nostalgic regret at the loss of an ancient culture seems shallow in hindsight.

A defining characteristic of imperialist nostalgia is that it routinely deflects personal responsibility for the decline of a colonised people. Referring to the two Bangerang clans that frequented his stations, Curr noted that during his ten years at Tongala 'a large and steady decrease took place in their numbers' from about 200 to 80.[24] Curr's use of the passive voice is illustrative: it obscures the fact that Bangerang mortality was, in one way or another, caused by the British invasion. Elsewhere, Curr gives a valuable account of the devastating effects of the pastoral occupation. His unwavering sense of racial superiority is clearly behind his comparative honesty on the issue of Aboriginal mortality; yet it did not inhibit his sense of nostalgic regret at the 'passing' of the Bangerang.

Curr claimed that during his decade of squatting 'but two individuals fell by the gun' and he attributed the Bangerang decline primarily to disease. He did, however, argue that disease was more prevalent than it might have been due to the demoralising effect of his own occupation:

> after my settlement in their country, the Bangerang gave up in great measure their wholesome and exhilarating practices of hunting and fishing, and took to hanging around our huts in a miserable objectless frame of mind and underfed condition, begging and doing trifling services of any sort.[25]

This change in lifestyle, suggested Curr, increased the Bangerang's susceptibility to disease. It is not an unreasonable assertion, but there is a misleading implication here that the Bangerang chose to abandon their healthy lifestyle.

---

22 Rosaldo 1989.
23 Curr 1883: 379.
24 Curr 1883: 235.
25 Curr 1883: 235.

This is despite the fact that, elsewhere, Curr recognised the ruinous effect of sheep grazing on traditional food sources.[26] He also described the process by which the Bangerang learnt that, if they chose to eat his sheep, they would be shot at or imprisoned.[27] In another passage Curr suggested that 'a certain listlessness and want of interest in life which sprung up under the pressure of our occupation had perhaps something to do with the reduction of the tribe.'[28] Here Curr admitted the significant effect of his occupation of Bangerang land, but he also implied a passive Bangerang response to the new colonial regime.

Curr regularly justified his invasion by characterising the Indigenous economy as unsophisticated and inefficient. He took great delight in describing the charming simplicity of Indigenous life, which he always contrasted with the complex ways of the British invaders. After recounting in fine detail the production of a bark canoe, Curr compared the Bangerang approach to boat building with that of the white man:

> The first, arriving at a stream, with the aid of a stone tomahawk provides himself in half-an-hour with a boat – frail and perishable, no doubt, but sufficient for the occasion, and passes over; whilst the white man, checked for the time, sits down deliberately, and after a long delay produces an article of wood or iron which may serve him for years.[29]

Although Curr expressed admiration for the skills of the boat builders, he nonetheless implied that the Bangerang method was less sophisticated compared to the efficient and forward thinking British way. Similarly, he argued that individual self-sufficiency among the Bangerang was a sign of their lack of civilisation. He noted that specialisation was not common: 'Each Black was master of everything known or performed by his tribe … no one ever got another to make a shield, climb a tree, or spear a fish for him'. For Curr such a state of affairs revealed a lack of economic development: 'They used often to joke [with] me and say that I could make neither a gun, nor a tomahawk, nor sugar, nor flour, nor anything else'.[30]

Curr's implication of primitive behaviour, according to a late nineteenth-century understanding, served to justify dispossession and define it as inevitable. Invasion also appeared more reasonable to the colonising mind if it could be shown that Indigenous people were wasteful or feckless in their use of natural resources. When describing the fishing practices of the Wongatpan, Curr noted that fish were so abundant that very little work was required to

---

26   Curr 1886, vol 1: 103.
27   Curr 1883: 190–206.
28   Curr 1883: 236.
29   Curr 1883: 89.
30   Curr 1883: 265.

keep the people fed: 'I often wondered how that sage people managed to pass their time before my party came and taught them to smoke.'[31] Importantly, by focussing on the plentiful supply of food, Curr characterised Bangerang life as simplistically appealing, but also provided an economic justification for invasion. For Curr, the Bangerang possessed enviable natural resources, but did not use them productively for the advancement of their society. Not only did they lack agriculture, but 'they never abstained from eating the whole of any food they had got with a view to the wants of the morrow.'[32]

In most of his nostalgic reminiscences Curr focussed on the apparent harmony of Bangerang life during the period immediately following his arrival. He did not quite replicate a 'noble savage' ideal in his descriptions, but he certainly tempered his disdain for certain 'savage' practices with a general belief that Bangerang society functioned in a healthy and harmonious way. He noted the 'simple sort of etiquette' that governed social interaction and stressed the bonds of friendship among the Bangerang: 'it always seemed to me that the bonds of friendship between blood relations were stronger, as a rule, with savages than amongst ourselves.' Reflecting his gendered approach, Curr suggested that Bangerang women quarrelled more, which he attributed to their not being related as they married into neighbouring clans. An overtly condescending tone characterises Curr's observations on these matters. Immediately following his compliment regarding Bangerang bonds of friendship, Curr is ironically nonchalant in his description of violence between women: 'Their little disagreements were settled with their yam sticks, without much injury being done, their husbands interfering with their clubs if matters went too far'.[33]

In a classic example of imperialist nostalgia, Curr wrote of the Bangerang: 'I believe that, on the whole, the blackfellow in his wild state suffered less and enjoyed life more than the majority of civilized men'.[34] Crucially, this observation reveals that Curr's nostalgic admiration for the Bangerang applied principally to the tribe in its 'savage' state. He regularly noted the corrupting effect of contact with the white invaders, such as in the following description of Aboriginal weapons:

> Their arms were wonderful productions, when it is remembered they were wrought with stone implements, pieces of shell, bone, &c.; and it is remarkable that, though their fabrication was enormously facilitated by the iron tools they got from us, they fell off in beauty, and got to have a sort of slop look about them.[35]

---

31 Curr 1883: 240.
32 Curr 1883: 262.
33 Curr 1883: 264, 274.
34 Curr 1883: 298.
35 Curr 1883: 279.

Curr also noted that the Bangerang tended to grow 'corpulent' when living with the whites, which was very rare 'in their wild state'.[36] The ideal of Aboriginality that Curr nostalgically admired was thus untouched by white influence. This is evident in Curr's recollection of the first corroboree he observed in 1842, which 'was gone through in a very different spirit from the tame exhibitions got up by our broken-spirited tribes during the last thirty years or more'. Curr observed that there was 'but a faint resemblance between the corroborees danced by the savage in his wild and subdued state' and insisted that after 1842 he never again saw a corroboree 'danced more successfully'.[37]

Curr exhibited a curious sort of respect for what he viewed as the authentic Aboriginal man: 'the blackfellow has decidedly something of the gentleman about him, when out of the reach of drunkenness and town influences.' He even implied that this gentlemanly status placed the traditional Bangerang man above the white labourer in the social world of the frontier:

> Like the gentleman reduced by circumstances to the necessities of menial service, he [the Bangerang man] was a good deal bullied by the white labourer, who lost no opportunity of asserting his superiority over him; whilst, on the other hand, he was generally treated by the educated squatter with a familiarity which argued something of equality, and in which the white labourer never shared.[38]

Ultimately, of course, Curr's nostalgic admiration for the pre-contact Aboriginal 'gentleman' paradoxically served to justify poor treatment of those Aborigines who survived. Curr expressed simple admiration for the 'wild' Aborigines, but disdain for the 'corrupted' and 'subdued' survivors; in doing so, he created an illusion of sympathetic understanding while simultaneously providing a permanent justification for the pastoral occupation. Invasion became almost a self-fulfilling prophecy.

Australian settler colonial endeavour relied fundamentally on land acquisition. While Indigenous labour was often utilised, it was not always essential to the success of the pastoral industry.[39] The abject lives of idle and dispirited Aboriginal survivors represented a challenge to the righteousness of the British colonies in Australia; they provided an ongoing reminder of the realities of invasion and dispossession. By characterising as dichotomous the 'wild' Aborigine and the 'subdued' Aborigine, Curr created a disjuncture between the traditional owners of the Australian continent and those Aborigines who remained; thus any challenge to the legitimacy of British sovereignty was stifled.

The best explanation for the internal logic of imperialist nostalgia, at least in Curr's version of it, is his routine assertion that Australian Aborigines were a childlike

---

36 Curr 1883: 287–288.
37 Curr 1883: 139–140.
38 Curr 1883: 298–299.
39 Wolfe 2001.

people. Curr wrote that the mind of the 'Australian savage' appeared 'to grow but little after twenty'. Furthermore, while he exhibited 'a latent capacity, moral and intellectual', there was little chance of this being developed: 'To cultivate this capacity to the highest standard would, no doubt, require time – perhaps a century or two – and favourable circumstance'.[40] Curr's nostalgic yearning for the Bangerang made sense because he viewed them with the same sentimental paternalism commonly applied to children in his own culture. In this way, he was able to reconcile the apparent charm and appeal of the Bangerang with the fact that he 'unceremoniously' dispossessed them. Ultimately, by recalling with fondness the 'sable companions' of his youth, Curr obscured his central role in the decimation of a people. This is perfectly illustrated by a passage from the closing pages of *Recollections of Squatting in Victoria*:

> But my pages are coming to an end, and I must have done with my sooty friends and their ways, of which I have, perhaps, said more than enough. So adieu, my Enbena, for I cannot even now, amidst the din of the city, forget thee, friend of my lone days. In truth, many a time when weary of books, with nothing to fill the vacant hour, right glad was I to see thee coming over the little plain at Thathumnera, with lubra, picaninni, and all thy belongings; to count with thee thy hunting spoil and listen to thy budget of small news, even though thou heldest an empty pipe somewhat prominently before me, or pressed on me thy longing for a share of the contents of my flour-bags. Many a time, too, I was glad to have thee as a companion in hunting and shooting, for a merry fellow thou wert, and a genial scamp! But our civilisation has rolled over thee, my Enbena, somewhat rudely since those times; ending alike, for the most part, thy merry ways and thy rascalities. Of thy tribe scarce one is left. Forest and swamp know thee no more. Adieu! Let the cry of the *jāāring** hurrying to the Murray to drink at sundown, and the loud laugh of the *wigilōpka*† from the towering river-gum, be thy memento; thy monument the lone *malōga*‡ grave, or the grass-grown oven which smokes no more; and the west wind, whistling through the streaming boughs of the oak, the dirge of a people who have passed away!
>
> * Cockatoo.   † Laughing Jackass.   ‡ Sandhill.[41]

Of course, Curr's euphemistic conclusion that 'our civilisation has rolled over thee' was his own nineteenth-century version of the 'tide of history', a problematic metaphor made famous by Justice Olney in his *Yorta Yorta* judgement.

---

40   Curr 1883: 292–293.
41   Curr 1883: 435–436.

12. The Tide of History

The publication of *The Australian Race* was Curr's last major achievement. On 3 August 1889 he died at Alma House and was buried alongside his wife in the St Kilda Cemetery. He had retired from his position as Chief Inspector of Stock only a few days earlier. In appreciation of Curr's outstanding service to the colony's pastoral industry, the Victorian Parliament voted him nine months' salary. His estate was valued at over £2,600 and was bequeathed entirely to his eldest son.[1] Using these funds, E.M.V. Curr consolidated his property 'Murrumbogie', near Trundle, New South Wales – by 1890 he owned over 5,000 acres of freehold land, most of which remains in the Curr family's possession to this day.[2]

Following Curr's death lengthy obituaries appeared in several Australian newspapers.[3] Unsurprisingly, they focussed on his professional achievements as Chief Inspector of Stock, hailing his successful program for eradicating scab from the Victorian flocks. His father's key role in achieving Victoria's separation from New South Wales also attracted considerable comment. One of the few observations about Curr's personal attributes appeared in the *Sydney Mail*: 'Those who knew him best regarded him as a good, earnest, honest man'.[4] Of Curr's published works, *Pure Saddle Horses* and *The Australian Race* were viewed as the most significant, while *Recollections of Squatting in Victoria* attracted little comment. Similarly, in his 1888 survey of *Victoria and its Metropolis*, Andrew Sutherland reserved special praise for Curr's ethnological writings: he certainly recognised the value of *Recollections of Squatting in Victoria* and its 'graphic account of the life of the early pioneers', but described *The Australian Race* as 'the most complete and judicious account ever given to the world in reference to this fast-vanishing race'.[5] Sutherland predicted that it would 'attain to an always increasing reputation'. As it turned out, Sutherland was wrong: in the fast-evolving discipline of anthropology Curr's ethnological work was quickly superseded. Increasingly, it was Curr's vast collection of ethnographic data that attracted the most praise, not his attempt to interpret this data.

As we have seen, *The Australian Race* created considerable controversy when it was first published, as ethnological rivals defended their own positions in response to Curr's bold criticisms. The most notable of these was A.W. Howitt, who responded to Curr in two articles, one of which was published in the

---

1   Edward M. Curr, Wills and Probate: PROV, VPRS 28/P2, Units 266, 494, Item 40/072; VPRS 7951/P2, Unit 150, Item 40/072.
2   Curr 1979: 69.
3   See, for example, *Australasian, Leader, Sydney Mail*, all on 10 August 1889.
4   Obituary: Edward M. Curr, *Sydney Mail*, 10 August 1889: 286.
5   Sutherland 1888: 502.

journal of the Anthropological Institute in London.[6] It seems likely that Howitt's influence ensured *The Australian Race* was not reviewed in the institute's journal; alternatively, James Dawson's scathing letter to the secretary of the Aborigines Protection Society, which was forwarded to the institute, might have exerted an influence.[7] A review of *The Australian Race* did appear in the journal of the Royal Geographical Society, written by the society's secretary John Scott Keltie, who briefly noted the value of Curr's work as an empirical resource: 'Mr. Curr states in his introduction that he has not made ethnology a study. There is, however, much fact (requiring sifting, no doubt) in these volumes, and little theory'.[8] Like W.H. Flower of the Anthropological Institute, who had reviewed Curr's work before publication, Keltie saw Curr's contribution primarily as a fact-gatherer.

In 1899 Spencer and Gillen dedicated their landmark work on *The Native Tribes of Central Australia* to Howitt and Fison, 'who laid the foundation of our knowledge of Australian anthropology'. In it they disputed Curr's view that Aboriginal society lacked a meaningful form of government; otherwise, their only mention of Curr was his description of sub-incision as 'the Terrible Rite', a term they thought 'may well be discarded'.[9] Five years later A.W. Howitt published *The Native Tribes of South-East Australia* (1904), in which he once again drew attention to Curr's errors regarding Aboriginal kinship terminology. He prefaced his comments with an observation of broader relevance to the difficulties of ethnological research:

> In order to grasp the true nature and bearing of the classificatory system of relationships, it is necessary not only to free oneself from misconceptions, as to the universal use of our own system, but also to have such an acquaintance with the nature of a savage as to be able to put oneself mentally into his place, think with his thoughts, and reason with his mind; unless this be done, the classificatory system will be a delusion and a snare.

Howitt insisted that a prevalent ignorance of kinship systems was 'strongly brought out in the late Mr. E. M. Curr's work' and cautioned his reader to use *The Australian Race* with care: 'It greatly detracts from the usefulness and value of Mr. Curr's work that he did not make himself aware of the native system of relationships'.[10]

---

6   Howitt 1891: 30–104.
7   James Dawson to F.W. Chesson, Secretary of the Society for the Protection of Aborigines, 11 November 1887, State Library of New South Wales, MLDOC 1747.
8   Keltie 1888: 254.
9   Spencer and Gillen 1899: 15, 263.
10 Howitt 1904: 157–158.

Not all of Curr's Australian contemporaries were so critical. In *Eaglehawk and Crow* (1899) John Mathew significantly revised Curr's theories regarding both Aboriginal racial origins and routes of migration, but he explained that he had been 'compelled by the logic of facts' to reject the conclusions of '[his] friend Mr. Curr'. He stressed that he was 'specially indebted' to Curr's work and referred often to *The Australian Race* in mounting his own theories.[11] As noted, Curr had published Mathew's account of the Kabi in *The Australian Race*, but had prefaced it with a back-handed compliment that attributed its fullness to Mathew's 'love of ethnological studies' rather than the 'ripe knowledge which results from long experience'.[12] Nevertheless, Mathew clearly retained some respect for Curr, who had mentored him during his early ethnological studies, and with whom he shared an interest in comparative philology.[13] The prolific anthropologist R.H. Mathews was also less critical than Howitt or Spencer. In an article in the *Journal of the Anthropological Institute* in 1896 he described *The Australia Race* as a 'valuable work', while two years later in *American Anthropologist* he quoted Curr regularly and with a level of trust not shared by some of his contemporaries.[14]

An ambivalent attitude to Curr is also evident in the international scholarly networks of the early twentieth century. The German ethnologist Fritz Graebner, who was interned in Australia during World War I, considered *The Australian Race* to be 'so worthless a book' that he chastised the sociologist Edward Westermarck for even quoting it. Westermarck resisted such prejudice, deferring to the assessment of his student Bronislaw Malinowski that Curr had 'especially good opportunities' to observe Aboriginal custom first hand. In his 1913 study of *The Family Among the Australian Aborigines*, Malinowski often cited Curr; in fact, he expressed more suspicion regarding the work of Howitt and Spencer, who, he suggested, did not adequately explain 'the way in which they obtained their information'.[15]

For much of the twentieth century the discipline of anthropology in Australia was associated with A.P. Elkin, who occupied the chair of anthropology at the University of Sydney from 1933. Elkin's assessment of Curr is worth considering in some detail. In *The Australian Aborigines* (1938) Elkin did not cite Curr directly, but he included *The Australian Race* in a recommended reading list at the back of his volume. Significantly, however, Curr was grouped in the category 'Older Books: Compilations' along with such contemporaries as Smyth and Taplin. In contrast, Howitt, Spencer and Mathew were included in

---

11 Mathew 1899: ix–x.
12 Curr 1886, vol 3: 120–121.
13 Prentis 1998: 76–77.
14 Mathews 1896: 145–163; Mathews 1898: 325–343.
15 Westermarck 1921: 13; Malinowski 1913: 22–23.

the category 'Older Books: The Classics'.[16] Ronald and Catherine Berndt later followed Elkin's lead, suggesting that Curr's key contribution was the wealth of material he compiled.[17] In 1938 Elkin had also edited a volume titled *Studies in Australian Linguistics*, in which he assessed the collected vocabularies of Curr and Smyth: 'Careful sieving reveals some material of value, but they are very inadequate. They tell us so little about the language, and almost nothing about its part in the culture as a whole'.[18] The pioneering Australian linguist A.A. Capell was similarly ambivalent, noting Curr's significant early contribution but stressing that he had 'no phonetic system at all'.[19] In the middle part of his career Elkin apparently placed little value on Curr's interpretive ability. Shortly after his retirement, however, Elkin moderated this stance and concluded that Curr deserved a more prominent place in the history of his discipline. During a presidential address to the Anthropological Society of New South Wales in 1958, Elkin insisted that Curr and similar contemporaries 'were not merely collators and editors', but contributed their own views and theories and (importantly) had 'gathered some of their information at first hand'.[20]

In his eighties Elkin published a two-part article in *Oceania*, the main purpose of which was to grant the prolific R.H. Mathews due credit for his remarkable but often-overlooked career.[21] Significantly, however, Elkin also included Curr in his list of the ten 'founders of social anthropology in Australia'. Elkin expressed gratitude that Curr had collected ethnographic data on such a broad scale, as 'most of the tribes concerned were already dying out in the 1880s'. More significantly, however, he added that Curr deserved recognition for 'his ethnological and theoretical study of the Aborigines, their language, culture and origin'. Although Elkin disputed Curr's narrow assumptions regarding cultural diffusion, he nonetheless took Curr's contribution seriously. Moreover, he praised Curr's 'critical discussion of marriage rules' and applauded his critique of Fison's theoretical approach to Aboriginal marriage custom. Describing Fison's research as 'positive and stimulating, but ... of the arm-chair variety', Elkin saw value in the fact that Curr personally collected at least some of his data. Moreover, Curr's preference for facts over theory had exposed many flaws in Fison's analysis. Elkin noted that Curr 'like many non-academics, was biased against such theorising', but insisted that Curr's critique was not superficial: 'We cannot but appreciate Curr's insight'. Following Malinowski, Elkin commended Curr's 'arithmetical proof' that James Dawson could not be correct in his assertions regarding 'the tribal chief and the number of his wives, children and attendants'. Finally, Elkin concluded that Curr 'had greater personal experience and sound observation

---

16 Elkin 1938b: 389.
17 Berndt and Berndt 1964: 537.
18 Elkin 1938a: 9.
19 Capell 1963: 151.
20 Elkin 1958: 226.
21 Elkin 1975; Thomas 2011: 83.

[of Aboriginal society] than possibly any other investigator up to his time'. One might speculate that nearly two decades after his retirement Elkin thought it was time to give proper recognition to the important early role of untrained amateurs like Curr, even if their influence was not as great as the towering figures of Howitt and Spencer.[22]

A Sympathetic Observer?

The republication of *Recollections of Squatting in Victoria* in 1965 introduced Curr's engaging prose to a new generation of readers and scholars in a period when interest in Australian history was growing. Widely available in libraries and written in accessible and lucid language, Curr's memoir quickly became a standard source, prompting the historian Marie Fels to describe it as 'almost a sacred text, with considerable power over the present'.[23] A common assumption in this period was that Curr was unusually sympathetic to Aboriginal people. This view derived from several nostalgic passages in Curr's own memoir, but certainly overlooked his prominent role in Aboriginal administration, where he pursued a policy of strict discipline for 'childlike' Aborigines. In his introduction to the 1965 abridged edition of *Recollections of Squatting in Victoria*, the schoolteacher and local historian Harley W. Forster wrote that Curr was 'one of the more sensitive participators in the birth of a colony'.[24] Reviewing Curr's memoir the following year, Russel Ward took a similar view, arguing that 'our ancestors were not uniquely wicked – or ignorant'.[25] To demonstrate his point, Ward quoted a passage from Curr's memoir:

> But notwithstanding many differences between the Black and the White man, their sympathies, likes, and dislikes were very much what ours would have been if similarly situated; so that a very limited experience enabled both parties to understand and appreciate the position of the other. This fact only gradually dawned on me, as I had somehow started with the idea that I should find the Blacks as different from the White man in mind as they are in colour.[26]

Ward not unreasonably concluded that Curr showed more empathy than many of his contemporaries, but by implying a marked sympathy for Aboriginal people he painted a simplistic picture. The same is true of Harley Forster's

---

22   Elkin 1975: 12–15.
23   Fels 1988: 159.
24   Forster 1965a: vii.
25   Russel Ward, 'An early study of Black and White', *Sydney Morning Herald*, 15 January 1966.
26   Curr 1883: 93 quoted in Ward 1966.

1969 entry for Curr in the *Australian Dictionary of Biography* (ADB), which has undoubtedly bolstered the credibility of Curr's writings on Aboriginal people. Forster's account featured the following conclusion regarding Curr's legacy:

> His portrayal of station life in the western Goulburn Valley and his work on the Aboriginals of Victoria are of merit. His approach to these people, now almost extinct, and to his fellow squatters reveals sympathetic understanding, and his writings increase the knowledge of early Victoria.[27]

By neglecting to mention Curr's role in Aboriginal administration, Forster and the ADB certainly missed an opportunity to provide a fuller account of his attitude to Aboriginal people.[28] Biographical dictionaries are an important resource for scholars engaged on broader projects: they have the potential to shape dominant views of individuals and to influence how significant historical texts are interpreted. This certainly seems to have been the case with Curr's entry in the *Australian Dictionary of Biography*, as many have accepted its broad conclusion regarding Curr's sympathetic understanding of Aboriginal people. As recently as 2004 the *Oxford Dictionary of National Biography* published a new account of Curr's life written by the historical geographer J.M. Powell, who further exaggerated Curr's concern for Aborigines: 'His later works are highly valued for their atypically sympathetic approach to the indigenous peoples'.[29]

Curr's role in Aboriginal administration suggests that his reputation for sympathy towards Aboriginal people requires reassessment and careful qualification. A related and arguably more important consideration is the extent of Curr's authority as an observer of Aboriginal custom. In *Triumph of the Nomads* (1975) Geoffrey Blainey described Curr as 'one of the sharpest observers of tribal life'.[30] With the rise in popularity of Aboriginal history in the 1980s a more complicated picture began to emerge. Some scholars continued to see considerable value in Curr's work, particularly his ethnological magnum opus *The Australian Race*. Henry Reynolds, for example, praised Curr's general overview of frontier violence, while Noel Butlin admired Curr's theories about Aboriginal population decline.[31] Meanwhile, the anthropologist and pioneer of Aboriginal history Diane Barwick began to pay closer attention to Curr's forgotten role in Aboriginal administration. She identified his leading part in the attempt of the Board for the Protection of Aborigines to close the Coranderrk

---

27 Forster 1969: 508.
28 It should be noted that the editor of the *Australian Dictionary of Biography* altered Forster's conclusion prior to its publication. An earlier draft read: 'The approach to his fellow squatters and to the aborigines shown in his writings was *generally* one of sympathetic understanding' (emphasis added). See the ADB file for Curr: 'Curr, Edward (1820–1889)', Australian National University Archives, ANU A 312, Box 153.
29 Powell 2004.
30 Blainey 1975: 97.
31 Reynolds 1982: 50; Butlin 1983: 129.

reserve and relocate its discontented residents. In particular, she drew attention to the evidence Curr gave to a Royal Commission on Aborigines in 1877 and a parliamentary inquiry in 1881, when he likened Aboriginal people to children or lunatics.[32]

Unlike earlier critics, Barwick identified the political and ideological dimensions of Curr's work.[33] Drawing a link between his ethnographic writings and the repressive regimes he advocated for Aboriginal people, she encouraged a more critical view of Curr than had previously been common. Others in the field of Aboriginal history, such as Marie Hansen Fels, soon expressed similar reservations about Curr's influence.[34] As a postcolonial view of Australia's past became more common, scholars increasingly began to question the underlying motives of those who wrote about Aboriginal people. This all came to a head following the *Yorta Yorta* native title case, when anthropologists, historians and legal scholars mounted a sustained scholarly critique, both of Curr writings on Aboriginal people, and of the way these writings were utilised in the *Yorta Yorta* case.

Edward M. Curr and the Yorta Yorta case

The *Yorta Yorta* native title case was one of the first to be heard by the Federal Court of Australia following the landmark Mabo judgement of 1992 and the *Native Title Act* of 1993. It was an important test case for native title law. Commencing in October 1996, the court sat for 114 days and heard from 211 witnesses. On 18 December 1998 Justice Howard Olney concluded that 'the tide of history has indeed washed away any real acknowledgment of their traditional laws and any real observance of their traditional customs'.[35] Many critics quickly disparaged Justice Olney's choice of words: one asked, 'Tide of History or Tsunami?'; while others suggested that the unsuccessful claimants were 'Awash in Colonialism'.[36] David Ritter has traced the genealogy of the 'tide of history' metaphor, noting its prevalence in religious, philosophical and historical discourse. In the Australian context, he cites A.W. Howitt as a notable proponent, who wrote of the 'tide' of settlement 'breaking the native tribes with its first waves and overwhelming their wrecks with its floods'.[37] For a similar metaphorical representation of the apparently inexorable process of

---

32 Barwick 1984: 100–131; Barwick 1998.
33 Barwick 1984: 103; Barwick 1998.
34 Fels 1988: 159.
35 *Members of the Yorta Yorta Aboriginal Community v Victoria* (1998) FCA 1606, [129].
36 Case 1998: 17–19; Kerruish and Perrin 1999: 3–8.
37 A.W. Howitt, quoted in Ritter 2004: 114.

colonisation, Ritter might also have looked to Edward M. Curr, who lamented the destruction of Aboriginal society in his 1883 memoir: 'our civilisation has rolled over thee ... somewhat rudely since those times'.[38]

The *Yorta Yorta* case demonstrated the important role of historical inquiry within the native title process: to establish the nature of the traditional laws and customs in which native title rights reside; and to decide if claimants have appropriately and continuously exercised those rights. As Ritter astutely observed, 'if applicants do not "win the historiography," they will lose the case'.[39] Consequently, historical methodology underpins many of the fundamental debates surrounding native title. A significant theme in these debates is the extent to which legal and historiographical standards diverge. This has led to a wealth of scholarship inquiring into the relationship between history and the law, and indeed, other relevant disciplines.[40] Edward M. Curr has loomed large in many of these discussions. During a cross-disciplinary conference of native title practitioners held in 2000, Curr's posthumous role in the *Yorta Yorta* case was a common point of reference in the wider debate.[41]

Many critics noted the extent to which the *Yorta Yorta* judgement privileged written evidence.[42] Ben Golder, for example, characterised Justice Olney's historiographical technique as 'prioritising the specious neutrality of the written word over the tendentious malleability of the oral'.[43] Justice Olney had argued that 'evidence based on oral tradition passed down from generation to generation does not gain in strength or credit through embellishment by the recipients of the tradition'. Moreover, he stated that an 'unfortunate aspect' of the Yorta Yorta evidence in the case was 'frequent, and in some instances, prolonged, outbursts of what can only be regarded as ... righteous indignation'. In contrast he concluded that Curr 'clearly established a degree of rapport with the local Aboriginal people and subsequently published two valuable works dealing with his experiences'. Following this reasoning, Justice Olney concluded that 'less weight should be accorded to [Yorta Yorta oral evidence] than to the information recorded by Curr'.[44] Although the judge's scepticism of oral history is not entirely misplaced, it must equally be recognised that written accounts such as Curr's, when republished or cited in historical articles and books, neither 'gain in strength or credit' as a result. Intelligent and nuanced

---

38 Curr 1883: 435–436.
39 Ritter 2002: 81.
40 Paul and Gray 2002; Toussaint 2004; Curthoys, Genovese and Reilly 2008.
41 Toussaint 2004: 3.
42 Pitty 1998: (41)–61; Finlayson 1998: 85–98; Kerruish and Perrin 1999; Choo 2004: 198.
43 Golder 2004: 51.
44 *Yorta Yorta v Victoria* (1998), [14, 21, 53, 106].

historical inquiry requires an appreciation of the strengths and weaknesses of oral history; similarly, however, a healthy scepticism of written evidence will help avoid the naïve simplicity of narrow-minded empiricism.

Edward M. Curr's written works fitted neatly into the particular historiographical framework with which Justice Olney was familiar. In *Rights and Redemption: History, Law and Indigenous Peoples*, Ann Curthoys, Ann Genovese and Alexander Reilly describe in detail the discipline of 'legal history' and identify its key points of divergence from wider historiographical practice.[45] They astutely observe that the law has not only a particular view of how historians study the past, but also 'an autonomous historical methodology of its own'. Legal history is 'a specific genre of history writing', routinely taught in law schools and pervasive in its influence on how lawyers perceive history more generally. The purview of legal history is circumscribed; it maps the development of sovereign law using the written sources that constitute its canon. Furthermore, the relationship between sovereign law and the society it governs are outside the scope of traditional legal history, which is 'internal' in its focus. The legitimate evidence of traditional legal history is thus both abundant and contained, in stark contrast to the diverse and sparse historical evidence often presented in native title cases. Curthoys, Genovese and Reilly explore the implications of this 'juridical frame' on various cases involving Indigenous peoples. They suggest that despite fruitful inter-disciplinary collaboration in the native title era the decisions of Australia's major courts continue to promote a narrow view of historiography that is typical of traditional legal history. They also report a pervasive mistrust of the historian as an expert witness, which has hampered a meaningful dialogue between history and the law surrounding the evidence used in native title courts. The role of Curr in the *Yorta Yorta* case is a clear example of how this common judicial approach to history differs from wider historiographical practice, particularly as it concerns Indigenous peoples.

Justice Olney's Use of Curr

Justice Olney assumed that Curr's written account was largely free from the bias he attributed to the oral testimony of the Yorta Yorta people. He stated that he was 'conscious of the need to avoid assuming the role of historian' but also rejected the contribution of various expert witnesses, whose evidence he found unhelpful.[46] As a result he concluded that 'the Court must have resort to

---

45 Curthoys, Genovese and Reilly 2008: 138–143.
46 *Yorta Yorta v Victoria* (1998), [26].

such credible primary evidence as is available and apply the normal processes of analysis and reason'.[47] These 'normal processes' appear, however, to be a poor guarantee of historical truth.

Justice Olney's most obvious error was his inadequate recognition of the lapse of time between Curr's years as a squatter and the publication of his memoir. For example, he misleadingly equated 'the recorded observations' of Curr and the Chief Protector of Aborigines, George Robinson.[48] There are fundamental differences between the written works of these two men: Robinson wrote his diaries in the 1840s and, in Justice Olney's own words, 'made no attempt to collate or interpret' the 'many details' that he recorded; in contrast, Curr wrote his book nearly four decades later, when he compiled a nostalgic memoir for the general entertainment of a British colonial readership. For Justice Olney, Robinson's journal was 'extremely hard to decipher', while Curr 'published two valuable works dealing with his experiences'.[49] It is clear that Justice Olney gauged the relative value of Curr and Robinson's writings by their clarity of written expression, rather than their likely accuracy. As a result, he readily accepted the nostalgic recollections of a squatter who had dispossessed the claimants, while shunning the unedited, day-to-day journal of a man whose job it was to observe Aborigines and to record ethnographic details.[50] Although Justice Olney recognised that Curr was 'not averse to a degree of speculation', he was confident he could distinguish Curr's speculation from 'his record of his own observations' simply by analysing the texts presented to him.[51] He did this, however, without the aid of historical and biographical context, which would have helped him to identify those moments when Curr's recollections distort the truth through selective presentation of material, through a failing memory, through nostalgia, not to mention through cultural bias.

In part, Justice Olney's reliance on Curr was motivated by a belief that he was sympathetic to the Aboriginal people he encountered. This view has been pervasive in Australian historiography, as we have seen, but by characterising Curr as a sympathetic pastoralist, Justice Olney glossed over Curr's status as a primary dispossessor of the Yorta Yorta people. For example, he wrote in his judgement: 'Even Curr, who generally enjoyed a good relationship with the indigenous people, on establishing an outstation on the northern side of the Murray had his shepherds attacked and sheep driven off'.[52] This is a curiously one-sided reference to an extended conflict between Curr and the Bangerang people in 1842–43, which resulted in the spearing of 200 of Curr's sheep,

---

47 *Yorta Yorta v Victoria* (1998), [62].
48 *Yorta Yorta v Victoria* (1998), [54].
49 *Yorta Yorta v Victoria* (1998), [53].
50 Pitty 1998: 48–49.
51 *Yorta Yorta v Victoria* (1998), [106].
52 *Yorta Yorta v Victoria* (1998), [34].

12. The Tide of History

the arbitrary murder by border police of a Bangerang man, the wounding of Captain Dana (Commander of the Native Police Corps) during a reprisal raid, and the subsequent imprisonment and farcical trial of the supposed Aboriginal 'ringleader'. In the 1880s Curr recounted this tale with some regret, but also with humour and irony.[53] As has been shown, however, the contemporary record paints a clearer picture of the dispute over land that was at the heart of the conflict.

Having judged Curr 'the most credible source of information concerning the traditional laws and customs' of the Yorta Yorta people, he proceeded to present a literal reading of several passages from *Recollections of Squatting in Victoria*.[54] In a discussion of 'Traditional Laws and Customs', for example, Justice Olney quoted in full Curr's recollection of 'purchasing' a portion of country from a young boy for a stick of tobacco:

> I recollect, on one occasion, a certain portion of country being pointed out to me as belonging exclusively to a boy who formed one of the party with which I was out hunting at the time. As the announcement was made to me with some little pride and ceremony by the boy's elder brother, ... I not only complimented the proprietor on his estate, *on which my sheep were daily feeding*, but, as I was always prone to fall in with the views of my sable neighbours when possible, I offered him on the spot, with the most serious face, a stick of tobacco for the fee-simple of his patrimonial property, which, after a short consultation with his elders, was accepted and paid. (Emphasis in original)[55]

In writing this passage, Curr aimed to amuse his readers by belittling the system of land tenure of his 'sable neighbours'. It reveals, first and foremost, a confident man armed with an Enlightenment discourse that justified (in his eyes) the theft of Indigenous land. For Justice Olney, Curr's passage constituted an important source of evidence regarding the nature of traditional Yorta Yorta land ownership: as the judge strangely put it, 'a useful basis from which to proceed'.[56]

Justice Olney quoted several more passages from Curr's memoir, which portray Aboriginal people in a predictably stereotypical way, but which the judge viewed as transparent evidence of traditional Yorta Yorta custom. He accepted at face value Curr's assertions regarding traditional gender roles: that the Bangerang man was 'despotic in his own mia-mia or hut' and closely controlled

---

53   Curr 1883: 193–206.
54   *Yorta Yorta v Victoria* (1998), [106].
55   Curr 1883: 243–244; quoted in *Yorta Yorta v Victoria* (1998), [111].
56   *Yorta Yorta v Victoria* (1998), [110].

the lives of his wife and daughters.[57] Indigenous women have condemned this deference to Curr: Monica Morgan observed that Justice Olney 'determined from a one liner from Curr that we were patrilineal'; similarly, Marcia Langton argued that the *Yorta Yorta* judgement perpetuated the gender bias inherent in Curr's account.[58] A more sophisticated analysis would recognise that Curr was writing in a gentlemanly genre, which routinely justified white bourgeois male privilege by pointing to the apparent delicacy of British gender relations compared to the 'savage' natives. Thus Curr's assertion of gender subservience among Bangerang women served implicitly to justify British patriarchy and, indeed, the colonial project itself.[59]

Portraying Aborigines as feckless and wasteful was another common way of justifying colonial invasion. In a crucial part of his judgement, Justice Olney quoted a passage from Curr's book, which suggested that traditional Yorta Yorta people were profligate in their use of natural resources:

> It is a noteworthy fact connected with the Bangerang, … that as they neither sowed nor reaped, so they never abstained from eating the whole of any food they had got with a view to the wants of the morrow. … So, also, they never spared a young animal with a view to its growing bigger. … I have often seen them, as an instance, land large quantities of fish with their nets and leave all the small ones to die within a yard of the water.[60]

After quoting this passage Justice Olney contrasted a modern Yorta Yorta practice with the wastefulness Curr described. Several Yorta Yorta witnesses had explained that conservation of food resources was 'consistent with traditional laws and customs' and that 'only such food as is necessary for immediate consumption' was taken from the land. In relation to these claims, Justice Olney concluded: 'This practice, commendable as it is, is not one which, according to Curr's observations, was adopted by the Aboriginal people with whom he came into contact and cannot be regarded as the continuation of a traditional custom'.[61]

The judge's reasoning on this issue helps create the view that evolution in Indigenous custom undermines native title in law. Even if Curr's charge of wastefulness is accepted as an accurate account of Bangerang custom during the 1840s, it remains perfectly believable that Yorta Yorta tradition later evolved to include conservation measures. Curr himself noted the abundant food supply

---

57   *Yorta Yorta v Victoria* (1998), [114]; see also Curr 1883: 247–249.
58   Morgan and Muir 2002: 9; Langton 1998: 109.
59   See Grimshaw and May 1994: 94.
60   Curr 1883: 262–263; quoted in *Yorta Yorta v Victoria* (1998), [115].
61   *Yorta Yorta v Victoria* (1998), [123].

enjoyed by the Bangerang in the early 1840s.[62] He also described the subsequent decimation of traditional food resources brought about by pastoralism.[63] In other words, Curr described a compelling motive for changes to Indigenous custom, which might explain the apparent disjuncture between the customs described by Curr and those of the Yorta Yorta claimants. If a tradition of sustainable environmental management evolved after (and in response to) British invasion, it is no less valid a tradition. Moreover, a literal reading of Curr's claim of fecklessness is problematic in itself. Deborah Bird Rose has argued that 'the evolutionary theory that the savage is only partially separated from nature … runs through Curr's work in a way that is so predictable as to be laughable'.[64] She rightly suggests that taking every word of Curr's book at face value is a dangerous historiographical approach.

Justice Olney's uncritical acceptance of Curr's writings indicates the extent to which the written word, granted special status as legal evidence, creates particularly devastating effects in native title proceedings. In his *Yorta Yorta* judgement Justice Olney posited Curr as the only acceptable evidence regarding the nature of traditional Yorta Yorta culture in the 1840s; he then consulted written evidence from the missionary Daniel Matthews as to the nature of local Indigenous culture in the 1870s. He concluded: 'The evidence is silent concerning the continued observance in Matthews' time of those aspects of traditional lifestyle to which reference is made in the passages quoted from Curr'.[65] The judge erred by viewing the writings of Curr and Matthews as transparent windows on historical reality. Moreover, he formed concrete conclusions about historical change based on highly selective and narrowly focussed documentary evidence. He presented two accounts of Yorta Yorta custom, both written by white men, and observed a disjuncture. It is a remarkably unimaginative and empirically flawed historical methodology, which has had a significant impact on subsequent native title jurisprudence.

The Appeal Courts

The Yorta Yorta claimants twice appealed the result of their native title claim, but both the full bench of the Federal Court and the High Court upheld Justice Olney's decision.[66] A key argument of the claimants was that Justice Olney had

---

62 Curr 1883: 240.
63 Curr 1886, vol 1: 103.
64 Rose 2002: 41.
65 *Yorta Yorta v Victoria* (1998), [118].
66 *Members of the Yorta Yorta Aboriginal Community v Victoria* (2001) 110 FCR 244 (FCA Black CJ, Branson and Katz JJ), Black CJ dissenting. *Members of the Yorta Yorta Aboriginal Community v Victoria* (2002) 214 CLR 442; 194 ALR 538; 77 ALJR 356 (HCA Gleeson CJ, Gaudron, McHugh, Gummow, Kirby, Hayne and Callinan JJ), Gaudron and Kirby JJ dissenting.

applied a 'frozen in time' test to Yorta Yorta tradition: that he had required present day Yorta Yorta tradition remain largely unchanged from pre-colonial times for native title to survive. Pursuing this line of argument Ron Castan QC told the Federal Court in 1999: 'There is no image of the Aborigine standing on the hill with a spear against the sunset that conditions the exercise of the native title jurisdiction'.[67] When making this remark, Castan might easily have had in mind one of Curr's nostalgic recollections of his 'sable companions'.[68]

Although the appeal courts rejected the 'frozen in time' argument, the dissenting judge in the first appeal case, Chief Justice Black, engaged in a meaningful way with pertinent issues of historical methodology. He recognised that to discern evolution in traditional law during a period of great change a broad view of history is necessary, warning that 'danger lies in what might be termed the historical snapshot of adventitious content, which may in any event reveal little or nothing of a process of adaptation and change then taking place'.[69] Chief Justice Black also defended the value of oral evidence and stressed the need 'to take fully into account the potential richness and strength of orally-based traditions as well as the inherent difficulties'. Moreover, he emphasised the danger of relying too strongly on written accounts such as Curr's *Recollections of Squatting in Victoria*:

> It is necessary too, to bear in mind the particular difficulties and limitations of historical assessments, not least those made by untrained observers, writing from their own cultural viewpoint and with their own cultural preconceptions and for their own purposes.[70]

Chief Justice Black was clearly looking for a way to accommodate Indigenous perspectives within the native title framework, but his views found little support at the High Court. In a joint judgement, Justices Gleeson, Gummow and Hayne rejected the view that Justice Olney implicitly privileged written evidence, arguing that he 'no doubt took account of the emphasis given and reliance placed by the claimants on the writings of Curr'.[71] In a separate judgement, Justice Callinan explicitly rejected Chief Justice Black's criticism and noted that the Yorta Yorta were disadvantaged by their 'lack of a written language'.[72] Justice Callinan also reasserted Justice Olney's suspicion of Yorta Yorta oral testimony:

---

67   Ron Castan QC, 19 August 1999, *Yorta Yorta v Victoria*, Full Court Appeal, quoted in Seidel 2004: 72.
68   See, for example, Curr 1883: 435–436.
69   *Yorta Yorta v Victoria* (2001), Black CJ, [59].
70   *Yorta Yorta v Victoria* (2001), Black CJ, [55].
71   *Yorta Yorta v Victoria* (2002), Gleeson CJ, Gummow and Hayne JJ, [63]. Lawyer for the Yorta Yorta Peter Seidel has disputed this view, arguing that Justice Olney favoured written evidence both 'explicitly' and 'inferentially'; see Seidel 2004: 73.
72   *Yorta Yorta v Victoria* (2002), Callinan J, [190].

human experience knows, [it] is at risk of being influenced and distorted in transmission through the generations, by, for example, fragility of recollection, intentional and unintentional exaggeration, embellishment, wishful thinking, justifiable sense of grievance, embroidery and self-interest.[73]

Clearly, the potential sources of corruption outlined above by Justice Callinan apply equally well to Curr's written text, with the possible exception of a 'justifiable sense of grievance'. Despite this, Justice Callinan strongly defended Justice Olney's reliance on Curr, and pointed to 'four relevant advantages' in Curr's account, one of which was the absurd claim that Curr had 'nothing to gain from his accounts' of Aboriginal people.[74] Curr's descriptions of Aboriginal people are deeply imbedded in a genre of colonial observation that contrasts the primitive 'savage' with the civilised British invader; they provide a philosophical justification for the theft of Aboriginal land and a rationale for the repressive colonial regimes that Curr championed as an Aboriginal administrator. In essence, Justice Callinan argued that Curr had 'nothing to gain' and simultaneously pointed to the 'self-interest' of the Yorta Yorta claimants; this is an overtly discriminatory approach, which also reveals a clear inability to interpret historical sources.

All of this leads to the conclusion that the decision of the courts in the *Yorta Yorta* case rests on a deeply flawed historiography. As the first native title case to go to court, the *Yorta Yorta* case was a major challenge – not only for the judiciary, but for all those involved in the native title process. Furthermore, the claim was characterised by an engagement between lawyers and historians, which was previously uncommon. Ultimately, the role of Curr in the *Yorta Yorta* case is symptomatic of fundamental differences between legal and historiographical approaches to studying the past.

History and Native Title

Following Justice Olney's *Yorta Yorta* judgement, many scholars advocated a more prominent role for historians as expert witnesses in native title cases.[75] It seemed clear to many, however, that the native title courts could not wholly accommodate the historian's craft. The situation was summarised nicely by Deborah Bird Rose, who argued that in the *Yorta Yorta* case 'scholarship collided with adversarial cross examination'.[76] It is perhaps inevitable that historical and

---

73   *Yorta Yorta v Victoria* (2002), Callinan J, [143].
74   *Yorta Yorta v Victoria* (2002), Callinan J, [155].
75   Ritter 1998: 7–8; Finlayson and Curthoys 1997.
76   Rose 2002: 35.

legal discourses will clash in this way. For several decades most historians have embraced the complexity and ambiguity that surrounds their scholarly pursuits. Conversely, lawyers and judges are wary of historical theories that undermine certainty, simply because the legal system is predicated on a commitment to factual findings. Curthoys, Genovese and Reilly described this disjuncture eloquently: 'where the courts must decide on one account being true, historians can and do live with alternative possible and competing accounts'.[77]

The historiographical flaws in the *Yorta Yorta* judgements might be seen as mirroring a more general malaise in the native title process of the early twenty-first century; specifically, the difficulties of reconciling ambiguity in historical understanding with strict legalism. Reilly and Genovese have argued that 'the law suffers from the illusion of a determinate past', which can be accessed objectively by consulting 'reliable' evidence.[78] Such a view presents a difficult dilemma regarding the usefulness of historians to the native title process, but it also has potential implications for the practice of history more generally. David Ritter has noted the 'reductionist' effect of native title on Aboriginal history: 'If the historiography is reduced to "they have it or they don't," then a more nuanced historiography, self-critically exploring the ambiguities of the past, will not develop'.[79] Importantly, such an environment affects not only the study of Aboriginal history, but also militates against a nuanced reading of Edward M. Curr's life. Sophisticated historical inquiry might, therefore, be irretrievably incompatible with the discourse of native title. Curr's role in the *Yorta Yorta* case revealed that the courts were reluctant to approach historical evidence critically, preferring to consider the written text as akin to a witness and, as Rose puts it, 'to find the truth but without the aid of cross-examination'.[80] Such an approach will always favour the written word over an oral account; this in turn promotes a deeply problematic view of the past and greatly disadvantages the majority of claimants in native title cases.

---

77 Curthoys, Genovese and Reilly 2008: 17.
78 Reilly and Genovese 2004: 36.
79 Ritter 2002: 81.
80 Rose 2002: 37.

Epilogue: 'The Ghost of Edward Curr'

Following the High Court decision in the *Yorta Yorta* case, a group of the claimants proclaimed that 'the Ghost of Edward Curr' had come back to haunt them.[1] An Indigenous playwright, Andrea James, subsequently developed this idea in a play titled *Yanagai! Yanagai!* – a theatrical exploration of her people's struggle for land justice.[2] James dramatised a memorable passage from Curr's *Recollections of Squatting in Victoria*, in which Curr recalled his first encounter with a Wongatpan fishing party in 1842.[3] In *Yanagai! Yanagai!* an ancestral spirit, Munarra, pursues the 'Ghost of Curr' and confronts him about his invasion of Yorta Yorta lands. Her conversations with Curr's ghost are juxtaposed with scenes from the native title case, where an insensitive barrister prevents Yorta Yorta people from explaining their cultural heritage during cross-examination. The implication is that Curr's invasion of Yorta Yorta lands and the decision of the High Court 160 years later are two parts of the same process of dispossession.

A ghost by definition transcends death. If Edward M. Curr achieved such a feat it was through his writing. When Russel Ward wrote a review of *Recollections of Squatting in Victoria* in 1966 he argued:

> Curr's name ... will be honoured by posterity more than those of his fellow pastoralists or even public service chiefs and politicians. He was more interested in life and people than in money or success, and he left us several books which are among the best of their kind written about important aspects of colonial life in the past century.[4]

Notwithstanding Ward's specious conclusion that Curr was indifferent to 'money or success', he correctly identified Curr's status in Australian historiography. He undeniably left a significant literary legacy. The empirical value of *Recollections of Squatting in Victoria* is severely undermined, however, if the social, cultural, political and philosophical views of its author are not adequately understood. Importantly, just as a ghost is disembodied from its terrestrial predecessor, Curr's book has developed a life of its own, apparently distinct from the man who wrote it. In legal historiography in particular, a tendency to consider the meaning of written documents as self-evident, without any consideration of context, has had profound implications on dominant understandings of Australia's past. This was illustrated very clearly by the role of Curr's writings in the *Yorta Yorta* case.

---

1 Fergus Shiel, 'Claim sunk by pen of a swordsman', *Age*, 13 December 2002.
2 James 2003.
3 Curr 1883: 176–179. See also Chapter 4 of this publication.
4 Russel Ward, 'An early study of Black and White', *Sydney Morning Herald*, 15 January 1966.

Figure 28: Edward M. Curr (c.1880).

Photograph courtesy of Ian G. Curr.

Curr regularly employed the trump card of bush experience to assert his authority in Aboriginal administration, in ethnology, and as a chronicler of the early history of the Port Phillip District. His pastoral experiences are, of course, a key reason why his work is so valuable to historians; but they also point to a major deficiency in his account, particularly as it concerns Aboriginal custom. Curr was integrally involved in the first phase of settler colonial endeavour, which involved the dispossession of Aboriginal people. His account of past events unsurprisingly affirms the righteousness of the colonial project and his own involvement in it. Curr's ethnographic account of the Yorta Yorta ancestors is deeply problematic because of his role as an invader of their lands.

In his New Zealand letters of 1855–56, Curr expressed quite clearly his attitude to colonial land acquisition.[5] He adhered to a Lockean view of private property, which immediately dismissed the legitimacy of Aboriginal land ownership. Curr enthusiastically entered into a colonial argument about productive land use, during which Indigenous land rights did not even feature; for Curr, such considerations were self-evidently irrelevant. It is not surprising that his only brief mention of Bangerang land tenure in *Recollections of Squatting in Victoria* involves his ironic 'purchase' of a part of his squatting run for a stick of tobacco.[6]

Recollections of Squatting in Victoria is shaped in a variety of ways by Curr's life experiences. For example, his nostalgia for the 1840s makes considerable sense when the overall trajectory of his life is understood. The wealth and social status of the Curr family reached a peak in 1850, when Edward Curr senior was proclaimed the 'Father of Separation' in the newly independent Colony of Victoria. Following the death of their father, Edward M. Curr and his brothers inherited a vast squatting empire comprising 300 square miles of prime pastoral land, but as Curr related in his private family memoir, his own personal wealth was all but lost by 1861. Despite his subsequent and successful public service career, it hardly seems surprising that Curr would look back favourably on the profitable 1840s. Importantly, in *Recollections of Squatting in Victoria* Curr was able to emphasise his pastoral successes, rather than his dismal failure on the Lachlan River when all his cattle died during a drought.

Curr's memoir evinces a form of imperialist nostalgia, whereby the path of settler colonialism is marked as inexorable. His own complicity in the decimation of Indigenous society is deflected in the many passages where he expresses regret at the passing of his 'sable companions'. Passages of this type have often prompted historians to argue that Curr was atypically sympathetic to Aborigines, but such an argument does not pay adequate attention to the wider context of his life. The official record of Curr's involvement in Aboriginal administration exposes

---

5   Curr 1856; see also Chapter 5 of this publication.
6   Curr 1883: 243–244.

the ideological preoccupations that shaped his descriptions of Aboriginal people. He was stubbornly committed to a policy of long-term incarceration for surviving Aborigines, whom he argued should be treated like 'children' or 'lunatics'. Advocating supreme authority for the Board for the Protection of the Aborigines, he rejected the emerging view of the 1880s that the Aboriginal race might be assimilated into the white population.

While Curr's biases must be considered and his authority on many topics questioned, it does not follow that *Recollections of Squatting in Victoria* should be discarded by historians. In so many ways, Curr's book offers an insight into early colonial Australia that is crucial to historical study: his detailed descriptions of landscape, his engaging anecdotes, and his humorous characterisation of the social world of the frontier are all of immense worth. Even his descriptions of Indigenous people remain valuable if used intelligently. Deborah Bird Rose, in her criticism of the *Yorta Yorta* judgement, suggested that it is possible to read between the lines of Curr's writings:

> One can set aside his evaluative tropes, examine his observations for probable truth value, and provide an ethnographic account of what he saw that takes into account the culture and social organisation of the people involved.[7]

Curr's books clearly need to be critiqued with care. Contextualisation of written sources is the essence of the historian's craft, but has not adequately been integrated into native title jurisprudence.

Curr's great skill as a writer elevated his status as an historical observer, while his engaging prose discouraged critical analysis of his writings. His influence on Australian historiography and native title illustrates clearly the unbridled power of written language in Western epistemology, a power captured neatly in 2002 by the *Age* headline: 'Claim sunk by pen of a swordsman'. The headline provided an appropriately figurative concluding remark for a native title case seemingly defined by metaphor. The story of Edward M. Curr, his life and legacy, is a compelling demonstration of how Western cultural knowledge and systems of law are embedded in a written discourse that disadvantages Indigenous peoples.

Encouragingly, the potential for written accounts to grow disproportionately in authority was recognised by Chief Justice Black in his dissenting judgement in the first *Yorta Yorta* appeal:

---

7   Rose 2002: 44.

The dangers inherent in giving particular authority to the written word, and more authority when it is repeated, need to be borne constantly in mind as well. The phenomenon of repetition strengthening authority is, of course, a familiar one, to be found in other areas of scholarship.[8]

Chief Justice Black's unique judgement provided hope that Australian native title law might, in the future, consider historical practice in a more nuanced way and recognise that written sources are not unproblematic. Only then might native title achieve something approaching its potential for redemptive justice within the Australian settler colonial state.

Edward M. Curr concluded *Recollections of Squatting in Victoria* with a quote from Lord Byron's epic poem *Lara*.[9] It seems appropriate to end this book with a passage from the same poem, which eloquently expresses the power of the written word to shape dominant understandings of the past. Byron describes the return of his brooding hero to his kingdom after a long exile. As Lara enters his ancestral halls, he views the superficially plausible signs and relics of the past:

> He turn'd within his solitary hall,
> And his high shadow shot along the wall;
> There were the painted forms of other times,
> 'Twas all they left of virtues or of crimes,
> Save vague tradition; and the gloomy vaults
> That hid their dust, their foibles, and their faults;
> And half a column of the pompous page,
> That speeds the specious tale from age to age:
> When history's pen its praise or blame supplies,
> And lies like truth, and still most truly lies.
>
> Lord Byron, *Lara*, Canto I, Part XI.

---

8 *Yorta Yorta v Victoria* (2001), Black CJ, [58].
9 'Kaled, Lara, Ezzelin are gone', see Curr 1883: 452. See also Chapter 7 of this publication.

Bibliography

Archives and Manuscripts

State Library of Victoria

Curr, Edward M. 'Memoranda Concerning Our Family' (1877), MS 8998.

Curr, Edward M. Catalogue of the Library of Edward Micklethwaite Curr, [c.1830–c.1850], MS 13897.

State Library of New South Wales

'Curr Family – Papers and Station Records, 1838–1937', MLMSS 2286.

Curr, Edward M. Letter to Hyde Clarke, 8 September 1880, MLDOC 2095.

Dawson, James, Letter to F. W. Chesson, 11 November 1887, MLDOC 1747.

Public Record Office (Victoria)

PROV, VA 473 Superintendent, Port Phillip District, VPRS 19 Inward Registered Correspondence (1838–1851).

PROV, VA 475 Chief Secretary's Department, VPRS 1189 Inward Registered Correspondence I (1851–1863).

PROV, VA 475 Chief Secretary's Department, VPRS 3991 Inward Registered Correspondence II (1864–1884).

PROV, VA 914 Supreme Court of N.S.W. for the District of Port Phillip, VPRS 7952 Wills and Probate and Administration Files, 1841–1852.

PROV, VA 2624 Master in Equity, Supreme Court, VPRS 28 Probate and Administration Files, 1852–1948.

PROV, VA 2878 Crown Lands Department, VPRS 5920 Pastoral Run Files.

National Archives of Australia

NAA: CA 2013 Central Board for the Protection of the Aborigines; B314 Minutes of meetings, single number series, 1869–1957.

The National Archives of the UK

Public Record Office (PRO), CO 280/1 Colonial Office: Tasmania, Original Correspondence, Van Diemen's Land Company, 1824–5.

Public Record Office (PRO), CO 201/332 Colonial Office: New South Wales Original Correspondence, Despatches (April 1843), Item 46, 'Annual Report on the State of the Aborigines for 1842'.

Public Record Office (PRO), CO 201/334 Colonial Office: New South Wales Original Correspondence, Despatches (July-August 1843), Item 68, 'Annual Report on the State of the Aborigines for 1843'.

The Australian National University Archives

Australian Dictionary of Biography, Subject Files, ANU A 312, Box 153, 'Curr, Edward (1820–89)' and 'Curr, Edward (1798–1850)'.

Murrumbogie Papers

Privately held by Ian G. Curr, Trundle NSW 2875.

E.M.V. Curr, 'Memoir' (1872–).

Constance Curr album (c.1905).

Correspondence, Edward M. Curr to E.M.V. Curr (1883).

Elizabeth Sarah Pennefather (née Curr), 'In the Early Days' (1911).

Florence Curr, Unpublished memoir, (undated).

Mary Margaret (Margery) Curr, 'History of the Curr Family (1798–1955)' (undated).

Government Records

Conference of the Chief Inspectors of Stock for the Several Australian Colonies. 'Report, Minutes of Proceedings, Resolutions, etc.' in Victoria, *Papers Presented to Parliament by Command*, Session 1875–6, Vol 2.

Victoria. Coranderrk Aboriginal Station. 'Report of the Board appointed to enquire into, and report upon, the present condition and management of the

Coranderrk Aboriginal Station, together with the minutes of evidence', in Parliament of Victoria, *Papers Presented to Parliament by Command*, Session 1882–3, Vol 3.

Victoria. *Parliamentary Debates*, Legislative Assembly.

Victoria. Royal Commission on the Aborigines (1877). 'Report of the Commissioners … together with Minutes of Evidence,' in Parliament of Victoria, *Papers Presented to Parliament by Command*, Session 1877–78, Vol 3.

Victoria. Royal Commission on Foot and Mouth Disease (1872). 'Progress Report of the Commission, with Minutes of Evidence' in Victoria, *Votes and Proceedings of the Legislative Assembly*, 1872, 3 (58).

Victoria. Royal Commission on Foot and Mouth Disease (1872). 'Report of the Commission' in Victoria, *Votes and Proceedings of the Legislative Assembly*, 1872, 3 (76).

Legal Cases and Judgements

Commonwealth v Yarmirr (1999) 101 FCR 171 (FCA Beaumont, von Doussa and Merkel JJ)

Mabo v Queensland [No. 2] (1992) 175 CLR 1; 107 ALR 1 (HCA Mason CJ, Brennan, Deane, Dawson, Toohey, Gaudron and McHugh JJ)

Members of the Yorta Yorta Aboriginal Community v Victoria (1998) FCA 1606 (FCA Olney J)

Members of the Yorta Yorta Aboriginal Community v Victoria (2001) 110 FCR 244 (FCA Black CJ, Branson and Katz JJ)

Members of the Yorta Yorta Aboriginal Community v Victoria (2002) 214 CLR 442; 194 ALR 538; 77 ALJR 356 (HCA Gleeson CJ, Gaudron, McHugh, Gummow, Kirby, Hayne and Callinan JJ)

Newspapers

Age (Melbourne)

Argus (Melbourne)

Australasian (Melbourne)

Economist (Melbourne)

Illustrated London News

Leader (Melbourne)

New Zealand Spectator

Port Phillip Herald

Queenslander

South Australian Advertiser

Sydney Mail

The Times

Wellington Independent

Published Sources

Anderson, Warwick 2002, *The Cultivation of Whiteness: Science, Health and Racial Destiny in Australia*. Carlton, Vic.: Melbourne University Press.

Atkinson, Wayne 2000, '"Not one iota": the Yorta Yorta struggle for land justice', PhD thesis, La Trobe University.

Barwick, Diane 1984, 'Mapping the past: an atlas of Victorian clans 1835–1904', *Aboriginal History* 8, no. 2: 100–131.

Barwick, Diane 1998, *Rebellion at Coranderrk*, edited by Laura E. Barwick and Richard E. Barwick. Canberra: Aboriginal History Inc.

Berndt, R.M. and C.H. Berndt 1964, *The World of the First Australians*. Sydney: Ure Smith.

Blainey, Geoffrey 1975, *Triumph of the Nomads: A History of Ancient Australia*. South Melbourne: Macmillan.

Bland, Fred 1930–31, 'John Curr, originator of Iron Tram Roads', *Transactions (The Newcomen Society)* XI: 121–130.

Bunn, C.M., M.G. Garner and R.M. Cannon 1998, 'The 1872 outbreak of foot-and-mouth disease in Australia – why didn't it become established?' *Australian Veterinary Journal* 76, no. 4: 262–269.

Burn, David 1973, *A Picture of Van Diemen's Land*. Hobart: Cat and Fiddle Press.

Butlin, Noel 1983, *Our Original Aggression: Aboriginal Populations of Southeastern Australia, 1788–1850*. Sydney: George Allen & Unwin.

Cannon, Michael 1990, *Who Killed the Koories?* Melbourne: William Heinemann.

Capell, A.A. 1963, 'Commentary', in *Australian Aboriginal Studies: a Symposium of Papers Presented at the 1961 Research Conference*, edited by Helen Sheils. Melbourne: Oxford University Press: 149–168.

Case, Natasha 1998, 'Tide of history or tsunami?' *Indigenous Law Bulletin* 4: 17–19.

Choo, Christine 2004, 'Working as a historian on the Miriuwung Gajerrong Native Title claim', in *Crossing Boundaries: Cultural, Legal, Historical and Practice Issues in Native Title*, edited by Sandy Toussaint. Carlton: Melbourne University Pres: 195–201.

Choo, Christine and Shawn Hollbach 1999, 'The role of the historian in native title litigation', *Indigenous Law Bulletin* 4, no. 17: 7–8.

Christie, Michael 1990, 'Aboriginal literacy and power: an historical case study', *Australian Journal of Adult and Community Education* 30, no. 2: 116–121.

Clark, Ian D. (ed.) 2000, *The Journals of George Augustus Robinson, Chief Protector, Port Phillip Aboriginal Protectorate*. 6 vols. Ballarat: Heritage Matters.

Clarke, Hyde 1878, 'Himalayan origin and connection of the Magyar and Ugrian', *The Journal of the Anthropological Institute of Great Britain and Ireland* 7 (January): 44–65.

Clarke, Hyde 1879, 'On the Yarra dialect and the languages of Australia in connexion with those of the Mozambique and Portuguese Africa', *Transactions and Proceedings of the Royal Society of Victoria*.

Clendinnen, Inga 1995, 'Reading Mr. Robinson', *Australian Book Review* 170: 34–42.

Corris, Peter 1972, 'Dawson, James (1806–1900)', *Australian Dictionary of Biography*, 4: 35–36.

Curr, Edward 1824, *An Account of the Colony of Van Diemen's Land Principally Designed for the Use of Emigrants*. London: George Cowie.

Curr, Edward 1834, *Three Years Residence in Van Diemen's Land*. London: George Cowie and Co.

Curr, Edward A. 1979, *Selected Stories from the Past for My Family and Friends*. 3rd ed. Parkes, N.S.W.: E.A. Curr.

Curr, Edward M. 1853, 'A bush fire in Australia: by an Australian squatter', *The Illustrated London News*, 7 May 1853.

Curr, Edward M. 1856, *The Waste Lands of the Province of Wellington, New Zealand: In a Series of Letters*. Wellington: New Zealand Spectator and Cook's Strait Guardian.

Curr, Edward M. 1863, *Pure Saddle-Horses and How to Breed Them in Australia: Together with a Consideration of the History and Merits of the English, Arab, Andalusian, & Australian Breeds of Horses*. Melbourne: Wilson & Mackinnon.

Curr, Edward M. 1865, *An Essay on Scab in Sheep: Its Causes, Symptoms, Pathology, Best Means of Treatment, and Practical Hints for Its Avoidance and Extermination, Etc.* Melbourne: John Ferres, Government Printer.

Curr, Edward M. 1868, *Des Bêtises = Frivolities / by E.M.C.* Melbourne: H.T. Dwight.

Curr, Edward M. 1883, *Recollections of Squatting in Victoria, Then Called the Port Phillip District (from 1841 to 1851)*. Melbourne: G. Robertson.

Curr, Edward M. 1886, *The Australian Race: Its Origin, Languages, Customs, Place of Landing in Australia, and the Routes by Which It Spread Itself over That Continent*. 4 vols. Melbourne: John Ferres, Govt. Printer.

Curr, Edward M. 1965, *Recollections of Squatting in Victoria, Then Called the Port Phillip District (from 1841 to 1851)*, edited by Harley W. Forster. Abridged ed. Carlton, Vic.: Melbourne University Press.

Curr, Edward M. 1968, *Recollections of Squatting in Victoria, Then Called the Port Phillip District (from 1841 to 1851)*. 2nd ed. Adelaide: Libraries Board of South Australia.

Curr, Edward M. 2001, *Recollections of Squatting in Victoria, Then Called the Port Phillip District (from 1841 to 1851)*. 3rd ed. Echuca, Vic.: Rich River Printers.

Curr, Edward M. 1887, *Veterinary Reports on Some Diseases of Stock Found in Victoria*. Melbourne: John Ferres, Government Printer.

Curr, Frederick Carlton 1998, *The Curr Family in Far North Queensland, 1862–1925*, edited by Eleanor E. Freeman. Sydney: Eleanor E. Freeman.

Curr, John 1797, *The Coal Viewer and Engine Builder's Practical Companion*. Sheffield: John Northall.

Curr, John 1847, *Railway Locomotion, and Steam Navigation: Their Principles and Practice*. London: John Williams and Co.

Curr, John 1970, *The Coal Viewer and Engine Builder's Practical Companion, 2nd Edition, with a New Introduction by Charles Lee*. London: Frank Cass & Co. Ltd.

Curr, Rev. Joseph 1829, *Familiar Instructions in the Faith and Morality of the Catholic Church, Adapted to the Use of Both Children and Adults*. Manchester: Robinson & Co.

Curthoys, Ann, Ann Genovese and Alexander Reilly 2008, *Rights and Redemption: History, Law and Indigenous Peoples*. Sydney: University of New South Wales Press.

Dawson, James 1881, *Australian Aborigines: The Languages and Customs of Several Tribes of Aborigines in the Western District of Victoria, Australia*. Melbourne: George Robertson.

de Serville, Paul 1980, *Port Phillip Gentlemen and Good Society in Melbourne Before the Gold Rushes*. Melbourne: Oxford University Press.

de Staël, Madame (Anna-Louise-Germaine) 1995, *Delphine: Translated and with an Introduction by Avriel H. Goldberger*. DeKalb, Illinois: Northern Illinois University Press.

Dingle, Tony 1996, *Gold and the Victorian Economy During the 1850s*. Collingwood, Vic.: HTAV.

Dixon, Robert M.W. 1980, *The Languages of Australia*. Cambridge: Cambridge University Press.

Dow, Hume 1972, 'Dow, John Lamont (1837–1923)', *Australian Dictionary of Biography* 4: 93–95.

Duxbury, Jennifer 1989, *Colonial Servitude: Indentured and Assigned Servants of the Van Diemen's Land Company*. Clayton: Monash Publications in History.

Edmonds, Penelope 2006. 'The Le Souëf Box: reflections on imperial nostalgia, material culture and exhibitionary practice in colonial Victoria', *Australian Historical Studies* 37, no. 127: 117–139.

Elkin, A.P. (ed.) 1938a. *Studies in Australian Linguistics*. Sydney: Australian National Research Council.

Elkin, A.P. 1938b, *The Australian Aborigines*. Sydney: Angus and Robertson.

Elkin, A.P. 1958, 'Anthropology in Australia: one chapter', *Mankind* 5, no. 6 (October): 225–242.

Elkin, A.P. 1970, 'The Aborigines of Australia: "one in thought, word and deed"', in *Pacific Linguistic Studies in Honour of Arthur Capell*, edited by S.A. Wurm and D.C. Laycock. Pacific Linguistics, Series C No. 13. Canberra: Linguistic Circle of Canberra.

Elkin, A.P. 1975, 'RH Mathews: his contribution to Aboriginal studies: Part I: the founders of Social Anthropology in Australia', *Oceania* 46, no. 1: 1–24.

Eyre, Edward John 1845, *Journals of Expeditions of Discovery into Central Australia, and Overland from Adelaide to King George's Sound, in the Years 1840–1*. 2 vols. London: T. and W. Boone.

Fearon, Frances 1969, 'Cuningham, Hastings (1825–1908)', *Australian Dictionary of Biography* 3: 506.

Fels, Marie Hansen 1988, *Good Men and True: The Aboriginal Police of the Port Phillip District 1837–1853*. Carlton: Melbourne University Press.

Finlayson, Julie 1998, 'Sustaining memories: the status of oral and written evidence in native title claims', in *Connections in Native Title: Genealogies, Kinship and Groups*, edited by J.D. Finlayson, B. Rigsby and H.J. Bek. Canberra: Centre for Aboriginal Economic Policy Research, The Australian National University: 85–98.

Finlayson, Julie and Ann Curthoys 1997, 'The proof of continuity of native title', *Land, Rights, Law: Issues of Native Title*, no. 18.

Finn, Edmund 1888, *The Chronicles of Early Melbourne, 1835 to 1852: Historical, Anecdotal and Personal, By 'Garryowen'*. 2 vols. Melbourne: Fergusson and Mitchell.

Fisher, J.R. 2000, 'Origins of animal quarantine in Australia', *Australian Veterinary Journal* 7, no. 7: 478–482.

Fison, Lorimer and A.W. Howitt 1880, *Kamilaroi and Kurnai: Group-Marriage and Relationship, and Marriage by Elopement, Drawn Chiefly from the Usage of the Australian Aborigines: Also the Kurnai Tribe, Their Customs in Peace and War*. Melbourne: George Robertson.

Forbes, J. 1999, 'Judicial tidy-up or takeover? Centralisms next stage', *Proceedings of the Samuel Griffiths Society* 11, no. 7: 6–8.

Forster, Harley W. 1965a. 'Foreword', in *Recollections of Squatting in Victoria*, edited by Harley W. Forster. Abridged edition. Carlton, Vic.: Melbourne University Press.

Forster, Harley W. 1965b. *Waranga, 1865–1965: A Shire History*. Melbourne: F.W. Cheshire.

Forster, Harley W. 1969, 'Curr, Edward Micklethwaite (1820–1889)', *Australian Dictionary of Biography* 3: 508.

Foster, Bernard John 1966, 'Featherstone, Dr Isaac Earl (1813–76)', in *An Encyclopaedia of New Zealand*, edited by A.H. McLintock. Wellington: Government Printer.

Furphy, Joseph 1903, *Such Is Life: Being Certain Extracts from the Diary of Tom Collins*. Sydney: The Bulletin Newspaper Company.

Furphy, Samuel 2002, 'British surveyors and Aboriginal place names: New South Wales and Port Phillip, 1828–1851', in *Writing Colonial Histories: Comparative Perspectives*, edited by Tracey Banivanua Mar and Julie Evans. Melbourne: R.M.I.T. Publishing: 23–38.

Furphy, Samuel 2013, 'The Trial of Warri: Aboriginal protection and settler self government in colonial Victoria', *Journal of Australian Colonial History* (forthcoming).

Gammage, Bill 2011, *The Biggest Estate on Earth: How Aborigines Made Australia*. Crows Nest, N.S.W.: Allen & Unwin.

Gerard, Rev. John 1881, *Memorials of Stonyhurst College*. London: Burns and Oates.

Golder, Ben 2004, 'Law, history, colonialism: an orientalist reading of Australian native title law', *Deakin Law Review* 9, no. 1: 41–60.

Goodman, David 1994, *Gold Seeking: Victoria and California in the 1850s*. St Leonards, N.S.W.: Allen & Unwin.

Griffiths, Tom 1996, *Hunters and Collectors: The Antiquarian Imagination in Australia*. Melbourne: Cambridge University Press.

Hadfield, Charles 1889, *A History of S. Marie's Mission and Church, Norfolk Row, Sheffield*. Sheffield: Pawson and Brailsford.

Henderson, Andrew 1986, *The Stone Phoenix: Stonyhurst College 1794–1894*. Worthing: Churchman.

Hoare, Michael 1976, 'Smyth, Robert Brough (1830–1889)', *Australian Dictionary of Biography* 6: 161–163.

Holroyd, J.P. 1976, 'Robertson, George (1825–1898)', *Australian Dictionary of Biography* 6: 37–38.

Howitt, A.W. 1889, 'On the organisation of the Australian tribes', *Proceedings of the Royal Society of Victoria* 1.

Howitt, A.W. 1891, 'The Dieri and other kindred tribes of Central Australia', *The Journal of the Anthropological Institute of Great Britain and Ireland* 20 (January): 30–104.

Howitt, A.W. 1904, *The Native Tribes of South-East Australia*. Macmillan and Co.

Irving, Washington 1832, *The Alhambra*. Philadelphia: Carey and Lea.

James, Andrea 2003, *Yanagai! Yanagai!* Sydney: Currency Press/Playbox Theatre.

Keltie, John Scott 1888, 'New geographical publications', *Proceedings of the Royal Geographical Society and Monthly Record of Geography* 10, no. 4 (April): 250–256.

Kerruish, Valerie and Colin Perrin 1999, 'Awash in colonialism: a critical analysis of the Federal Court decision in the matter of the members of the Yorta Yorta Aboriginal Community v the State of Victoria and Ors (1998)', *Alternative Law Journal* 24: 3–8.

Kiddle, Margaret 1967, *Men of Yesterday: A Social History of the Western District of Victoria, 1834–1890*. Carlton, Vic.: Melbourne University Press.

Land, Clare 2002, 'Representations of gender in E. M. Curr's *Recollections of Squatting in Victoria*: implications for land justice through the native title process', *Indigenous Law Bulletin* 5, no. 19: 6–9.

Langton, Marcia 1998, 'Grandmother's law, company business and succession in Aboriginal land tenure systems', in *Traditional Aboriginal Society*, edited by W.H. Edwards. South Melbourne: Macmillan.

Leader, Robert Eadon 1901, *Sheffield in the Eighteenth Century*. Sheffield: The Sheffield Independent Press.

Lee, Ida (ed.) 1927, *The Voyage of the Caroline, from England to Van Diemen's Land and Batavia in 1827–28 by Rosalie Hare with Chapters on the Early History of Northern Tasmania, Java, Mauritius and St. Helena*. London: Longmans, Green and Co. Ltd.

Lennox, Geoff 1990, 'The Van Diemen's Land Company and the Tasmanian Aborigines: a reappraisal', *Papers and Proceedings (Tasmanian Historical Research Association)* 37, no. 4: 165–208.

Lucas, Percy Hylton Craig 1966, 'Land settlement', in *An Encyclopaedia of New Zealand*, edited by A.H. McLintock. Wellington: Government Printer.

Macwhirter, P.J. 1997, 'Shifting paradigms: the hard road to acceptance of the contagion principle in Australia', *Australian Veterinary Journal* 75, no. 7: 515–519.

McEvey, Allan 1975, 'Le Souëf, Albert Alexander Cochrane (1828–1902)', *Australian Dictionary of Biography* 5: 80–81.

McFarlane, Ian 2003, 'Cape Grim', in *Whitewash: On Keith Windschuttle's Fabrication of Aboriginal History*, edited by Robert Manne. Melbourne: Black Inc.: 277–298.

McGrath, Ann 2003, 'History and land rights', in *Proof and Truth: The Humanist as Expert*, edited by Iain McCalman and Ann McGrath. Canberra: Australian Academy of the Humanities: 233–250.

McGregor, Russell 1997, *Imagined Destinies: Aboriginal Australians and the Doomed Race Theory, 1880–1939*. Carlton: Melbourne University Press.

McLaren, Ian F. 1972, 'Dwight, Henry Tolman (1823? – 1871)', *Australian Dictionary of Biography* 4: 121–122.

Malinowski, Bronislaw 1913, *The Family Among the Australian Aborigines: a Sociological Study*. London: University of London Press.

Manne, Robert (ed.) 2003, *Whitewash: On Keith Windschuttle's Fabrication of Aboriginal History*. Melbourne: Black Inc.

Massy, Charles 2007, *The Australian Merino: The Story of a Nation*. Sydney: Random House.

Mathew, John 1899, *Eaglehawk and Crow: a Study of the Australian Aborigines, Including an Inquiry into Their Origin and a Survey of Australian Languages*. London: D. Nutt.

Mathews, R.H. 1896, 'The rock paintings and carvings of the Australian Aborigines', *The Journal of the Anthropological Institute of Great Britain and Ireland* 25 (January): 145–163.

Mathews, R.H. 1898, 'The Victorian Aborigines: their initiation ceremonies and divisional systems', *American Anthropologist* 11, no. 11 (November): 325–343.

Medlicott, Ian R. 1983, 'John Curr and the development of the Sheffield collieries, 1781–1805', *Transactions of the Hunter Archaeological Society* 12: 51–60.

Medlicott, Ian R. 1999, 'John Curr, 1756–1823, mining engineer and viewer', in *Aspects of Sheffield 2: Discovering Local History*, edited by Melvyn Jones. Wiltshire, Great Britain: Wharncliffe Publishing Ltd: 63–78.

Monks, Linda 1966, 'Conolly, Phillip (1786–1839)', *Australian Dictionary of Biography* 1: 241–242.

Moreton-Robinson, Aileen 2004, 'The possessive logic of patriarchal white sovereignty: the High Court and the Yorta Yorta decision', *Borderlands e-journal* 3, no. 2.

Morgan, Monica and Jan Muir 2002, 'Yorta Yorta: the community's perspective on the treatment of oral history', in *Through a Smoky Mirror: History and Native Title*, edited by Mandy Paul and Geoffrey G. Gray. Canberra: Aboriginal Studies Press: 1–10.

Morrell, William Parker 1966, 'Wakefield, Edward Gibbon (1796–1862)', in *An Encyclopaedia of New Zealand*, edited by A.H. McLintock. Wellington: Government Printer.

Moss, David J. 2004, 'Wakefield, Edward Gibbon (1796–1862)', in *Oxford Dictionary of National Biography*. Oxford: Oxford University Press.

Mott, R.A. 1969, 'Tramroads of the eighteenth century and their originator: John Curr', *Transactions: The Newcomen Society for the Study of the History of Engineering and Technology* XLII: 1–23.

Mullaly, Paul 2008, *Crime in the Port Phillip District 1835-51*. Ormond, VIC: Hybrid Publishers.

Paul, Mandy 2004, 'Reflecting on past practice: the Alice Springs Arrernte claim', in *Crossing Boundaries: Cultural, Legal, Historical and Practice Issues in Native Title*, edited by Sandy Toussaint. Carlton: Melbourne University Press: 142–151.

Paul, Mandy and Geoffrey G. Gray (eds) 2002, *Through a Smoky Mirror: History and Native Title*. Canberra: Aboriginal Studies Press.

Pike, D.H. 1966, 'Curr, Edward (1798–1850)', *Australian Dictionary of Biography* 1: 269–272.

Pink, Kerry and Gill Vowles 1998, *Against the Tide: A Maritime History of Circular Head*. Hobart: Hobart Ports Corporation.

Pitty, Roderic 1999, 'A poverty of evidence: abusing law and history in Yorta Yorta v Victoria (1998)', *Australian Journal of Legal History* 5, no. 1: (41)–61.

Plomley, N.J.B. (ed.) 1966, *Friendly Mission: The Tasmanian Journals of George Augustus Robinson, 1829–1834*. Kingsgrove, N.S.W.: Tasmanian Historical Research Association.

Powell, J.M. 2004, 'Curr, Edward (1798–1850)', in *Oxford Dictionary of National Biography*, edited by H.C.G. Matthew and Brian Harrison. Oxford: Oxford University Press.

Prentis, Malcolm 1998, *Science, Race and Faith: A Life of John Mathew*. Sydney: Centre for the Study of Australian Christianity.

Pyne, Stephen J. 1991, *Burning Bush: A Fire History of Australia*. New York: Henry Holt and Company.

Rainger, Ronald 1978, 'Race, politics, and science: the Anthropological Society of London in the 1860s', *Victorian Studies* 22, no. 1 (October): 51–70.

Reilly, Alexander 2000, 'The ghost of Truganini: use of historical evidence as proof of native title', *Federal Law Review* 28: 453–475.

Reilly, Alexander and Ann Genovese 2004, 'Claiming the past: historical understanding in Australian native title jurisprudence', *Indigenous Law Journal* 3: 19–42.

Reynolds, Henry 1989, *Dispossession: Black Australians and White Invaders*. Sydney: Allen & Unwin.

Reynolds, Henry 1982, *The Other Side of the Frontier: Aboriginal Resistance to the European Invasion of Australia*. Ringwood, Vic.: Penguin.

Ridler, Ann Margaret 2004, 'Latham, Robert Gordon (1812–1888)', *Oxford Dictionary of National Biography*. <http://www.oxforddnb.com/view/article/16094>

Ritter, David 1998, 'Whither the historians?: The case for historians in the native title process', *Indigenous Law Bulletin* 4, no. 17: 4–6.

Ritter, David 2002, 'No title without history', in *Through a Smoky Mirror: History and Native Title*, edited by Mandy Paul and Geoffrey G. Gray. Canberra: Aboriginal Studies Press.

Ritter, David 2004, 'The Judgement of the world: the Yorta Yorta case and the "tide of history"', *Australian Historical Studies* 35, no. 123: 106–121.

Robson, Lloyd 1983, *A History of Tasmania: Volume I, Van Diemen's Land from the Earliest Times to 1855*. Melbourne: Oxford University Press.

Rosaldo, Renato 1989, 'Imperialist nostalgia', *Representations* 26: 107–122.

Rose, Deborah Bird 2002, 'Reflections on the use of historical evidence in the Yorta Yorta case', in *Through a Smoky Mirror: History and Native Title*, edited by Mandy Paul and Geoffrey G. Gray. Canberra: Aboriginal Studies Press: 35–47.

Scott, Peter 1967, 'O'Brien, Henry (1793–1866)', *Australian Dictionary of Biography* 2: 292–293.

Seidel, Peter 2004, 'The struggle for justice for the Yorta Yorta Nation', *Alternative Law Journal* 29, no. 2: 70–74.

Shaw, A.G.L. (ed.) 1989, *Gipps–La Trobe Correspondence 1839–46*. Carlton: Melbourne University Press.

Shaw, A.G.L. 1996, *A History of the Port Phillip District: Victoria before Separation*. Carlton: Melbourne University Press.

Smyth, R. Brough 1878, *The Aborigines of Victoria: With Notes Relating to the Habits of the Natives of Other Parts of Australia and Tasmania*. 2 vols. Melbourne: John Ferres, Govt. Printer.

Spencer, Baldwin, and F.J. Gillen 1899, *The Native Tribes of Central Australia*. London: Macmillan.

Stanner, W.E.H. 1969, *After the Dreaming*. Sydney: Australian Broadcasting Commission.

Stanner, W.E.H. 1972a. 'Fison, Lorimer (1832–1907)', *Australian Dictionary of Biography* 4: 175–176.

Stanner, W.E.H. 1972b. 'Howitt, Alfred William (1830–1908)', *Australian Dictionary of Biography* 4: 432–435.

Stephens, Marguerita 2003, 'White without soap: philanthropy caste and exclusion in colonial Victoria 1835–1888, a political economy of race', PhD thesis, The University of Melbourne.

Stern, Bernhard J. 1930, 'Selections from the letters of Lorimer Fison and A. W. Howitt to Lewis Henry Morgan (concluded)', *American Anthropologist* 32, no. 3 (July): 419–453.

Stocking, George 1987, *Victorian Anthropology*. New York: Free Press.

Stocking, George 1996, *After Tylor: British Social Anthropology, 1888–1951*. London: Athlone.

Sutherland, Andrew 1888, *Victoria and Its Metropolis, Past and Present*. 2 vols. Melbourne: McCarron, Bird & Co.

Thomas, Martin 2011, *The Many Worlds of R. H. Mathews: In Search of an Australian Anthropologist*. Crows Nest, N.S.W.: Allen & Unwin.

Toussaint, Sandy (ed.) 2004, *Crossing Boundaries: Cultural, Legal, Historical and Practice Issues in Native Title*. Carlton: Melbourne University Press.

Van Toorn, Penny 1999, 'Authors, scribes and owners: the sociology of nineteenth-century Aboriginal writing on Coranderrk and Lake Condah reserves', *Continuum: Journal of Media and Cultural Studies* 13, no. 2: 333–343.

Van Toorn, Penny 2006, *Writing Never Arrives Naked: Early Aboriginal Cultures of Writing in Australia*. Canberra: Aboriginal Studies Press.

Von Stieglitz, K.R. 1952, *A Short History of Circular Head and Its Pioneers, Also of the V.D.L. Company*. Launceston: Telegraph Printery.

Wakefield, Edward Gibbon 1829, *A Letter from Sydney, the Principal Town of Australasia, Together with the Outline of a System of Colonization*, edited by Robert Gouger. London: Joseph Cross.

Walker, Mary Howitt 1971, *Come Wind, Come Weather: a Biography of Alfred Howitt*. Carlton: Melbourne University Press.

Ward, Russel 1966, 'An early study of Black and White', *Sydney Morning Herald*, 15 January 1966.

Westermarck, Edward 1921, *The History Of Human Marriage*. Vol. 1. 3 vols. London: Macmillan and Co.

Windschuttle, Keith 2002, *The Fabrication of Aboriginal History. Vol. 1, Van Diemen's Land 1803–1847*. Paddington, N.S.W.: Macleay Press.

Wolfe, Patrick 1999, *Settler Colonialism and the Transformation of Anthropology: The Politics and Poetics of an Ethnographic Event*. London: Cassell.

Wolfe, Patrick 2001, 'Land, labor, and difference: elementary structures of race', *American Historical Review* 106, no. 3: 866–905.

Wood, J.D. (ed.) 1879, *The Native Tribes of South Australia*. Adelaide: E.S. Wigg.

Index

Aboriginal people
  language xi, 37, 54, 68, 73, 145, 147-49, 151, 153, 155-56, 159, 168, 173-75, 188
  racial origins 148-49, 151, 153, 156, 173-74, 187
  migration 145, 149, 155-56, 173-74, 187
  government 160-62, 168-69, 175-76, 186
  marriage 147, 152, 163-66, 168, 171
  marital relations 166, 176, 195-96
  kinship systems 168, 168, 186
  mortality 171, 179
  prostitution 166, 168
  corroborees 54-55, 182
  numeracy 160
  circumcision 155
  sub-incision 155, 186
  as childlike 40, 58, 74, 136, 139-40, 144, 170, 182-83, 189, 191, 204
  reserves (Victoria) xi, 127, 136-37, 141, 143, 147-48, 167, 170-71, 190-91
  protest 60-61, 128, 131, 137, 160, 170
  assimilation 134, 137, 141-43, 169-71, 204
  protection 31-32, 57, 127, 134, 141-42, 169-70
  'half-castes' 128, 137, 141, 143, 170-71
  dying race 142, 148, 185, 188
  Royal Commission on Aborigines (Victoria, 1877) 136-37, 142-44, 170-71, 191
  Aborigines Protection Act (1886) 141, 170
Aborigines Protection Society 163, 186
Adelaide, SA 28, 86
Age (Melbourne) xi, 133-34, 204
alcohol 26, 43, 51-52, 100, 119, 124, 182
Alhambra palace 78-79
Anthropological Institute of Great Britain and Ireland 147, 149, 151, 154, 163, 168, 186-87

Anthropological Society of London 151, 154
Anthropological Society of Washington 184
anthropology xv, 147, 151-57, 165, 169, 185-88
Ardpatrick (pastoral station) 32
Argus (Melbourne) 49, 94-97, 103, 106-8, 111, 123-24, 133-34, 145, 149-50, 153, 162-63
Arthur, George 7-8, 11-13
Austral Downs (pastoral station) 110
Australia Felix 31
Australian Dictionary of Biography xv, 57, 190

Baala Creek, VIC 58-59
Baillieston, VIC 32
Ballarat, VIC 76
Bangerang language 145, 173-74
Bangerang people xi, 37-44, 51, 54, 58-63, 70, 72, 74, 88, 124, 127, 145, 173-83, 194-97, 203
Barak, William 134-36, 138, 141, 170
bark canoes 40, 59, 62, 119, 180
Barmah, VIC 59
Barwick, Diane xv, 134, 143, 171, 190-91
Bathurst, Lord 6-8
Batman, John 24, 48
Bendigo, VIC 75, 100
Berndt, Ronald and Catherine 188
Berry, Graham 131, 134, 136-38, 143
biography xiii-xvi, 57, 72, 190
birds 54, 60
Black Thursday bushfire 80
Black, Chief Justice Michael 198, 204
Blainey, Geoffrey xv, 190
Board for the Protection of Aborigines (Victoria) xi, xv, 127-45, 169-71, 190, 204
Boldrewood, Rolf xv, 122
Bon, Ann 134, 138-40
border police 62, 64, 195
Brazil 5, 7
Brisbane Courier 123

223

Brisbane, QLD 89
Brixham cave 152
Broken Creek *see* Baala Creek
Bruce, Alexander 106
Brussels 79
bullocks 26-8, 31-34
Bulmer, John 167
Burn, David 8
Burramboot ranges, VIC 34
Bush Inn (Gisborne, VIC) 25, 28
Butlin, Noel 190
Byron, George Gordon 118, 120-22, 205

Cadiz, Spain 77
Callinan, Justice 198-99
Cameron, E.H. 138, 140
Campbell, Thomas 120
Cape Grim Massacre 10-12, 28
Capell, A.A. 188
Castan, Ron 198
catarrh 97, 105
Catholicism xi, 1, 4-6, 16, 47, 50, 77, 101, 109, 117
cattle 32, 89-91, 104-5, 142-43, 160, 178, 203
Chamberlain, Charles 10-11
Chesson, F.W. 163
Christie, Michael 134
Circular Head (Stanley, TAS) 8, 11, 13, 15-16, 20-21, 23-24
Clarke, Hyde 147-48, 154, 159, 163,
Clarke, Marcus 122
classical languages 119
Colbinabbin (patoral station) 34-35, 45-46, 51-52, 75-76
Collins Street (Melbourne, VIC) 53, 76
Collins, David 157
Collins, Tom *see* Furphy, Joseph
Colonial and Indian Exhibition (1886) 149
Commissioner of Crown Lands 43, 45, 62, 72-73, 161, 173
communal marriage 163-66, 168, 171, 188
comparative philology 151-56, 173-74, 187
Condell, Henry 47
Conolly, Fr Philip 6
conservation 196
Constance Downs (pastoral station) 110

convicts 10, 23, 26, 33-34, 48-49, 51-52, 57, 124, 177
Coragorag (pastoral station) 34, 44-46, 53
Coranderrk Aboriginal Reserve xi, 127-29, 131-41, 143, 147-48, 159-60, 170-71, 190-91
Corop (pastoral station) 46, 77, 82
Cunningham, Hastings 89, 110
Curr, Agnes 13, 17, 89
Curr, Arthur 13
Curr, Augusta 13, 17
Curr, Charles (brother) 13, 41, 75-76, 83, 89-90, 120, 176
Curr, Charles (cousin) 17
Curr, Contance 80, 89, 117
Curr, Edward (senior)
   youth 4-5
   mercantile activities 5-7
   An Account of the Colony of Van Diemen's Land 6
   and Van Diemen's Land Company 7-10, 17, 23-24
   and Cape Grim Massacre 11-13
   political career xi, 6-7, 41, 47-50, 203
   campaign for Victoria's separation from NSW 47-48, 50, 82, 93, 122, 185, 203
   death and legacy 46, 49, 75-77, 82, 203
Curr, Edward M.
   childhood 13-20
   education 4, 16-20, 24, 27, 53, 97
   fencing xi, 19, 204
   journal 18-20, 89-90
   family memoir xiii, 23, 50, 93, 109, 177
   marriage 81, 109
   parenting 109-11
   library 51, 78, 88, 109, 111
   employees 26-28, 31, 33-34, 39, 49, 50-53, 55, 61-65, 167, 118, 124, 177, 194
   inheritance 75-77, 81-82, 203
   Mediterranean Tour 77-79
   horse trading 84-85, 91, 94, 113-16
   Inspector of Sheep 10, 98-103
   Chief Inspector of Stock xi, 46, 91, 93, 97, 104-8, 142, 185
   letter writing 83-89, 94, 98-99, 110-13, 203

poetry 19, 78, 116-18, 121
literary inspiration 17-19, 118-122
ethnology xi, xiii, 54, 71-72, 124, 127, 145-48, 151, 153-55, 173, 175, 178, 185, 186, 188, 190, 203
paternalism xi, xv, 39-40, 60, 134, 139, 141-42, 169, 183
nostalgia 93, 178, 181, 194, 203
sympathy for Aboriginal people xv, 57, 72-73, 137, 139, 182, 189-90, 194, 203
use of Aboriginal place names 37, 44, 46
Pure Saddle Horses 95-97, 106, 112-13, 118, 185
Recollections of Squatting in Victoria xi, xiii-xiv, 24-25, 27, 42, 55, 57-58, 71, 85, 93, 109, 119-24, 144, 157, 174-75, 179, 185, 189, 198, 201, 203-4
The Australian Race xiii, xv, 71, 74, 124, 127, 145, 148-53, 157, 163, 167-71, 173-75, 185-87, 190
Essay on Scab in Sheep xiii, 46, 101-2, 108, 112, 118
the ghost of xvi, 201
Curr, Edward M.V. 85, 91, 109-11, 122, 145, 155, 185
Curr, Ela 93, 109, 117
Curr, Elizabeth (née Micklethwaite) 3, 5-6, 13-14, 80
Curr, Elizabeth jnr, *see* Pennefather, Elizabeth
Curr, Ernest xiv, 93, 109-10
Curr, Florence 13, 75, 80, 117,
Curr, Geraldine 13
Curr, Hannah (née Wilson) 3, 17
Curr, Hubert 93, 109-10
Curr, John (cousin) 17
Curr, John (grandfather) 1-4, 6, 93, 111
Curr, John (uncle) 4, 17, 111
Curr, Joseph 4, 17, 111
Curr, Julia 13, 20
Curr, Julius 13, 20, 89, 91, 110
Curr, Justin 93, 109-10, 117

Curr, Mabel 93, 117
Curr, Margaret (née Vaughan) 81-83, 89, 91, 93, 109-10, 117, 177, 185
Curr, Maria 81, 91
Curr, Marmaduke 13, 20, 110
Curr, Montagu 13, 20, 77, 89, 110, 145-46
Curr, Richard 6, 13, 16-17, 41, 43-45, 52, 54, 58, 62, 65, 75-76, 81-83, 91
Curr, Walter 13, 17, 41, 75-76, 83
Curr, Wilfred 91
Curr, William 13, 16-17, 41, 46, 77
Curthoys, Ann 193, 200

Dana, Captain Henry 48, 62-65, 67, 74, 195
Daniel, George 7
Darling River tribes 173-74
Darwin, Charles 151-52, 156, 165
Dawson, James 157, 160-63, 166, 171, 186, 188
de Staël, Madame 116
Deakin, Alfred 138-39, 141
Dieyeri (Dieri) people 168-69
discipline 16-17, 29-40, 70, 110, 131, 136, 141, 170, 189
dogs 30, 39, 53, 62-63, 67, 120
Dow, John Lamont 133-34, 137-40, 143
drought 45, 76, 91, 93, 127, 203
Dublin 79, 81
Duffy, Charles 105
Dunolly, Thomas 134-35, 170
Dwight, Henry 117
Economist (Melbourne) 113-16
Elkin, A.P. xv, 147, 155, 187-89
Embling, Thomas 139-40
Emu Bay, TAS 12, 24
Ethnological Society of London 151, 153-54
ethnology (*see also* Curr, Edward M.) 151-55
exploration 86, 94, 111
Eyre, Edward John 157, 162

Featherstone, Isaac 87
Federal Court of Australia 191, 197-98
Fels, Marie Hansen 63, 189, 191

Fiji 164, 166
Finn, Edmund (Garryowen) 44, 49
fire xiii, xv, 45, 80, 124
Fisher J.R. 106
fishing 37, 54, 59, 60, 132, 179-80, 196, 201
Fison, Lorimer 157, 163-69, 171, 186, 188
flood plains 43-45, 58, 61
Flower, W.H. 149, 154, 186
foot-and-mouth disease 104-6
foot-rot 27, 98
Forster, Harley xv, 45, 57, 189-90
Francis, James 105
French (language) 16, 18, 19, 77, 116-18
Furphy, Joseph 112-13

Gammage, Bill xv
Garryowen *see* Finn, Edmund
Gason, Samuel 168
Gellibrand, Joseph 24
Genovese, Ann 193, 200
Gillen, Francis James 186
Gillies, Duncan 149
Gipps, George 48
Gippsland 166-67
Gleeson, Justice 198
Gobongo (pastoral station) 89-90, 160
Godfrey, Frederick Race 129-34, 136-37
gold 45, 49-50, 55, 75-76, 82, 86, 122, 171
Golder, Ben xv, 192
Goldie, Alexander 11-12
Goulburn River xi, 27, 31-32, 34-35, 37, 43-44, 64, 70, 79, 119, 121, 129, 133, 144, 190
Graebner, Fritz 187
Grant, J.M. 138
Great Exhibition (1851) 77
Green, John 127-29, 131, 133, 137-38, 140, 147, 159-60, 170
Grey, George 83, 94, 148, 157
group marriage, *see* communal marriage
Gummow, Justice 198

Hare, Rosalie 11, 13, 15-16
Hawdon, Joseph 28

Hawke's Bay, NZ 83, 87
Hayne, Justice 198
Healesville, VIC xi, 127, 138
High Court of Australia xi, 197-99, 201
Highfield House 13, 15, 20-21
Hobart Mercury xiv
Hobart, TAS xi, 5-7, 9, 11, 13, 23
hops 128, 131, 133
Horne, Richard 117
horse breeding xiii, 95-97, 107, 111-12
horses 5, 26, 43, 47, 51, 53, 71, 79, 82, 91, 94-97, 112-16
Howitt, A.W. xv, 154, 157, 163-69, 171, 185-87, 189, 191
Hunter, John 157
hunting 53-55, 94, 121, 179, 183, 195
Huxley, T.H. 152, 154, 156

Illustrated London News 79-80
imperialist nostalgia 179-83
importation of livestock 106-7
Irving, Washington 78-79
Italian (language) 77

James, Andrea 201
Jennings, Henry 137, 139
Jesuits 16, 77, 109
Jimmy-Jack (Aboriginal servant) 51

Kabi (Gubbi Gubbi) people 160, 187
Kamilaroi people 164-65
Keltie, John Scott 186
Kerr, John 105
Kiddle, Margaret 96-97
Kilmore, VIC 41, 58, 80, 100
Kimberley region, WA 155
Kulin people 127, 131, 134, 141, 170
Kulkyne, VIC 132
Kurnai people 164-67

La Trobe, Charles 48, 63, 65, 70
Lachlan River 76, 91, 93, 203
Lake Tyers Aboriginal reserve 167
Lang, John Dunmore 47-48
Langton, Marcia 196

Latham, R.G. 153
Le Souëf, Albert A.C. 129-34, 137-38, 142, 169, 171
Le Souëf, Caroline 130
Le Souëf, William 65, 67
Leader (Melbourne) 133, 136
legal history 193
Legislative Council (New South Wales) 47-48, 76, 98
Legislative Council (Van Diemen's Land) 7
Legislative Council (Victoria) 76, 98
Levien, Jonas Felix 149
Liverpool, England 4, 81
Lockhart, C.G.N. 173
London 6-7, 11, 23, 47-48, 77, 79-81, 85, 149, 151, 153, 163, 186
Looker, William 76
Lubbock, John 156

MacBain, James 133
Macpherson, James 119-20
Macwhirter, P.J. 108
Madeira 13
Madowla lagoon 58
Major's Line 31-32
Malinowski, Bronislaw 187-88
Maori people 83
Mason, Horatio William 6
Mathew, John 160, 187
Mathews, R.H. 188
Matthews, Daniel 197
McCrae, George 117
McCulloch, James 99
McFarlane, Ian 10-11
Melbourne Intercolonial Exhibition (1866) 130
Melbourne, VIC 24-26, 28-29, 31, 33, 41, 45, 47-50, 66-67, 70, 75-76, 80-81, 83, 86, 89-94, 97, 100, 102, 109-10, 117-19, 122, 129, 131, 138, 147, 157, 163-64, 171
Merino sheep 10, 142
Micklethwaite, Benjamin 5
Micklethwaite, Elizabeth, *see* Curr, Elizabeth
Micklethwaite, Richard 5

Micklethwaite, Sarah (née Lister) 5
Milton, John 20, 120-21
missionaries 131-32, 145, 157, 162, 165, 167, 197
Mitchell, Major Thomas 31, 94, 157
Moira (pastoral station) 37, 43-44, 46, 53, 57-65, 70, 74, 174
Moitheriban clan 37, 59
monogenism 151-52
Morgan, Lewis H. 163-66
Morgan, Monica 196
Mozambique 147
Müller, Max 152-53, 156
Mundy, Alfred 28
Mungalella Creek, QLD 174
Murphy, James 76
Murray River xi, 32, 34, 37, 43, 58-59, 61, 64, 119, 132, 136, 141, 144, 162, 174, 183, 194
Murrumbogie, (pastoral station) 111, 185

Narre Narre Warren 68, 70
native police force (Port Phillip) 62-64, 195
native police force (Queensland) 71
native title
  Mabo judgement 191
  Yorta Yorta case xi, xiii, xvi, 57, 175, 183, 191-201, 204
  and history xiii, 192-93, 199-200
  and legal history 193
  and the written word xi, xvi, 139, 192-93, 197-201, 204-5
  and oral testimony xvi, 192-93, 198, 200
  historians as expert witnesses 193, 199
  frozen in time 198
New Zealand 6, 83-88, 94, 111, 114, 148, 203
New Zealand Spectator 85-86, 111
Newcastle, NSW 84, 114
Ngooraialum people 37, 41, 54, 88, 121, 145
Noah (biblical figure) 151

O'Brien, Henry 43
O'Loghlen, Bryan 138, 141
Ogilvie, Christian 132-33
Old Crossing Place (Goulburn River) 32
Olney, Justice Howard xiv, 57, 175, 183, 191-99
Oxford Dictionary of National Biography 72, 190

Pama (*see* Barmah, VIC)
Paris, France 79
penal labour 48-49
Pennefather, Elizabeth (née Curr) 5, 20, 47, 53, 75
Pentonville Prison, London 48-49
Phillip, Arthur 157
pigs 53, 104-5
Pike, D.H. 7, 48
Pink, Kerry 23
polygenism 151
Port Phillip District (NSW) xi, 24, 33, 43-44, 47-49, 62, 85, 88, 122, 162, 171, 203
Portuguese (language) 5, 119, 153
Portuguese Africa 147, 159
Powell, J.M. 190
Powlett, F.A. 43, 62
Prahran, VIC 93, 97, 122
Prichard, James Cowles 151-55
Pyne, Stephen xv

quarantine 99, 102, 106-7

Raine, John 5
Reilly, Alexander 193, 200
Reynolds, Henry 70-72, 192
Ridley, William 157
Riley, James 100
Rio de Janeiro 13, 76
Ritter, David 191-92, 200
Robertson, George 122, 157
Robinson, George Augustus 10, 62-63, 67-68, 177, 194
Rome 79, 109, 112
Rosaldo, Renato 179

Rose, Deborah Bird 175, 177, 197, 199-200, 204
Royal Geographical Society 186
Royal Society of Victoria 147, 163, 168-69

scab (sheep disease) xiii, 26-27, 45-46, 97-108, 185
Search, Frederick 128
Seville, Spain 77-79
Shakespeare, William 118-19
Shaw, Thomas 107
Sheffield, England 1-4
Shelley, Percy Bysshe 120-21
shepherds 10, 11, 26-28, 31, 33-34, 39-40, 49, 51-53, 61-65, 67, 72, 75, 124, 177, 194
Sheppard, Sherbourne 133
Smith, Adam 87-88
Smith, G.P. 103
Smithsonian Institution 163-64
Smyth, R. Brough 69, 127, 129, 131-33, 147, 154, 157-60, 162, 170-71, 187-88
Sorell, William 6-7
Spain 7, 77-79
Spanish (language) 77, 153
Spencer, Walter Baldwin 186-87, 189
squatters xi, xiii, 37, 48-49, 52-53, 71, 76, 85-86, 94, 122, 124, 161, 190
St Edmunds College, Douai, France 17-19
St Germains (pastoral station) 32
St Heliers, Abbotsford, VIC 42, 47, 76
St Kilda, VIC 91, 109-10, 122, 185
Stähle, Johann 131-32
Stanley, TAS *see* Circular Head
Stanner, W.E.H. 72, 169
Stocking, George 151
Stonyhurst College, Lancashire 16-17, 19, 24, 77, 111, 148
Strickland, Frederick 137
Surrey Hills, TAS 24
Sutherland, Andrew 185
Swan Hill, VIC 145
Sydney Mail 185
Sydney, NSW xiii, 5, 47-48, 86, 89-90, 107, 119

Syme, David 133
Syme, George 133, 136

Table Cape, TAS 91
tallow 43-44, 76
Tallygaroopna (pastoral station) 133
Taplin, George 157, 162-64
Thomas, William 67-70
Threlkeld, Lancelot Edward 157
tide of history xvi, 183, 191
Tommy (Aboriginal guide) 59-61
Tongala (pastoral station) 27, 37, 40-46, 51, 53, 54, 58-59, 63, 65, 67-68, 70, 74-75, 78, 80, 88, 98, 111, 119, 121, 133, 178-79
Toolamba (pastoral station) 32
Toomcul (pastoral station) 89-90
Tower of Babel 151
Towroonban clan 37
Trundle, NSW 111, 185
Tylor, E.B. 156, 164

Uabba (pastoral station) 91, 93, 127
Undyārning (Aboriginal girl) 60

Vale, William 120
Van Diemen's Land Company 7-12, 23-24
Van Toorn, Penny 141
Von Stieglitz, K.R. 7, 9
Vowles, Gill 23

Wakefield, Edward Gibbon 83, 87
Wandin, Robert 134, 170
Ward, Russel 189, 201
Warri (Aboriginal prisioner) 61, 64-70
Weld, Frederick A. 148
Wellington Independent 85
Westermarck, Edward 187
Wild Duck Creek (pastoral station), *see* Wolfscrag
Willis, Justice 47, 67
Windschuttle, Keith 10
Winter, John 76
Wolfscrag (pastoral station) 24-32, 44, 55, 98, 118

Wongatpan clan 37, 59, 63, 119-20, 201
Wyndham, George 84
Wyuna (pastoral station) 32, 57

Xavier College, Melbourne VIC 109-10

Yanagai! Yanagai! 201
Yarra River 47, 118, 136
Yass, NSW 44
Yorta Yorta people xi, xvi, 37, 127, 175, 193-94, 201

Zoological and Acclimatisation Society (Victoria) 130

www.ingramcontent.com/pod-product-compliance
Lightning Source LLC
Chambersburg PA
CBHW060929170426
43192CB00031B/2875